W. B. YEATS AND

THE THEATRE OF

DESOLATE REALITY

W. B. YEATS AND THE THEATRE OF DESOLATE REALITY

EXPANDED EDITION, INCLUDING

Vivien and Time,
The Irish National Theatre,
AND *The Poet and the Actress*

BY W. B. YEATS

BY DAVID R. CLARK *with Rosalind Clark*

The Catholic University of America Press
WASHINGTON, D.C.

The paper used in this publication meets the minimum
requirements of American National Standards for Information
Science—Permanence of Paper for Printed Library Materials,
ANSI z39.48-1984.
∞

LIBRARY OF CONGRESS CATALOGING-IN-
PUBLICATION DATA
Clark, David R.
   W. B. Yeats and the theatre of desolate reality / by David R.
Clark, with Rosalind Clark. Expanded edition, including Vivien
and time, The Irish National Theatre, and The Poet and the
actress / by W. B. Yeats.
      p.   cm. — (Critical Studies in Irish literature ; v. 3)
   Includes bibliographical references and index.
   1. Yeats, W. B. (William Butler), 1865–1939—Dramatic
works.   2. Theater—Ireland—History.   3. Ireland in
literature.   I. Clark, Rosalind.   II. Title.   III. Series.
PR5908.D7C56   1993
822'.8—dc 20
      ISBN 0-8132-0773-8. — ISBN 0-8132-0774-6 (pbk.)
CIP

To My Wife
who gave immeasurable help

Com' anima gentil, che non fa scusa,
ma fa sua voglia della voglia altrui,
tost ch' ell' e per segno fuor dischiusa . . .

Contents

Illustrations

Foreword

Few countries of Ireland's size, beset with "troubles" for centuries, can claim as many major literary voices as Ireland, but this has been especially true of the Classic Modern Period, approximately the time between the waning decades of the nineteenth century and the greater part of the twentieth. Oscar Wilde, George Moore, Bernard Shaw, W. B. Yeats, James Joyce, Æ, Lady Gregory, Sean O'Casey, and Samuel Beckett—Anglo-Irish literature would be impoverished without them. Critical Studies in Irish Literature undertakes to publish some of the best books on such Irish writers and related literary movements that have, for one reason or another, gone out of print.

Our Editorial Advisory Board consists of specialists and bibliographers on major and minor writers and various literary movements in Ireland. The criteria for selection are the excellence of the critical study and its continued usefulness for research and teaching. Older studies, if they meet that test, will be considered in addition to more recent titles.

It is our aim to keep alive the best critical work on Irish literature in the Classic Modern Period, for we believe that the richness, beauty, and importance of that literature need continued sustenance by its best interpreters.

Originally a Yale dissertation, published as a slim volume during Yeats's centenary year (1965) by two small presses as *W. B. Yeats and the Theatre of Desolate Reality,* David Clark's book is seeing new life co-authored with Rosalind Clark. This volume was originally selected for this series because it met all the criteria for being included. Clark's book was admired when first published for its clarity and insights; and like so many researchers in the fifties and sixties, Clark had benefited from the generosity of Mrs. Yeats by having access to Yeats's manuscripts.

What is new in this expanded edition is the inclusion of the text (and an analysis of it) of Yeats's first play, *Vivien and Time,* a work that hovers between juvenilia and the emerging young poet; *The Irish National Theatre;* and *The Poet and the Actress. Vivien and Time,* reprinted here in its entirety, gives us valuable glimpses into the emerging mind of the poet. The analysis following the text explores its "Themes, Images, and Forms" and sheds new light on the earliest phase of Yeats's career, and it also provides hints of the plays to come—even the dance plays.

Before returning to the narrative of the original book, Clark first inserts a previously uncollected essay, *The Irish National Theatre,* delivered during a congress in Rome in 1934, and attended by such luminaries as Maurice Maeterlinck and Luigi Pirandello. While the essay may not break new ground, its tone as a retrospective is properly that of reminiscence and elegy.

The Poet and the Actress (1916) is an elaboration of Yeats's dramatic theories of the Mask and his opposition to Ibsenian Realism.

Clark's expanded volume is, therefore, not merely a reprint of the original book with corrections or minor additions. Rather, with tact and ingenuity, Clark has folded in, as it were, snapshots into the album to create a more resonant, a more complete, and more rewarding volume.

EDWARD ENGELBERG
General Editor

Preface
W. B. Yeats: A Dramatist First and Last

". . . I need a theatre," declared the poet W. B. Yeats, "I believe myself to be a dramatist; I desire to show events and not merely tell of them; . . . and I seem to myself most alive at the moment when a room full of people share the one lofty emotion."[1] And he was a dramatist: in 1884 when, at eighteen, he finished his first play and probably played in it at a neighbour's house; in 1899 when the Irish Literary Theatre began with a production of his *The Countess Cathleen;* in 1904 when the Abbey Theatre opened and began to present his formally constructed plays in verse, the Racine-like *"Deirdre"* (1907) being, perhaps, the most beautiful; in 1916 when, once again in the drawing rooms of friends, he began experiments with dance plays, coming closest to a Japanese Noh play model in *The Dreaming of the Bones* (1919); in the twenties and thirties when he perfected dramatic speech in prose again for the stage, *The Words upon the Window-pane* (1934) being the most masterful; in his last years when he perfected dramatic speech in verse, especially in *Purgatory* (1939); in his last days when, on his death-bed, he corrected the dialogue of his last play.

Deirdre, The Dreaming of the Bones, The Words upon the Window-pane and *Purgatory* were analyzed in detail and made to illustrate the course of Yeats's development as a dramatist in the first edition of *W. B. Yeats and the Theatre of Desolate Reality.*[2] I could not, at this late date, have revised what had appeared in 1965 and had been written still earlier as part of my 1955 Yale dissertation—back when no book had appeared on Yeats's plays. I could, however, expand it by adding both other work of my own and illustrative primary material, previously unpublished or uncollected work by Yeats.

1. "Notes" to *At the Hawk's Well, Variorum Plays,* p. 415.
2. David R. Clark, *W. B. Yeats and the Theatre of Desolate Reality* (Dublin: The Dolmen Press; Chester Springs, Penna.: Dufour Editions, 1965).

The book now begins with Part One, "The Young Yeats." It includes Yeats's first play, *Vivien and Time*. Amateurish and slight, literary rather than dramatic, this play nevertheless introduces themes perennial with Yeats, the fascination with medievalism, magic, and myth, the wandering poet-singer in endless search for a phantom "glimmering girl," symbols like the laurel, butterflies, swans, fountains, dark groves. Yet in January of 1884 Yeats's orientation is still English, not Irish. He had not yet met John O'Leary, A.E., Maud Gonne. Therefore his myth is Arthurian, his magic from Scott and Shelley, his loyalty to Irish subject matter not aroused. Yet his love is already a "Leanhaun Shee," leading the poet a phantom chase.[3] Much of the later integral development and exfoliation of Yeats's work is implicit in this small seed, *Vivien and Time*.

The second section, "The Abbey Dramatist," gives us Yeats the writer of plays for the Irish national theatre and is introduced appropriately by Yeats's address on that subject to the *Convegno di Lettere* at Rome. Though he says very little about his own work in this talk, he does give a fascinating, brief, popular and anecdotal history of the theatre, its origin, founding, and chief figures—the Fays, Miss Horniman, Lady Gregory, Synge, O'Casey, and Lennox Robinson. From Yeats's general account I move to my own survey of the course of Yeats's development as a dramatist and my analyses of two of his most effective plays for his Irish national theatre: *The Countess Cathleen* and *Deirdre*.

The third section, "The Mask Maker," deals with Yeats's temporary abandonment of the stage for the drawing room dance play, the "theatre of beauty"—"Verse, ritual, music, and dance in association with action. . . ."[4] The use of masks is the mark of this type of play—

3. "*The Leanhaun Shee* (fairy mistress), seeks the love of mortals. If they refuse, she must be their slave; if they consent, they are hers, and can only escape by finding another to take their place. The fairy lives on their life, and they waste away. Death is no escape from her. She is the Gaelic muse, for she gives inspiration to those she persecutes. The Gaelic poets die young, for she is restless, and will not let them remain long on earth—this malignant phantom" (*Fairy and Folk Tales*, p. 76).

4. *Essays and Introductions*, pp. 228, 224.

even though not all the dance plays require masks—and the section begins with Yeats's *The Poet and the Actress* (1916), a dialogue in which the poet tries to persuade an actress successful in Ibsen's *A Doll's House* and *Hedda Gabler* to cover "her expressive face with a mask."[5] Here, Yeats develops the anti-realistic principles of his dance plays and points to the Noh theatre of Japan as his model. There follows my analysis of *The Dreaming of the Bones,* the Yeats play most obviously indebted to the Noh drama.

Finally, in a section called "The Later Yeats," are my analysis of his play on Jonathan Swift, *The Words upon the Window-pane,* in which he turned to prose and back to the stage, and my analysis of *Purgatory,* which he wrote within a year of his death, marking his greatest prosodic achievement in dramatic verse.

These studies of six plays demonstrate Yeats's striking consistency in theme and his even more striking evolution in form over the fifty-four years of his development. With the new primary material—an early play, a middle-period dialogue, and a late address—they demonstrate that Yeats was a dramatist, first and last.

5. *Variorum Plays,* p. 991. Yeats uses the phrase, and the idea, nineteen years later in dedicating *The King of the Great Clock Tower* to Ninette de Valois, who played the Queen.

Acknowledgments

The poem I use as an epigraph was found by the late Professor Fred B. Millett among the papers of Carl Carlson, my fellow student at Wesleyan University, a *non*-Irish airman killed in action in World War II. The poem, not copyrighted, was published by Millett in a small collection called *From the Poems of Carl Carlson 1920–1943* (Whitman, Massachusetts: The Washington Street Press, 1969). I have corrected two typographical errors by reference to a typescript of the poem among Carlson's papers in the Wesleyan University Library. My thanks to librarian and University archivist Elizabeth A. Swaim for her help. Burton Carlson has kindly granted permission for the use of his brother's poem.

Time and the Witch Vivien by W. B. Yeats, Yeats's previously unpublished early play *Vivien and Time,* his previously unpublished 1916 dialogue *The Poet and the Actress,* and his previously uncollected 1934 address to the Volta Congress in Rome, "The Irish National Theatre," are included by the permission of A. P. Watt Ltd on behalf of Michael Yeats and Anne Yeats. Roy Foster, author of the forthcoming official biography, has also given his permission.

My thanks are due the Yeats family for many kindnesses and courtesies, beginning in 1957 when Mrs. W. B. Yeats first showed me Yeats's early unpublished plays and encouraged me in "sorting them out."

Extracts from various works of W. B. Yeats still in copyright are reprinted by permission of A. P. Watt Ltd on behalf of Anne Yeats and Michael Yeats and, for publication within the United States of America, by permission of the Macmillan Publishing Company, New York.

Excerpts are reprinted with permission of Macmillan Publishing Company from *Essays and Introductions* by W. B. Yeats. Copyright © Mrs. W. B. Yeats, 1961.

Excerpts are reprinted with permission of Macmillan Publishing

Company from *The Variorum Edition of the Poems of W. B. Yeats,* edited by Peter Allt and Russell K. Alspach. Copyright 1918, 1919, 1924, 1928, by Macmillan Publishing Company, renewed 1946, 1947, 1952, 1956, by Bertha Georgie Yeats. Copyright 1940 by Georgie Yeats, renewed 1968 by Bertha Georgie Yeats, Michael Butler Yeats, and Anne Yeats.

Excerpts are reprinted with permission of Macmillan Publishing Company from *The Variorum Edition of the Plays of W. B. Yeats,* edited by Russell K. Alspach. Copyright 1934, 1952 by Macmillan Publishing Company. Copyrights renewed 1962 by Bertha Georgie Yeats, and 1980 by Anne Yeats. Copyright © Russell K. Alspach and Bertha Georgie Yeats, 1966.

Excerpts are reprinted with permission of Macmillan Publishing Company from *Autobiography of W. B. Yeats.* Copyright 1916, 1936 by Macmillan Publishing Company, renewed 1944, 1964 by Bertha Georgia Yeats.

Brief excerpts are reprinted with permission of Macmillan Publishing Company from the following works of W. B. Yeats:

Explorations (Copyright © Mrs. W. B. Yeats 1962)

A Vision (Copyright 1937 by W. B. Yeats, renewed 1965 by Bertha Georgie Yeats and Anne Butler Yeats)

Mythologies (© Mrs. W. B. Yeats 1959)

Fairy and Folk Tales of Ireland, with Foreword by Kathleen Raine (New York: Macmillan, 1973)

Quotations from *The Letters of W. B. Yeats,* ed. Allen Wade (London: Rupert Hart-Davies; New York: Macmillan, 1954), are reprinted by permission of Oxford University Press. John Kelly, editor of the multi-volume *The Collected Letters of W. B. Yeats,* has also given his permission.

The courtesy of A. P. Watt & Son and of the Macmillan Press Ltd, is greatly appreciated.

"Vision and Revision: Yeats's *The Countess Cathleen*" is reprinted from *The World of W. B. Yeats,* edited by Robin Skelton and Ann Saddlemyer, published for the University of Victoria by the Adelphi Bookshop Limited, Victoria, British Columbia, 1965. Copyright 1965 Robin Skelton and Ann Saddlemyer and reprinted with their permission.

Part One, "The Young Yeats," first appeared in *Yeats,* V (1987), as "Sailing from Avalon: Yeats's First Play, *Vivien and Time,*" copyright 1987 by David R. Clark and Rosalind Clark, and is reprinted by courtesy of editor Richard J. Finneran and the UMI Research Press. *Vivien and Time* and all previously unpublished materials by W. B. Yeats copyright 1987 by Anne Yeats and Michael Butler Yeats.

" 'The Poet and the Actress': An Unpublished Dialogue by W. B. Yeats" first appeared in *Yeats Annual No. 8* (1991), edited by Warwick Gould, copyright The Macmillan Press Ltd., 1991, and is reprinted by permission. *The Poet and the Actress* by W. B. Yeats is copyright 1993 by Anne Yeats and Michael Butler Yeats.

I renew my thanks to those mentioned in "Acknowledgments in the First Edition" and particularly to Robin Skelton, without whom the book would not have been published. I am very grateful to those who encouraged me in the making of this expanded edition: Edward Engelberg, Richard Finneran, Robert Mahony, and David J. McGonagle, and earlier the late Liam Miller, who suggested it, Richard Fallis, and Mrs. Arpena Mesrobian. Richard Weber, of the National College of Art, Dublin, helped me find pictures. He and Sigrid Weber read Part One of the book, as did Roy and Erika Leslie, for which I thank them all. They didn't say much, and perhaps I should thank them for that too![1] Warwick Gould made suggestions about presenting *The Poet and the Actress* and *The Irish National Theatre.*

I thank Director Patricia Donlon, former Directors Patrick Henchy, Alf Mac Lochlainn, and Michael Hewson, and the staff of the National Library of Ireland, for much help. I also thank the staff of the British Library, London. At the William Butler Yeats Archives, State University of New York at Stony Brook, Evert Volkersz, Lewis Lusardi, Arthur F. Sniffen, and Peggy McMullen have helped me at various periods, and Narayan Hegde has done so over many years. I have been helped by the staffs of several libraries: in Amherst, the University of Massachusetts Library, the Amherst College Library, the Mead Art Gallery Library, and the Jones Library; in Northampton, Massachu-

---

1. Since I wrote this, I have been saddened by the death of Roy F. Leslie, distinguished Arthurian scholar and my good friend.

setts, the Smith College Library and the Hillyer Art Library; in Notre Dame, Indiana, the St. Mary's College Library and the University of Notre Dame Library.

The American Philosophical Society, the American Council of Learned Societies, and the University of Massachusetts Research Council have aided me with recent grants, and I thank them.

I thank my co-author, Rosalind Clark, whose paper "Yeats and the Witch Vivien: Arthurian Sources in Yeats's First Play" we have expanded into Part One of this book.

My wife has always functioned as chief reader and editor, and the book is dedicated to her.

Acknowledgments in the
First Edition

I should like to thank those who have encouraged and helped me both in this book and in my closely related continuing work. The present book has come out of my Yale Ph.D. dissertation on W. B. Yeats's development as a dramatist. It sets forth my idea of Yeats's aims and the direction of his development. I am at work on another book which will, in the light of a study of the manuscripts, more extensively demonstrate the *process* of his development.

I owe a debt of gratitude to William G. O'Donnell who first suggested my subject to me, to Cleanth Brooks and especially to Louis L. Martz for criticism and guidance, to Arthur W. Hoffman for years of (now too infrequent) conversation, often on Yeats, and to Robin Skelton for shared interests and specific encouragement. Obviously, I owe a debt to Francis Fergusson for having written that central book, *The Idea of a Theater,* which has provided me with a framework for my interpretation of Yeats.

I thank Russell K. Alspach and W. Denis Johnston for prompt and authoritative answers to my various queries. Curtis Bradford supplied me with copies of his own work on Yeats's manuscripts. Harlow Shapley, the astronomer, helped me in many practical ways and furnished me a much appreciated introduction to President Eamon de Valera. Among many Irish friends I should like to mention particularly Roger McHugh and Liam Miller. To Pearse and Mary O'Malley I am indebted for much hospitality and for opportunities to see the Lyric Players' Theatre in rehearsal and performance of Yeats's plays. Mr. and Mrs. Wilfred Lamb and Mr. and Mrs. Robert Magill were most kind to my family while we were in Dublin. Captain Patrick Hone introduced me to Yeats's biographer, the late Joseph Hone.

I should like most especially to thank Mrs. W. B. Yeats for her great kindness, not only in allowing me to examine manuscripts of

Yeats's plays and poems in her home frequently during the autumn of 1957 but also in granting me many pleasant, informative and memorable conversations. It is a privilege of a very special sort to have this memory.

I thank the National Library, Dublin, especially Dr. R. J. Hayes, Director, and Mr. A. MacLochlainn, Assistant Keeper of Manuscripts, for allowing me to use the manuscript collection and for cooperating with my work on the many manuscripts of Yeats's plays which Mrs. Yeats gave to the Library in 1957.

The American Philosophical Society, the American Council of Learned Societies, the Bollingen Foundation, and the Modern Language Association have all supported my investigation of the manuscripts, and I thank them.

I thank the University of Massachusetts Research Council for a number of grants in support of my research and the English Department and the School of Arts and Sciences for their generosity in granting me released time. I thank the University of Massachusetts Press for a subsidy in aid of publication. I thank Richard Haven for the use of his books.

Portions of this book appeared in "W. B. Yeats and the Drama of Vision," *The Arizona Quarterly* XX, 2 (Summer 1964), pp. 127–141 and in "Yeats and the Modern Theatre," *Threshold,* IV, 2 (Autumn/Winter, 1960), 36–56. The latter had been given as a lecture at the First Yeats International Summer School, sponsored by The Yeats Society, Sligo, in August 1960. Chapter II is a longer version of "W. B. Yeats's *Deirdre:* The Rigour of Logic" which appeared in *The Dublin Magazine,* XXXIII, 1 (January–March, 1958), 13–21. Chapter III on *The Dreaming of the Bones* appeared in *Modern Drama,* VII, 2 (September, 1964). These essays are reprinted by permission.

Several able and important studies of Yeats's plays have recently appeared: F. A. C. Wilson, *W. B. Yeats and Tradition* (London, 1958), and *Yeats's Iconography* (London, 1960); Peter Ure, *Yeats the Playwright* (London, 1963); and Helen Hennessy Vendler, *Yeats's* Vision *and the Later Plays* (Cambridge, Massachusetts, 1963). My work was done before these books came out (in my unpublished dissertation *The Theatre of Desolate Reality,* Yale, 1955). I have indicated in the notes those points at which my work crosses that of others, but I have been heartened to discover that my analyses have values of their own.

Lear is dead & Blake is dead,
The rod has lost its butting head
And Wm. Butler Yeats is laid
In his stony bed.

He was a stubborn man who made
No bones about th love he paid[1]
His Ireland or th debt he owed
To subtle Plato's shade.

He was a passionate man who strode
So grimly his elected road,
An old man shook his head & cried:
"Th black dog is his goad!"

He for his sin no penance did,
Which was the mortal sin of pride,
But was firm-handed & cold-eyed
Until th Day he died.

—CARL CARLSON, 1920–1943

1. "Paid" is my emendation of "said."

PART ONE

The Young Yeats: Yeats's First Play

DAVID R. CLARK AND ROSALIND CLARK

❧ "I've built a dreaming palace"

EATS WAS A dramatist first. "I had begun to write poetry in imitation of Shelley and of Edmund Spenser, play after play—for my father exalted dramatic poetry above all other kinds—and I invented fantastic and incoherent plots."[1] The oddness of imitating a great non-dramatic poet in "play after play" escapes Yeats, possibly because Shelley too had imitated Spenser in dramatic poems, but Spenser, if listening in from his poetic immortality, may have been startled by Yeats's statement. Only one who indeed felt himself to be a dramatist could have written with such unconscious contradiction. In "The Young Yeats" is presented *Vivien and Time,* the earliest of the works to which Yeats refers, one that antedates any published poem or play by Yeats.

Readers in 1889 of Yeats's brief dramatic sketch *Time and the Witch Vivien,* published in *The Wanderings of Oisin and Other Poems,*[2] were unaware, as are readers of it today in *The Variorum Edition of the Poems of W. B. Yeats* or *The Poems* (1989),[3] that this playlet was salvaged from a play of two acts, *Vivien and Time,* which Yeats wrote sometime between the autumn of 1882 and the very beginning of 1884.[4] Although it

---

1. *Autobiographies,* pp. 66–67.

2. *"The Wanderings of Oisin" and Other Poems* (London: Kegan Paul, Trench & Co., 1889). Cf. Richard J. Finneran, "Farewell, 'Ha, ha!': "New Revisions to Some Early Poems by W. B. Yeats," *Yeats* 8 (1990), p. 325, for an unpublished revision of "Ha, ha! ha, ha, ha!" (l. 15) to "So then it is you."

3. *Variorum Poems,* pp. 720–22; cf. *Poems,* pp. 517–20.

4. The "Dedication" of *Vivien and Time* is dated "January the 8th/1884." There is no sign that the dedication is of a different date from the rest of the play. On the cover of the notebook containing the play appears "Viven [sic] and Time / a dramatic poem / January the 8th / 1884." On January 7th J. B. Yeats wrote to Edward Dowden asking for the return of the manuscript. January 7, 1884, then is the late date for the finishing of the play. However, J. B. Yeats reported that his son was "sixteen years old" when he wrote *Vivien and Time.* Marguerite Wilkinson, "A Talk with John Butler Yeats about His Son William

survived in the 1892 reissue of the volume in which it had appeared, the playlet was not reprinted in *Poems* (1895), which contained "all the writer cares to preserve out of his previous volumes of verse."[5] Nor was it included in any other collection during Yeats's lifetime. Now we see the published *Time and the Witch Vivien* as part of the unpublished *Vivien and Time,* which Yeats himself identified as "my first play."[6]

Vivien and Time is Yeats's starting point. Here begins the great evolution of his total work, of which no step is irrelevant or unconnected. Not just the isolated greatness of particular works but the unity of all has pushed Yeats's reputation steadily upward during this century. By the sixties Yeats was recognized as "one of the established writers in the history of English poetry," "the greatest modern poet." Today he has risen "From Great Modern Poet to Canonical Classic."[7] To see Yeats's work as a whole, to distinguish his essential development, we perhaps need to return to the very beginning.

Yeats's reputation is secure. It will not suffer from the publication here of this his first hesitant attempt at drama. The full play will illuminate the fragment, *Time and the Witch Vivien.* It will also illuminate later works by showing that certain themes and images were perennial with Yeats—and certain forms, as well. It is interesting that his first play, like his middle-period dance plays, was in form a drawing-room drama of which the highpoint is the manifestation of a spirit, in this case the figure of Time.

Principally the play is of value in showing us the Yeats who had not

---

Butler Yeats," *Touchstone* 6 (Oct. 1919), pp. 10–17. Quoted in Murphy, *Prodigal Father,* p. 569, n. 42. WBY was sixteen on June 13, 1881. He wrote the play for Laura Armstrong at Howth and the Yeats family did not move to Howth until the end of 1881 (Murphy, p. 123). That leaves 1882 and 1883 for the writing. Murphy (p. 132) says it was in the autumn of 1882 that Yeats met Laura. Autumn 1882, then, is the earliest date that Yeats could have written *Vivien and Time.* The dating "1882–3" for the writing of the play will refer to the period between Autumn 1882 and January 7, 1884. We will respect Yeats's date of January 8, 1884, for the play's completion.

5. *Poems* (London: T. Fisher Unwin, 1895), p. v; *Variorum Poems,* p. 845.

6. *Letters,* p. 117; cf. *CL1,* p. 155.

7. Thomas Parkinson, "Some Recent Work on Yeats: From Great Modern Poet to Canonical Classic," *Southern Review,* 15, No. 3 (July 1979), 742–52 esp. p. 748.

yet found his ostensible "subject matter," his "theme." In it Yeats's perennial preoccupations appear in their pre-Irish form. Under the heading "Subject-matter" Yeats wrote in 1937, "It was through the old Fenian leader John O'Leary I found my theme."[8] O'Leary did not return to Ireland from exile until late in 1884.[9] *Vivien and Time* was completed before January 7, 1884, on which date Yeats's proud father, who had lent a manuscript of the play to Professor Edward Dowden of Trinity College, wrote asking for its return.[10] The copy published here has the date "January the 8th, 1884" both on its cover and after the "Dedication" poem.

Dowden's influence was strong on Yeats at this time, and Dowden thought Irish subject matter confining.[11] At least a year would go by before Yeats could come under the influence of O'Leary, be sent to O'Curry, discover Standish O'Grady, and discover the "great tapestry" hanging behind all Irish history. "Nobody looking at its dim folds can say where Christianity begins and Druidism ends."[12] When Yeats wrote *Vivien and Time* he had not yet been persuaded by John O'Leary to admire the Young Ireland poets who, however bad their poetry, "spoke or tried to speak out of a people to a people." Yet he already longed "to get back to Homer, to those that fed at his table," "to cry as all men cried, to laugh as all men laughed."[13] He "read nothing but romantic literature," knew himself "vague and incoherent."[14] Though he had learned Irish folk tales at his mother's knee, the folklore behind *Vivien and Time* comes from the brothers Grimm.[15] O'Leary had not yet sanctioned Irish folklore as material for Irish writers.[16] Yeats's witch Vivien, though in some ways a recognizable sister of later enchantresses like Niamh in *The Wanderings of Oisin* or the Woman of the Sidhe in *The Only Jealousy of Emer,* is not Irish. She comes from the Arthurian literature as treated by Tennyson.

8. *Essays and Introductions,* p. 510.   9. Ellmann, *Man and Masks,* p. 45.
10. Hone, p. 43.   11. Ellmann, *Man and Masks,* p. 47.
12. *Essays and Introductions,* pp. 513–14.   13. *Ibid.,* pp. 510–11.
14. *Ibid.,* p. 510.   15. *Autobiographies,* p. 47.
16. Ellmann, *Man and Masks,* p. 46.

Nor had Yeats's interest in the occult well begun. He was not to meet his "mystical friend"[17] George Russell, who probably introduced him to Eastern and Theosophical literature,[18] until he entered the Metropolitan School of Art in May 1884.[19] Meeting Russell gave Yeats confidence that, as Ellmann puts it, "the dream of the magician was no longer an absurdity."[20] Up to that point Yeats's interest in magic was little more than a literary pose out of Scott,[21] Byron, and Shelley.[22] *Vivien and Time* shows us Yeats as he was before Ireland and the occult possessed him.

Nor had love possessed him, although his feeling for the prototype of "Vivien" indicated the kind of relationship that would dominate much of his later life. It was not until 1889 that that "classical impersonation of the Spring" Maud Gonne walked like a goddess into the Yeats house.[23]

Yeats begins *Vivien and Time* with a dedicatory poem to the girl who suggested the character of Vivien. Among the "many statues fair" standing in the "dreaming palace" of Yeats's imagination—statues of the heroines of Elizabethan tragedy—is one before which he casts "a wayward play." The figure that receives his "Dedication"

> . . . is a pale elf statue
>   With sweet Titania's grace
> But black's the hair, as though it were
>   The peeping pansy's face.
>
> The eyes as the wine are bright
>   in Circe's charmèd cup:
> O dark are the eyes as the morning skies
>   When scarce the day is up.
>   [SB23(3p163)][24]

---

17. Dedication to *Fairy and Folk Tales of the Irish Peasantry*, ed. W. B. Yeats (London: Walter Scott; New York: Thomas Whittaker; Toronto: W. Gage and Co., 1888).

18. Mary Catherine Flannery, *Yeats and Magic: The Earlier Works* (New York: Barnes & Noble, 1978), p. 16.

19. Ellmann, *Man and Masks*, p. 31.   20. *Ibid.*, p. 32.

21. *Autobiographies*, p. 46.   22. *Ibid.*, p. 64.

23. *Ibid.*, p. 123.

24. The number means that this page may be found in Reel 23 Volume 3, Page 163 of

The description is like that of Naschina in *The Island of Statues*:

> Oh, more dark thy gleaming hair is
> Than the peeping pansy's face,
> And thine eyes more bright than faery's,
> Dancing in some moony place . . .[25]

In *Reveries over Childhood and Youth* (1916) Yeats tells how he first met Laura Armstrong, a distant cousin related to him through the Corbet family.[26]

> I was climbing up a hill at Howth when I heard wheels behind me and a pony-carriage drew up beside me. A pretty girl was driving alone and without a hat. She told me her name and said we had friends in common and asked me to ride beside her. After that I saw a great deal of her and was soon in love. I did not tell her I was in love, however, because she was engaged. She had chosen me for her confidant and I learned all about her quarrels with her lover. Several times he broke the engagement off, and she fell ill, and friends had to make peace. Sometimes she would write to him three times a day, but she could not do without a confidant. She was a wild creature, a fine mimic, and given to bursts of religion. I had known her to weep at a sermon, call herself a sinful woman, and mimic it after. I wrote her some bad poems and had more than one sleepless night through anger with her betrothed.[27]

It was for this creature, a combined Titania and Circe, that Yeats wrote *Vivien and Time*. Apparently the play was performed, with Laura in the title role and probably Yeats as the knight Clarin. J. B. Yeats's January 7, 1884, letter to Dowden, asking for the return of the manuscript, says that his son "wants it for a rehearsal which is to come off immediately."[28] Ellmann bases on a letter from Laura Armstrong (not necessarily the letter quoted below) and on a conversation with John Eglinton (Yeats's schoolfellow) the information that *"Vivien and Time* was rehearsed and possibly presented by Yeats and a group of his friends at the home of a Judge Wright at Howth. The girl who played

---

the William Butler Yeats Archives, State University of New York at Stony Brook. This is the most accurate way of numbering Yeats's manuscripts at present.

25. *Variorum Poems*, p. 647; cf. *Poems*, p. 455.
26. *Letters*, p. 117; cf. *CL1*, p. 155.
27. *Autobiographies*, p. 76.   28. Hone, p. 43.

Vivien, Laura Armstrong, appears to have been the boy's first love."[29]
Laura was herself a judge's child, "the youngest and prettiest of the
daughters of Sergeant Richard Armstrong, a distinguished Dublin
barrister who had gone mad years before," as Murphy puts it.[30]

That this "Vivien" was indeed a tantalizing witch is shown by her
one surviving letter to Yeats, dated from Dublin a few months later:

60 STEPHEN'S GREEN

DUBLIN.

10.8.84

My dear Clarin, What can I say to you for having been so rude to you—in not
being at home when you called and I had asked you? I am really very sorry
about it. I hope you will forgive me. It so happened that I was positively
obliged to go out at the hour I had appointed for you to come but it was only
to a house quite close here—and I had told our maid to send me over word
when you *came*—she did so (but I find since it was just before you *went!*) and
I was rising to leave the room—I looked out of the window and to my great
disappointment saw my Clarin leaving No. 60. It was too bad—and I am
indeed sorry I missed you.—I like your poems more than I can say—but I
should like to hear you read them. I have not nearly finished them. Could you
come some afternoon—and read a little to me—I shall be in all Tuesday
afternoon. *I promise!* so can you come? I should have written to you sooner
but I have been away from home. Pray excuse my silence. Trusting to see "the
poet"—! and with kind regards. Believe me Ever yours "Vivien."[31]

She liked the poems more than she could say, but had not nearly
finished reading them! Obviously the poetry held little interest except
as a means for dangling the poet! Wade reprints a poem of this period
which seems a response to further dangling.

> A double moon or more ago
>   I writ you a long letter, lady,
>   It went astray or vexed you, maybe,
> And I would know now yes or no.
>
> Then dying summer on his throne

29. Ellmann, *Man and Masks,* p. 35.

30. Murphy, p. 132. Murphy cites John Butler Yeats's letter to John Quinn of December 3, 1917, in the Berg Collection of the New York Public Library.

31. *Letters,* p. 117n; cf. *CLI,* p. 155.

Faded in hushed and quiet singing;
 Now winter's arrow's winging, winging,
And autumn's yellow leaves are flown.

Ah we poor poets in our pride
 Tread the bare song road all our summer,
 To wake on lips of some newcomer
"A poor man lived here once and died."

How could we trudge on mile by mile
 If from red lips like quicken berry,
 At some odd times to make us merry,
Came nowise half of half a smile?

And surely therefore would I know
 What manner fared my letter, lady,
 It went astray or vexed you, maybe,
A double moon or more ago.[32]

Little more than a month after writing her dangling letter to Yeats, Edith Laura Armstrong married Henry Morgan Byrne in St. Peter's Church, Dublin, 17 September 1884.[33] Later in life she married a Welsh gardener, "'a very decent and intelligent man,'" whom she nagged until he left her. She "was taken by whims which she insisted on exercising, such as suddenly altering all the furniture on the spot."[34]

In Yeats's semi-autobiographical novel *John Sherman,* written in 1888,[35] Laura Armstrong appears as "Margaret Leland, the flighty and inconsiderate heroine,"[36] who "wore the most fascinating hats," read Bulwer-Lytton, and hated frogs.[37] Like Laura, Margaret had difficult engagements. She "had been jilted and was in despair, had taken to her bed with every resolution to die, and was growing paler and paler."

32. *Ibid.*
33. Murphy, p. 569, note 43.
34. *Ibid.,* p. 569, note 44. Murphy cites letters of John Butler Yeats to Lily Yeats of December 24, 1915, and to W. B. Yeats of February 12, 1916, presumably in the collection of Michael Yeats.
35. First published in Ganconah, *John Sherman and Dhoya* (London: T. Fisher Unwin, 1891). Here quoted from William Butler Yeats, *John Sherman & Dhoya* (Detroit: Wayne State University Press, 1969), p. 10.
36. Murphy, p. 573, note 19.
37. *John Sherman,* p. 62.

Her fiancé's sister, however, thought it "was temper that ailed Margaret, and she was a little vixen, and that if she had not flirted with everybody the engagement would never have been broken off."[38]

Margaret's lively spirit, not her mere face, attracts John Sherman, as Laura's "wild dash of half-insane genius" attracted Yeats.[39] "She was a pretty girl with quite irregular features, who though not really more than pretty, had so much manner, so much of an air, that every one called her a beauty: a trefoil with the fragrance of a rose."[40] "As Margaret darted about at the tennis, a red feather in her cap seemed to rejoice with its wearer. Everything was at once gay and tranquil. The whole world had that unreal air it assumes at beautiful moments, as though it might vanish at a touch like an iridescent soap-bubble."[41]

The Reverend William Howard also finds a contrast between Margaret's features and the spirit that animates them. "As he was shown in he noticed, with a momentary shock, that her features were quite commonplace. Then she saw him, and at once seemed to vanish wrapped in an exulting flame of life." If Laura, as in Yeats's "Dedication" to *Vivien and Time*, mixed the qualities of Titania and Circe, it was her Circe-like qualities that Yeats allowed Howard to see in Margaret Leland. Or perhaps her Lilith-like qualities. "As she spoke her face quivered with excitement. The exulting flame of life seemed spreading from her to the other things in the room. To Howard's eyes it seemed as though the bright pots and stuffed birds and plush curtains began to glow with a light not of this world—to glimmer like the strange and chaotic colours the mystic Blake imagined upon the scaled serpent of Eden."[42] Margaret Leland is a fairy for Sherman and a witch for Howard!

Like Vivien, Margaret is vain and jealous. Before discovering her limitations, Sherman proposes marriage and is accepted. But he cannot understand his difficulty in writing the news of his engagement to a friend back home, Mary Carton. Margaret insists that he write and

38. *Ibid.*, p. 63.
40. *John Sherman*, p. 64.
42. *Ibid.*, p. 97.

39. *Letters*, p. 117; cf. *CLi*, p. 155.
41. *Ibid.*, p. 65.

exults when he promises to do so. " 'If I were in her place I know what I would like to do when I got the letter. I know who I would like to kill!'—this with a laugh as she went over and looked at herself in the mirror on the mantlepiece."[43] Vivien's jealousy, too, evokes murderous thoughts, and she attempts to kill her rival Asphodel, because of her beauty.

Murder and mirrors! Vivien repeatedly consults a magic mirror in *Vivien and Time* and watches her image in the pool of a fountain in "Time and the Witch Vivien." One wonders if Laura, prototype of both heroines, was noticeably fascinated by her own reflection. But this subjective, self-dramatizing quality is not presented as entirely negative in *John Sherman*. Here, as in Yeats's characterizations of Richard II and Henry IV in his essay "Stratford-on-Avon" (1901),[44] we have an early example of his sympathetic analysis of the subjective type of person versus the objective type:

After a little Margaret said she was tired, and, sitting on a garden-seat among the bushes, began telling him the plots of novels lately read by her. Suddenly she cried: "The novel-writers were all serious people like you. They are so hard on people like me. They always make us come to a bad end. They *say* we are always acting, acting, acting; and what else do you serious people do? You act before the world. I think, do you know, *we* act before ourselves. All the old foolish kings and queens in history were like us. They laughed and beckoned and went to the block for no very good purpose. I daresay the headsmen were like you."
"We would never cut off so pretty a head."
"Oh, yes, you would—you would cut off mine to-morrow." All this she said vehemently, piercing him with her bright eyes. "You would cut off my head to-morrow," she repeated, almost fiercely; "I tell you you would."[45]

Sherman is the objective man of Yeats's view of personality (later explained in the "system" of *A Vision*) as Margaret and William Howard are subjective.

Margaret's piercingly bright eyes are another feature deriving from Laura/Vivien, whose eyes in the "Dedication" to the play are bright as

43. *Ibid.*, pp. 75–76.   44. *Essays and Introductions*, pp. 96–110.
45. *John Sherman*, pp. 65–66.

the wine in "Circe's charmèd cup" and yet dark "as the morning skies /
When scarce the day is up" [SB23(3p165)]. Both Margaret's lovers are
affected by her eyes. "Several times she gazed at [William Howard]
with those large dark eyes of hers, of which the pupils to-day seemed
larger than usual. They made him feel dizzy and clutch tightly the arm
of his chair."[46] John Sherman, too, before his disillusionment, was
subject to those eyes: "The next day and the day after, Sherman was
followed by those bright eyes. When he opened a letter at his desk they
seemed to gaze at him from the open paper . . ." (JSD 66). However,
like his author, the dangled poet, Sherman has his awakening:

> One evening he said to his mother, "Miss Leland has beautiful eyes."
> "My dear, she puts belladonna in them."[47]

Ultimately, John Sherman turns away from Margaret towards Mary
Carton, as in *Vivien and Time* Clarin turns away from Vivien towards
Asphodel. John explains to Mary, "Margaret glitters and glitters and
glitters, but she is not of my kind."[48] Yeats's letter of March 21, 1889, to
Katharine Tynan (whom William Murphy believes to be the model for
Mary Carton) takes a similar apologetic tone, not only about Laura,
but also about Maud Gonne:

> Who told you that I am "taken up with Miss Gonne"? I think she is very
> good-looking and that is all I think about her. What you say of her fondness
> for sensation is probably true. I sympathise with her love of the national idea
> rather than any secondary land movement, but care not much for the kind of
> Red Indian feathers in which she has trapped out that idea. We had some talk
> as to the possibility of getting my "Countess O'Shea" acted by amateurs in
> Dublin and she felt inclined to help, indeed suggested the attempt herself if I
> remember rightly. I hardly expect it will ever get outside the world of plans.
> As for the rest, she had a borrowed interest, reminding me of Laura Arm-
> strong without Laura's wild dash of half-insane genius. Laura is to me always
> a pleasant memory. She woke me from the metallic sleep of science and set
> me writing my first play.
> Do not mistake me, she is only as a myth and a symbol. Will you forgive
> me for having talked of her? She interests me far more than Miss Gonne does

46. *Ibid.*, p. 97.   47. *Ibid.*, p. 66.
48. *Ibid.*, p. 106.

and yet is only as a myth and a symbol. I heard from her about two years ago and am trying to find out where she is now in order to send her *Oisin.* "Time and the Witch Vivien" was written for her to act. The "Island of Statues" was begun with the same notion, though it soon grew beyond the scope of drawing-room acting. The part of the enchantress in both poems was written for her. She used to sign her letters Vivien.[49]

Clearly the fate of being supplanted, which had overtaken the enchantresses of *Vivien and Time,* of "The Island of Statues," and of *John Sherman,* had caught up with Laura Armstrong. Certain future poetic dramas would model their heroines after a new enchantress, or be dedicated to her, or even be written for her to act. Time's skill proved powerless to defeat Maud Gonne's reign in Yeats's poetry. She stands there without a shadow.

Yeats almost certainly got the name "Vivien" from Tennyson's "Merlin and Vivien," though Arnold in his "Tristram and Iseult" uses "Vivian." She was "Nimuë" in Tennyson's 1857 version, but in 1858 Burne-Jones suggested the change to "Vivien" when "he found that the poet in his idyll had modernised and altered the character while preserving the ancient name."[50] According to Lucy Allen Paton, "Niniane" is probably the original name of the Lady of the Lake in the romances, but there are many variants, and "Viviane" is found in *Merlin* (1528), II, cxxvi, cxxvii; *Vulgate Merlin,* throughout; and Paris, *Les Romans de la Table Ronde,* throughout.[51]

The name "Sir Clarin of Tadmor" may be Yeats's own invention, but "Clarin" is indeed listed in G. D. West's *An Index of Proper Names in French Arthurian Prose Romances.*[52] A "Clarin" is "Mordrain's godson" and "Castellan d'Evalachin" in the *Histoire de Grimaud.*[53] An-

49. *Letters,* pp. 116–18; cf. *CL1,* pp. 154–55.

50. *Burne-Jones,* p. 27.

51. Paton, p. 247.

52. G. D. West, *An Index of Proper Names in French Arthurian Prose Romances* (Toronto, Buffalo, London: University of Toronto Press, 1978), p. 81.

53. *Histoire de Grimaud,* ed. Eugène Hucher, in *Le Saint-Graal* (3 vols.; Paris: Le Mans, 1875–8), III, 593, 595, 598, 600.

other Clarin is a knight entitled le Noir whose castle is besieged by Karados in *Guiron le Courtois* and in *Les Prophecies de Merlin*.[54] Clarin is listed in Langlois, *Table des noms propres de toute nature compris dans les Chansons de Geste,* as appearing in *Rolant* and in *Anseis de Cartage*.[55] Yeats may have found the name in some contemporary retelling of a romance or chanson de geste.

"Tadmor" is the old name for Palmyra, 150 miles northeast of Damascus, an ancient city, very powerful until reduced by Aurelian in A.D. 272 after Zenobia's revolt against Rome. It remained wealthy through the period of the Crusades and into the fourteenth century. The ruins were known to the West in the eighteenth century and the inscriptions in the nineteenth. A great fiscal inscription was discovered by Prince Abamalek Lazarew in 1882, less than two years before the date given on the manuscript of *Vivien and Time*.[56]

"Asphodel" has, of course, been the immortal pale flower of the other world ever since Homer showed the shade of Achilles striding proudly along the meadows of Erebus.[57] Sabrina, in Milton's *Comus,* was, as part of her "quick immortal change" into "Goddess of the River" Severn, bathed "In nectar'd lavers strew'd with Asphodel" (lines 838–42). Pope, in his "Ode on St. Cecilia's Day," has Orpheus intercede with Proserpine "By those happy souls, who dwell / In yellow meads of Asphodel." Shelley's "Arethusa," in her new life after union with Alpheus, flows with him through "meadows of Asphodel." Tennyson's "Lotos-Eaters" enjoy in advance the rewards of the dead who "in Elysian valleys dwell, / Resting weary limbs at last on beds of Asphodel" (lines 170–71). It is hard, however, to think of a work prior

54. Roger Lathuillère, *Guiron le Courtois, Étude de la tradition manuscrit et analyse critique.* (Publications romanes et français 86; Genève, 1966), section 262; and *Les Prophécies de Merlin,* ed. from MS 593 in the Bibliothèque Municipale of Rennes by Lucy Allen Paton (The Modern Language Association of America Monograph Series I; 2 vols.; New York, 1926–27, reprinted 1966), 394, 400.

55. Ernest Langlois, *Table des noms propres de toute nature compris dans les Chansons de Geste* (Paris, 1904), lists "Clarin" as appearing in *Rolant,* ed. Stengel, p. 63, 504b, and in *Anseis de Cartage* 5684.

56. "Palmyra," *Encyclopaedia Britannica* (1962), XVII, 163.

57. *Odyssey,* XI, 539. See also XXIV, 1.

to Yeats's *Vivien and Time* in which "Asphodel" is used as the name of a character.

The connection between the play *Vivien and Time* and the published playlet *Time and the Witch Vivien* is obvious, and not only from the close correspondence between their titles, characters, and themes. Several pages are separated from the manuscript of the play in act II, scene 2. These torn out pages contain one of the most important episodes of the plot, the death of Vivien.[58] Her death is the subject of the published playlet. *Time and the Witch Vivien* is a revision of the pages torn from *Vivien and Time*. But before we note the extent and nature of that revision we should take a look at the whole play.

Here is the plot into which act II, scene 2, and *Time and the Witch Vivien* both fit. Queen Vivien loves Clarin the poet, but her love changes to hatred when she realises he is indifferent to her and loves Countess Asphodel. Vivien asks her magic mirror if she is the fairest (Yeats borrows heavily from the story of Snow White), but the mirror replies that Asphodel is fairer. Vivien orders her soldiers to slay Asphodel. She then puts a spell on Clarin so that he will wander, a prey to spirits of unrest until he dies. Then she learns that the soldiers had pity on Asphodel and that she is not dead but is hiding in a cottage in the desert. Vivien disguises herself as a gypsy (again like the queen in "Snow White") and goes to the cottage. She tricks Asphodel into smelling a magic flower. Asphodel falls to the ground. She is not dead, however, but will lie in a trance as long as Clarin lives, then rise and be driven by the same spirits of unrest until she dies.

Clarin learns of Asphodel's enchantment and gathers a fairy army to avenge himself on Vivien. Next comes the crucial scene, in which Time kills Vivien. Then Clarin comes in, too late to take his own vengeance. When he discovers Vivien lying apparently dead on stage, he says, "That mighty shade [i.e., Time] has been before." He then remembers that the grey pedlar foretold that he (Clarin) would kill the queen and die soon afterward: he "would meet / A great queen whom

---

58. Ellmann, *Man and Masks*, p. 35, quotes the opening passage of act II, scene 2.

I'd slay with mine own hand / O scarce survive her for a minute's space" [SB23(3pp190–91)]. As it is Time, not Clarin, who kills Vivien in both the published and the unpublished scene, the prophecy does not exactly correspond to the plot. Either this is an oversight of the author, which seems unlikely, or there is a mistake in the manuscript. Perhaps "O" was meant to be "Or"—Clarin would slay Vivien "O[r] scarce survive her. . . ." The prophecy would then be accurate, as Clarin dies at the end of the scene. Asphodel returns to consciousness in the desert and begins her restless wanderings.

Though revised to stand by itself, *Time and the Witch Vivien* retains most of the links with the total play that the original scene had. In the published version, Vivien first looks at her reflection in the fountain, admiring both her own beauty and her skill as an enchantress. Time, an old pedlar with a bag, scythe, and hour-glass, enters. Vivien plays at dice with him, trying to win his hour-glass. She loses, and then plays chess for triumph in her many plots. She loses again; defeat is death, and as the scene ends, she dies. In the unpublished play, Vivien is found before, not a fountain, but a magic mirror which is lit by a taper. Some of the imagery is different, many of the lines are less polished than in the published playlet, and Vivien's death is less climactic (since it is not the end). Otherwise the action is the same, and the linkages with the rest of *Vivien and Time* are the same. Time is a central character in both plays.

In *Vivien and Time,* although Time appears only in act II, scene 2, he has an importance out of all proportion to the brevity of his appearance. Time is listed fourth in the "Dramatis Personae." He is mentioned often as the grey pedlar, and every reference to him is an ominous foreshadowing of Vivien's fate. The "Dedication" poem tells the subject matter of the play: "a goblin queen, and a goblin dream / And a pedlar grey" [SB23(3p163)].

In act I, scene 1, Clarin reads a ballad "Bought from a pedlar with a bag and scythe" [SB23(3p167)]. The ballad is about Time—a hoary old man who holds an hour-glass. The ballad echoes the plot: "In life love hath ended / Old Time hath descended . . ." [SB23(3p168)]. Asphodel rebukes Clarin for his choice of a ballad, for she says, "Our only enemy is withered time" [SB23(3p168)]. Vivien, in love with Clarin, ceases to love him and plots against him. Figuratively speaking, she is "playing against Time" to succeed in her many plots before Time catches up with her. At her birth the augurs foretold that "lame-footed fate would o'ertake me / When the tide of my strength was full." She is always trying to keep one step ahead of the prophecy and hopes to "mock the dread presage that came / From the hollow cave of the gray dreamers" [SB23(3p177)]. Time, the pedlar, is mentioned again—the Page sees him pursuing Clarin on his restless wanderings, a sign that Clarin's death is near. Thus the scene is set for Time's actual appearance as a character in act II, scene 2.

Not only the theme of Time but also allusions to Merlin connect the published scene with the full-length play. In the latter, the magic mirror swears by "dread Merlin's self" that Asphodel is fairest [SB23(3p170)]. Vivien finds the spell of unrest in Merlin's book, a huge magic book which grows fiery hot when the spell is read aloud. Although she uses his magic, Vivien is scornful of Merlin. When the Page asks about the spell, Vivien calls it "the wild poem of a wild old man" [SB23(3p175)], a strange foreshadowing of the "wild old wicked man"[59] who is a persona in Yeats's late poetry. Although Vivien intends to deceive the Page by convincing him that the spell is harmless, she deceives herself also. She believes that she herself is greater than Merlin. The allusions to Merlin in the complete play form a context for Vivien's dialogue with Time. In both the published scene and the manuscript she compares Time to Merlin: "Yet whiter beard have you than Merlin had." She reminds him of the story of Merlin and Nimuë: "young girls' wits are better / Than old men's any day, as Merlin found."[60] Vivien must be first in everything. Looking into the fountain, she says "Where moves there any beautiful as I, / Save . . . / My image yonder? . . . / . . . / No; nor is there one / Of equal power in spells and secret rites."[61] She, like Circe, is an enchantress; like Circe, she is finally

59. *Variorum Poems*, p. 587; cf. *Poems*, p. 310.
60. *Ibid.*, p. 721; cf. *Poems*, p. 519.
61. *Ibid.*, p. 720; cf. *Poems*, p. 517.

overcome by a wily old man. In act II, scene 2, Vivien claims that she is greater than Circe:

> *Vivien.* Great Circe, Circe, now thy fame is fled
>   Since mine was born that shall have wing until . . .
> *Mirror.* Until the fountains on the steeps have rest
>   And 'fore the sun the flowers' lips are closed.
> *Vivien.* And that is forever.

[SB23(3p175)]

She believes that the mirror foretells her triumph, but in the end a bitter frost in fairyland freezes the fountains and flowers, and the mirror's prophecy is fulfilled as she dies.

In act II, scene 2, the two main themes of the play, the pride and power of the enchantress and the idea of Time, are brought forward in a dramatic confrontation between the two great antagonists. The main point of the play is that power, both temporal and magical, must yield to Time, and this is the scene in which that happens.

The theme of peace is an important link between *Time and the Witch Vivien* and *Vivien and Time.* In the published scene, peace is mentioned twice. In Time's bag are "mellow thoughts / Where dwell the minds of old men having peace. . . ." Vivien says to Time, "I do not need your scythe. May that bring peace / To those your 'mellow' wares have wearied out."[62] Vivien equates peace with the scythe, or death. In the unpublished play, act I, scene 4, Vivien, disguised as the gypsy, tells Asphodel's fortune. She looks at her palm and says, "The line of peace is wondrous deep and long: / . . . / Most instant and most deep the peace shall be" [SB23(3p185)]. Asphodel falls into a peaceful magic sleep. But it is not Vivien's wish to give her peace forever. Peaceful sleep or death is not her idea of revenge: "Die not, for that were but a weak revenge" [SB23(3p185)]. Vivien's spells make the lovers wander until death, drawn on by spirits of unrest:

> Him whom I name
> Wrap him like flame

62. *Ibid.,* p. 722; cf. *Poems,* p. 518.

Ye souls of unrest
. . . .
Arise, arise
   Rest on his eyes
   See that they weep
   See they ne'er sleep
Till he dies, dies. . . .
     [SB23(3pp173–74)]

So runs the spell in Merlin's book. At Clarin's death Asphodel wakes, her "whole soul bitterly athirst for peace" [SB23(3p192)], but she is now doomed to wander in her turn. As the play ends, two voices lead her on, promising peace:

First voice. Peace in the end you shall have
   And your o'erworn heart shall have rest
Second voice. When the yew and the cypress wave
   In the cold earth over your breast.
     [SB23(3p194)]

Having pointed to the linkages between the published *Time and the Witch Vivien* and other scenes of the unpublished parent play, we now mention, though briefly, because they will be evident to the reader's eyes, the revisions, their nature and extent. The scene torn from the manuscript was altered to make it suitable for publication on its own. References to specific settings, characters, or incidents that would have been unintelligible to readers of the single scene were removed. In the original scene, for example, Vivien's opening speech contains a reference to the earlier prophecy by the magic mirror that Vivien cannot die until the fountains cease to flow, as well as a reference to Asphodel that was meant to show the passage of time between acts I and II: "The lily-wristed Asphodel has slept / These summers three" [SB22(3p65)]. These references are removed and a new opening speech written which concentrates on Vivien's pride in her beauty and skill rather than on her lust for power.

However, the end to Vivien's soliloquy is almost the same in the two versions. In *Vivien and Time*

Some great spirit passes in the desert.
Turning it enters by the city gate.
. . . .
Now 't'as passed the sentries; 'tis at the door;
It is here.

[SB22(3p66)]

In *Time and the Witch Vivien*

Some fierce magician flies or walks
Beyond the gateway—by the sentries now. . . .

In *Time and the Witch Vivien* the scene takes place in Vivien's magic room. The description of the room, "*A marble-flagged, pillared room. Magical instruments in one corner. A fountain in the center,*" is different from that in the unpublished play. There, in act II, scene 2, the setting is described as "*Room in the castle as in Scenes 2 and 3 of Act I. Time night, a pale taper burning before the Magic Mirror*" [SB22(3p65)]. The description of Vivien's room in act I, scene 2, is "*A room in the castle. Magic mirror to R. surmounted by a skull in the background. A subdued light over everything*" [SB23(3p170)]. In the published version Yeats has emphasized the fountain not the magic mirror. Vivien admires her reflection in the water just as she looks at herself in the mirror in act I, scene 2. Perhaps Yeats stressed the fountain setting because he felt the mirror was too obviously borrowed from "Snow White," though Vivien uses the fountain for almost the same purpose: "Where moves there any beautiful as I . . . ?"[63] she asks the fountain. In the unpublished version the mirror laughs at the deaths of Vivien and Clarin successively as the scene closes.

The published scene ends abruptly. Time wins the chess game and says

Time.   Mate thus.
Vivien.   Already?
     Chance hath a skill!   [*She dies.*][64]

63. *Ibid.,* p. 720; cf. *Poems,* p. 517.
64. *Ibid.,* p. 722; cf. *Poems,* p. 520.

In the manuscript the end of the game is marked by Time's laugh and the fall of the curtain. When the curtain rises, Vivien is left alone to die at her leisure, a less effective end, but, after all, the unpublished play does not end there.

And not all is gain in Yeats's revisions. The swan image, for instance, which is so important elsewhere in *Vivien and Time* and was to become one of the most striking images in Yeats's later work, appears only in the manuscript:

> *Queen.* The wild swan has sunk from the blinding blue.
>   No more I trouble with my wayward life.
>   Old dreaming night, O hungry oblivion,
>   O sister death, I take thy hand, I come. (*She dies.*)
>   [SB22(3p70)]

In the following pages *Vivien and Time* is printed entire, with the six separated pages containing most of act II, scene 2, restored. Those restored pages are printed together with *Time and the Witch Vivien* so that the reader may make comparisons.

A Note on the Transcription of *Vivien and Time*

See "A Description of the Manuscript of *Vivien and Time*," pages 267–68 of this book, for National Library of Ireland Ms. 30,357, a maroon notebook bearing the inscription "Viven [*sic*] and Time / a dramatic poem / January the 8th / 1884," and for Ms. 30,460, the six pages that have been restored.

What follows here is not a diplomatic transcription but a reading text. Styling of act, scene, and speaker indications as well as of stage directions has been silently normalized. Cancelled words and letters are not reproduced. Yeats's revisions and additions are silently inserted. Compound or hyphenated words that Yeats gives as two separate words have been silently joined. Spelling and capitalization are normalized. Punctuation has not usually been supplied to the lyrics, except for end stops. Elsewhere the editors have made a more liberal use than did Yeats of punctuation, including dashes, semicolons, and colons. An attempt has been made to preserve both possible meanings of ambiguous expressions. Where an ambiguous passage is difficult to read, clarifying punctuation and spelling have been supplied, but the original text is given in the notes, sometimes with an alternative interpretation. Where an ambiguous passage is readily readable, however, Yeats's punctuation (as well as his ambiguity) is preserved.

Material in square brackets has been added by the editors. Quotations from Yeats's text are italicized in the textual notes. Each page of Yeats's manuscript is identified by its Stony Brook number. The citation is placed at the start of each page. The styling of the stage directions in the manuscript of *Vivien and Time* is highly inconsistent. We have placed them all in round brackets and, for ease of comparison, done the same with *Time and the Witch Vivien*.

The text of *Vivien and Time* that follows was transcribed and edited by Rosalind Clark.

In the notes words in italics are spelled and punctuated as in Yeats's manuscripts.

Vivien and Time

BY W. B. YEATS

Dramatis Personae

Vivien, The Goblin Queen	Time
Asphodel	Page
Clarin	

Dedication

I've built a dreaming palace
   With stones from out the old
And singing days, within their graves
   Now lying calm and cold.

Of the dreamland marble
   Are all the silent walls
That grimly stand, a phantom band,
   About the phantom halls.

There among the pillars
   Are many statues fair
Made of the dreamland marble
   Cut by the dreamer's[1] care,

And there I see a statue
   Among the maids of old
On either hand, a goodly band,
   So calmly wise and cold.

On one side is Miranda
   For virgin beauty famed

1. *dreamers*

Nearby is Penthea
   As she was fitly named—

O most fair and sad was she
   Of the fairest saddest pages
Of all the burning dramas
   Of the great Eliza's sages.

But there this image is
   Mid fair and pearly light
From the dreamland marble
   Like unto hawthorn white.

It is a pale elf statue
   With sweet Titania's grace
But black's the hair, as though it were
   The peeping pansy's face.

The eyes as the wine are bright   [SB23(3p165)]
   In Circe's charmèd[2] cup:
O dark are the eyes as the morning skies[3]
   When scarce the day is up.

And here I down before it
   Cast a wayward play
Of a goblin queen, and a goblin dream
   And a pedlar grey,

Of a speaking magic mirror
   Of a sad and heartless queen
Of young Asphodel and Clarin
   With his harp of lyric teen.

W. B. Yeats, January the 8th, 1884

---

2. *charmèd* By mistake Yeats used the acute instead of the grave accent, "charmèd," to give syllabic value to "-ed."

3. *sky s* Yeats may have meant "sky's," but "skies" seems more likely.

Act I

[SB23(3p166)]

SCENE I

A laurel grove. Time night. Clarin, zittar in hand, sitting on a large oak chair over the back of which hangs a leopard skin.

Clarin. I find no solitude by wood or stream
    For a radiant shadow haunting me.
    Hear you the southwest wind in the branches?
    It is calling, 'Asphodel, O Asphodel!'

(Enter to R. Vivien and Asphodel, behind, arm-in-arm, the first with a mask in her hand, the second masked.)

    The enamoured nightingale hath stolen
    For a chorus thy name, my disturber,[4]
    And the laurel fondles the sound in joy.
    What other note hath the sounding zittar?
Vivien. A most wondrous! Say, Sir Melancholy,
    Of the immortals who is favoured so?
    No lower than great Dian' Clarin looks:
    Surely it is the moon, no lower thing.
Clarin. Being supremely wise you've rightly guessed:
    I spoke but of the moon personified, [SB23(3p167)]
    As was the fashion in those ancient days
    When sea-built Troy the duchess Helen knew.
    But thou, being learned 'fore all ladies,
    Know all this.
Vivien.   I am weary with the dance.
    Have you any pleasant tale to tell
    Of pale Helen or of Menelaus,
    The stern old duke, or Paris, for I'm tired.
Clarin. Why, what wonder of the song-worn dead
    Have not the phantoms taught thee, goblin queen?

    4. *For a chorus, thy name my disturber*

But here's a ballad bought this very hour
From a lean pedlar with a bag and scythe.
Vivien (troubled). Bought from a pedlar with a bag and scythe?[5]
Clarin (reads).

Two shining drops of gracious dew
Two sprigs of rosemary and rue
　　Two loving friends there are
　　None fairer in story   [SB23(3p168)]
　　But yonder is hoary
Time on a whirling star
　　Falling are the golden sands
　　In the glass in his old, old hands.

The rosemary dead and the rue
In the monsoon burnt and the dew
Faints 'mid sunbeams that ban it
　　In life love hath ended
　　Old Time hath descended
From his far-circling planet.[6]
　　Falling are the silent sands
　　In the glass in his old old hands—

Asphodel. A most uncourtier song, for know you not
　　Our only enemy is withered time
　　Here in the Castle Joyeuse, Sir Clarin?
Clarin. If mirth you need, why sought you the laurel?
　　The flood tide of joy is full in the hall.
Vivien. If sang you of us, well say who's fairer
　　Of us who care not for the shadow'd[7] dead   [SB23(3p169)]
　　Of empty story—so between us judge.
　　　　(Asphodel unmasks.)
Asphodel. Gladly from such a contest I'd withdraw.
Clarin. Always the queen in her own right hath claim
　　Of victory *(He recognises Asphodel.)* Yet troubadours always

5. *scythe*   6. *planet* (no end stop)
7. *shadow'ed*

Are free to judge in wilful wise, so then
　My verdict is for Countess Asphodel.
Asphodel. O Sir Clarin—
Clarin.　　　　　　　Hear you! Again they dance!
　So, Countess Asphodel, a measure, pray!
Vivien. The sad moon, Sir Clarin hath deserted.
　That wan mistress shall die of jealousy.
　　(Exeunt to R. Clarin and Asphodel.)
　Slighted *(she sits in Clarin's chair)* in person and in royalty!
　The woman and the queen both are slighted,
　Doubly dangerous to those who slight them.　　　[SB23(3p170)]

SCENE 2

*A room in the castle. Magic mirror to R. surmounted by a skull in the
background. A subdued light over everything. Enter to R. Vivien, the mask
being still in her hand. She stands before the glass.*

Vivien. O glass, glass, glass, I come to ask of thee
　If I am not the fairest in the land,
　For, glass, I have been most sadly slighted.
Mirror.
　In each house I've an eye
　To be damned and die
　A thousand shapes have I,
　But by dread Merlin's self I swear
　Never have I aught as fair
　As Asphodel the Countess seen.
　O no not Dido that sad queen
　Had so majestical a mien.
Vivien. O glass, you are a sorry comforter;　　　[SB23(3p171)]
　But ne'er to brook a rival I have sworn.
　　(Writes on her tablets.)
　And now I sign her death warrant.
　When the rosemary's dead the rue shall live
　So much more in the sun. O Asphodel,

It is not well to be so fair! Clarin's so loved
By all the nobles that[8] him I cannot touch,
Unless with owlish wisdom in the dark.
> *(A Page appears at the door to R., carefully enclosing something in both his hands.)*

Page. Look, look you here!

Vivien.   What have you there, my child?
> *(The Page shows a large tropical butterfly. The Queen lays it on the table.)*

'Tis dead—you should not slay these sunny things;
They say they're souls of long dead fairies.
> *(The Page begins to cry.)*

Do not cry, my child, they're dying always—
The cold nights slay and all birds slay them.
What matter if you or I slay also?
> *(Puts the child sitting on the table, close by Merlin's book.)*

Page. Why is that book so large?   [SB23(3p172)]
> *(Tries to open it.)*

Vivien.   Can you read, child?

Page. Yes, quite fast, for Asphodel has taught me.
> *(The Queen opens the book.)*

Vivien. Read then.

Page *(reads with difficulty).*
> Him whom I name
> Wrap him like flame
> Souls of unrest

Vivien. Stay, stay—*(aside)* these charms of Merlin's have most might
When said by sinless children's lips;
But I must make him repeat Clarin's name.
> *(Aloud.)* My most dear child, whom love you best in the world?

Page. Why, Asphodel, of course. Don't you?

Vivien.   Whom next?

---

8. *that* The word seems accidentally blotted rather than cancelled.

Page. Clarin, for he showed me a squirrel's[9] dray.
Vivien. What's his full name—Clarin's full name? Speak loud!

[SB23(3p173)]

Page. Sir Clarin of Tadmor, as all men know.
Vivien. Now read.
Page (reads. As he reads the Queen grows more and more excited).
    Him whom I name
    Wrap him like flame
    Ye souls of unrest
    Who dwell on the crest
        Of the wind-worn waves—
        —In emerald caves
        Where the salt foam raves
    O cease ye to rest—
    See, a blue flame played on the book just then! O let me stop!
Vivien. No, you but dream. Read, read!
Page (reads).
    Him whom I name
    Wrap him like flame
    Arise, arise   [SB23(3p174)]
        Rest on his eyes
        See that they weep
        See they ne'er sleep
    Till he dies, dies
        Let his body burn
    Till his ash lies
        In his mural urn
    Let his whole brain melt
    As a cloudy belt
    Till he dies, dies—
    The book is fiery hot.
Vivien.   Read, read!

---

9. *squirrels* A "dray" is a squirrel's nest.

Page (reads in fear).
   Him whom I name   [SB23(3p175)]
   Wrap him like flame
   Things that were fair
   As Eve's bright hair
     To Adam of old
     Grow formless and cold
   To his weary stare.
   That is all. O what is it, your Majesty?
Vivien. 'Tis the wild poem of a wild old man.
   Here, bear these tablets to the seneschal.
   Begone, I'd be alone.
     (Exit Page to R. She takes the butterflies and says excitedly)
   O butterflies, butterflies ruined by a child,
   What did the laughter of thy wings for thee?
   What did the people's favour do for thee,
   Or all the fancies of thine idle harp?
   Beneath some evil star ye twain were born.
   Great Circe, Circe, now thy fame is fled
   Since mine was born that shall have wing until . . .
Mirror. Until the fountains on the steeps have rest
   And 'fore the sun the flowers' lips are closed.
Vivien. And that is forever.   [SB23(3p176)]

SCENE 3

A room in the castle. The queen Vivien, arranging flowers in a large antique vase, thus begins to speak:

[*Vivien.*] I triumph, for Asphodel is slain
   Where the shadowy pool in the desert
   Leers upon heaven like a demon's[10] eye,
   Where again the echoes by this are still

---

10. *deamons* It is more likely that Yeats meant the eye of a "demon" or devil than the eye of a "daemon" in the sense of a god, attendant spirit, or the genius of a place.

So little of noise does a murder make.
I think she now wanders a whimp'ring ghost.

     *   *   *

Men saw in the heaven when I was born
When a wild swan passed in the blinding blue
Great was the might and the mirth of his wings
Down 'fore their feet fell he dead in the way.
Then wan-faced augured the gray sign-tellers
That my life should have might like that wild wing   [SB23(3p177)]
That had for a soul the powers of night
For 'twas no common bird, those old men said,
But that lame-footed fate would o'ertake me
When the tide of my strength was full.
So evil augured the grey sign-tellers;
But Clarin whom alone I feared of men
Has journeyed forth to find new lands of woe,
Lands which the wild soul of his zittar e'en
That was 'fore all sage things in sorrow versed
Knew not even in its tuneful heart.
Sir Clarin the wild singer of wild songs
I had a fancy for him once of old
Till his indifference—*(to a flower)* lie there
Among thy sister mummers of the year
O pale Narcissus—till his indifference
Roused hate. So now he's gone and I grown bold
May mock the dread presage that came
From the hollow cave of the gray dreamers.

> *(Enter Page, who carefully avoids the great book of Merlin that lies on
> a side table. In one hand he has a letter, in the other a mourning
> wreath.)*

Page. A letter, your Majesty.
Vivien.   Ho, killer   [SB23(3p179)]
    Of butterflies! *(Takes the letter.)* What news have you today?
    *(She takes flowers from the vase and begins arranging them in his
    dress.)*

Page. Last week when I was walking down the path
    Having just been here I met Sir Clarin.
    His eyes were wild and he grasped at the air
    As though he too were chasing butterflies.
    He muttered to himself and saw me not
    Though I called and threw my cap at him.
    A world-worn pedlar with a bag and scythe
    Trod close behind. *(The queen shivers.)* Poor Clarin also dies.
Vivien. He is a strange man and has strange fancies.
    (Sees wreath.)
    That wreath—
Page. 'Tis of some snowy blossoms made
    That for tears stand or for some tearful thing.
    So read my sister from a little book,
    Weaving this wreath that I go now to hang
    Upon the column by the river's marge
    That is for memory of Asphodel.
    'Twas very kind of you to build it there—   [SB23(3p178)]
    Bright are the waters and golden their tongue
    And there the tufted sedge is pendulous.
Vivien. Pay honour to the dead always, my child.
    (Opens the letter, starts, and mutters excitedly.)
    Not dead! What! has the deep and hungry pool
    Ungorged its prey? What! Are the dead uncharneled?
    (She continues to read. Starts and drops it.)
    As the law is, O traitors, shall ye die,
    False soldiers and still falser seneschal!
    She lives and through the desert wanders safe.
    To one, she resembled his own dead child,
    To one old man, one whom in youth he knew
    And danced with on some old world village green,
    That growing weak they could not slay this child.
    Am I not queen? And live they not but by my breath?
Page. Do not so grieve for Asphodel that's dead;
    My mother says she's better off above

Amongst the merry saints than here on earth.
Vivien. 'Twas not for her I grieve. What, do you think
  The whole world pivots round dead Asphodel? [SB23(3p181)]
    (Turns to him.)
  Some of my subjects must die by the law
  And like Rachel I weep for my children.
  —Ha, ha, I have a thought: she shall not live!
  The wild swan soars!

SCENE 4

Before a cottage in the desert. Enter to R. Clarin. Through the cottage door Asphodel is seen sitting spinning, her back turned.

Clarin. By day and night crying aloud her name
  On hills and in the sombre forest
  Where shuddereth eternal night I seek
  Where pensive streamlets muse forever
  Like children in a dream so still they are
  Ever I follow the flying shadow
  But yet it flies and I must seek, still seek.
  Yonder it is on the hillside glowing
  While I live I follow without ceasing.
  I come, I come, shadow of Asphodel!
    (Exit to L. Asphodel turns round and says) [SB23(3p180)]
[*Asphodel.*] Did someone cry my name? No, I had dozed.
    (Turns back to her wheel. Enter Gypsy.) [SB23(3p181)]
Gypsy (singing on a guitar). [SB23(3p182)]
  O an evil thing
    I suffered of you
  Has withered my heart
    Right unto the core

  Spirits of doom
    Plagues of a feather
  Trooping as one
    Gather together

My voice sinks down
  To the country lone
Where each one sits
  On a blood-red throne

My voice sank down
  And each one started
Up on his throne
  And earthward darted.

(Asphodel comes slowly to the door while she is singing.) [SB23(3p175)]
Asphodel. Have you any news of the world, gypsy?
Gypsy (not seeing her). What! Claim I not most strict obedience
  From noble and from beggar all alike?
  Yet these dead dogs in impudence[11]
  Waked proud and spoke of mercy to the queen!
  But now their wrinkled heads can beg it from
  The sombre crows upon the castle gate.
Asphodel. My poor woman, some grief is burning thee.
  I caught not thy words but they seem troubled.
Gypsy. Once in dead of night two genii fought,
  A good one and an evil, for my soul.
  The genie of evil slew the other,
  And therefore I mutter, being possessed.
Asphodel. O pray to the good saints! Their love is great.
  (She sits beside her.)   [SB23(3p184)]
Gypsy. No, the angel of evil would kill me.
  He's by me now, standing invisible.
Asphodel. To holy Mary I will pray for thee.
  But come within, you're weary of travel,
  And we'll exchange stories with each other.
  I'm hiding from a queen who seeks my life.
  Yes, I too have known sorrow, so come in.

11. *imputence* Yeats probably means "impudence" rather than "impotence" or "impatience."

(The Gypsy stands up.)
Gypsy *(seeing a horseshoe that [hangs] over the door).*
  I may not go in; I may not linger.
  Close in the desert my tribe is waiting.
  I sat but by your door to rest this form
  That is a weary weed of womanhood,
  A frail wreck of its beauty and old strength.
  But 'fore I go, of me take this flower
  I give in gratitude for gracious words.
Asphodel. O one of autumn's passionate children,
  When scarcely tuned is the wild harp of spring!   [SB23(3p185)]
  Stand back, stand back—I fear thee!
    (She steps back. The Gypsy advances.)
Gypsy.   We gypsies,
  As you know, do deal with things above mankind.
  But let me tell thy fortune, holy maid.
    (She takes her hand. Asphodel tries to draw it away.)
  The line of peace is wondrous deep and long:
  Ne'er saw I such a line on mortal hand.
  Most instant and most deep the peace shall be.
  Smell the flower.
Asphodel.   I seem to know your voice.
    (She smells the flower and falls back in a trance.)
Gypsy. Die not, for that were but a weak revenge,
  But till thy lover Clarin dies, sleep, sleep;
  And when he breathes his last live breath on earth—
  Be it today, tomorrow, or the next,
  Next year or in a thousand thousand years,
  At morning or at noontide or at night—
  Awake and let thy soul see only then
  (Born of the o'erworn embers of thy sleep)   [SB23(3p186)]
  A deadly phantom that shall lead thee on
  From land to land as Clarin wanders now,
  Haggard-eyed with his dear phantom flying.
  But tender it is as the winged dew

Or as the lady Hope herself, by thine.
So doth the fever pass like racket ball
From you to him, from him to you.
                    Poor fools!
Poor racket ball in Vivien's driving bat!
   (Throws off her disguise and stands revealed the Queen.)
Vivien. Shine, sun, and blow, ye summer winds,
   Sweet vagrants, for I'm glad with triumphing.
      (Sings)
            Every flower bows his head
            Passion worn and passion fed
         Green and gold and lustrous yellow
            Glutted with excess of sun
            All the flowers quire as one
         Now where is the wild swan's fellow?
      (Exit.)

Act II   [SB23(3p188)]

SCENE I

Clarin comes in supporting his failing steps on a boar[12] *spear, his hair gray before its time with grief.*

Clarin. Conscience, a little longer be thou still!
   Write not upon thy books O yet, recorder;
   O write not yet Clarin hath slain his queen!
   My oath of fealty is spotless still.
   Planets, you pale mariners of night,
   Have pity on a fellow wanderer!
   Look all as ye were wont of old to look
   When oft I wooed you in this laurel copse.
   O disturb me not with your wan faces!
   Why seem ye all, pale ones, so lustreless?

---

12. *boar* An alternative reading is "bone."

I kiss my hand to you as heretofore:
Be fair to me as once ye were of old.
Wanderers, I tell you I am guiltless
Of great Vivien's blood!
                  My meddling harp,
Why won[13] thou from the fairy king his forces
That shall in viewless combat on this night
O'erthrow the goblin servants of the queen   [SB23(3p189)]
That I may slay her and my fame in one
And be a knight for endless time disgraced
For a broken oath? No more shall bards
Sing of the deeds of Clarin, for a crime
Shall quench his fame tonight, rather my soul.
Fairies, I cannot slay her now. A voice!
I think a voice said 'Asphodel!' just then.
   (He listens.)
Young Asphodel in thy magic trance
Hid in a secret cavern by the sea,
For her, for her—Oh hear, ye fairy things—
We storm the castle at the dawn of day.
   (Exit.)

[Here follow the six pages restored to manuscript NLI 30,357 from manuscript NLI 30,460. They are printed together with *Time and the Witch Vivien* for comparison.]

---

13. *wone* Probably Yeats's spelling of "won," not "wone" meaning "moan."

[Manuscript NLI 30,460, from *Vivien and Time*]

Act II   [SB22(3p65)]

SCENE 2

Room in the castle as in Scenes 2 and 3 of Act I. Time night, a pale taper
burning before the Magic Mirror. Queen alone.

Queen. The lily wristed Asphodel has slept
    These summers three, and I have quaffed full deep
    The glorious cup of magic, till in drinking
    That dread forbidden wine that once I dreamt
    And read of only my soul grows
    The image of the mighty. viewless ones.
    No 'tis changed, sweet metamorphosis,
    To one great throbbing string that throbbing calls
    Only one wild word, one wild word,
    Power, power, outspeeding envy self,
    The only drink for my unceasing thirst.
    O word, as the song of the sea to streams
    Art thou to me; in thee I'd lose myself,
    Outgrowing human sense and human thought.
    As I have pity for the fleeting race
    Of men who bend to every sudden blast
    Of joy or grief or scorn, and as they bend
    Say it is human thus to bend, well then   [SB22(3p66)]
    So much less human I who shall not bend
    Until upon the steeps the fountains rest
    And 'fore the sun the flowers' lips are closed.
        (She starts and trembles.)
    Some great spirit passes in the desert.
    Turning it enters by the city gate.
    I felt its influence through all my veins.
    'Tis swifter far than swiftest dream.
    Now 't'as passed the sentries; 'tis at the door;
    It is here.

[*Time and the Witch Vivien* from *The Wanderings of Oisin and Other Poems*, 1889 (*Variorum Poems*, pp. 720–22; cf. *Poems*, pp. 517–20)]

Time and the Witch Vivien

A marble-flagged, pillared room. Magical instruments in one corner. A fountain in the centre.

Vivien (looking down into the fountain). Where moves there any beauti-
    ful as I,
  Save, with the little golden greedy carp,
  Gold unto gold, a gleam in its long hair,
  My image yonder? *(Spreading her hand over the water.)* Ah, my
    beautiful,
  What roseate fingers! *(Turning away.)* No; nor is there one
  Of equal power in spells and secret rites.
  The proudest or most coy of spirit things,
  Hide where he will, in wave or wrinkled moon,
  Obeys.
           Some fierce magician flies or walks
  Beyond the gateway—by the sentries now—
  Close and more close—I feel him in my heart—
  Some great one. No; I hear the wavering steps
  Without there of a little, light old man;
  I dreamt some great one. *(Catching sight of her image, and spreading
    her hand over the water.)*
               Ah, my beautiful,
What roseate fingers!

(Enter an old pedlar with a black bag, a scythe, and an hour-glass.)
    No check are bolted doors for thee,
Thou wrinkled squanderer of human gold.
 (She laughs.)
But come, come sit thee down. I'd buy of thee.
Come, father.
Father Time. No, I never sit nor rest.
Queen. Well then, to business. What is in thy bag?
 *(Putting the bag and hour-glass on the table. Time rests on his
 scythe.)*
Father Time. Gray hairs and crutches for old age hath Time

            [SB22(3p67)]

And stately mansions of mild mellow thoughts
Where dwell the souls of old men having peace.
Such are the ripe fruits Time hath in his bag.
Queen (with a motion of disgust).
 No. None of these for me, old father wrinkles.
Time. Someday mayhap you'll buy.
Queen.   Never.
Time.   Never? *(Laughs.)*
Queen. You laugh. Why?
Time.   Best laugh is last. I laugh last always.
Queen (lays the glass on one side. Time puts it up again).
 Your scythe I do not need. Let that bring peace
 Unto those men your "mellow" gifts have wearied.
 I'd buy your glass.   [SB22(3p68)]
Time.   And that I will not sell.
 Without my glass I'd be a sorry clown.
Queen. Yet whiter beard have you than Merlin had.
Time. For slumber 'neath an oak I have no taste.
Queen. How old are you?
 (She lays the glass down.)
Time.   Before thy granddame Eve I was.
 (Puts standing upright again.)
Queen. Oh I am weary of that foolish tale.

(*Enter* Time *as an old pedlar, with a scythe, an hour-glass, and a black bag.*)

                    Ha, ha! ha, ha, ha!
The wrinkled squanderer of human wealth.
  Come here. Be seated now; I'd buy of you.
  Come, father.
Time.   Lady, I nor rest nor sit.
Vivien. Well then, to business; what is in your bag?
Time (*putting the bag and hour-glass on the table and resting on his scythe*). Grey hairs and crutches, crutches and grey hairs,
  Mansions of memories and mellow thoughts
  Where dwell the minds of old men having peace,
  And—
Vivien. No; I'll none of these, old Father Wrinkles.
Time. Some day you'll buy them, maybe.
Vivien.   Never!
Time (*laughing*).   Never?
Vivien. Why do you laugh?
Time.   I laugh the last always.
    (*She lays the hour-glass on one side. Time rights it again.*)
Vivien. I do not need your scythe. May that bring peace
  To those your 'mellow' wares have wearied out.
  I'd buy your glass.
Time.   My glass I will not sell.
  Without my glass I'd be a sorry clown.
Vivien. Yet whiter beard have you than Merlin had.
Time. No taste have I for slumber 'neath an oak.
Vivien. When were you born?
Time.   Before your grandam Eve.
Vivien. Oh, I am weary of that foolish tale.

'Tis said 'mong men you are a gambler, Time.
So come, I'd play thee for thine hour-glass.
I like such things about me; they are food
For antiquarian meditation *(fetches the dice)*.
Time. The best of three shall win the glass.
Queen (throws). Three-six.
Time (throws). Four-six.   [SB22(3p69)]
Queen. By one point thou art first *(throws)*. Five-six. Ha.
Time *(throws)*. Six-six.
Queen. O I have lost. They're loaded dice as always
    Are the dice time playeth with, but father,
    Another chance. I'd play thee at the chess;
    For a young girl's wits against a bent old man's
    Are mated any day as Merlin found.
      (Wheels over the chess men.)
    The passing of those little grains is snow
    Upon my soul, old Time.
      (She lays the hour-glass upon its side.)
Time.   No, thus it stands.
      (Puts it up again.)
      (The Queen sits at the chess-board.)
Time. You've lost the glass. For other stakes we play.
Queen. Well then, for triumph in my many plots.
Time. Defeat is death. *(They play.)*
Queen.   To fail in plotting is to die.   [SB22(3p70)]
    Thus play we first with pawns, small things and weak,
    And then the great ones come, and last the king.
    So men in life and I in magic play,
    First dreams and goblins and the lesser sprites,
    But now with Father Time I'm face to face.
Time (laughs).
      (The curtain falls for a moment. The curtain rises. The Queen
    alone, her head on her hands, gazing at the chess-board.)
A Voice. Lost.
The Mirror.   Lost.

They say you are a gambler and a player
At chances and at moments with mankind.
I'll play you for your old hour-glass. *(Pointing to the instruments of
   magic.)*   You see
I keep such things about me; they are food
For antiquarian meditation.   *(Brings dice.)*
Time.   Ay,
   We throw three times.
Vivien. Three-six.
Time. Four-six.
Vivien. Five-six. Ha, Time!
Time. Double sixes!
Vivien. I lose! They're loaded dice. Time always plays
   With loaded dice. Another chance! Come, father;
   Come to the chess, for young girls' wits are better
   Than old men's any day, as Merlin found.
      (Places the chess-board on her knees.)
   The passing of those little grains is snow
   Upon my soul, old Time.
      (She lays the hour-glass on its side.)
Time.   No; thus it stands. *(Rights it again.)*
   For other stakes we play. You lost the glass.
Vivien. Then give me triumph in my many plots.
Time. Defeat is death.
Vivien.   Should my plots fail I'd die. *(They play.)*
   Thus play we first with pawns, poor things and weak;
   And then the great ones come, and last the king.
   So men in life and I in magic play;
   First dreams, and goblins, and the lesser sprites,
   And now with Father Time I'm face to face.
                                        (They play.)

   I trap you.
Time.   Check.
Vivien.   I do miscalculate.
   I am dull to-day, or you were now all lost.

Queen. The wild swan has sunk from the blinding blue.
   No more I trouble with my wayward life.
   Old dreaming night, O hungry oblivion,
   O sister death, I take thy hand, I come.

(She dies.)

Chance, and not skill, has favoured you, old father!

(She plays.)

Time. Check.

Vivien. Ah! how bright your eyes. How swift your moves.
How still it is! I hear the carp go splash,
And now and then a bubble rise. I hear
A bird walk on the doorstep.   *(She plays.)*

Time.   Check once more.

Vivien. I must be careful now. I have such plots—
Such war plots, peace plots, love plots—every side;
I cannot go into the bloodless land
Among the whimpering ghosts.

Time.   Mate thus.

Vivien.   Already?
Chance hath a skill!   *(She dies.)*

[Manuscript NLI 30,357 of *Vivien and Time,* continued]

Both Voices (laugh).   [SB23(3p190)]
The Page (speaking without).
 Keep back, strange pale man! This is the Queen's room.
  (A struggle; a cry.)
Clarin (rushing in with a drawn sword).
 Now vengeance on the Queen, and then to seek
 A potent spell in Merlin's stolen book
 To rouse young Asphodel from magic trance.
  (He sees the Queen lying dead; goes over and touches her.)
 Dead. Dead. That mighty shade has been before.
  (Turns to the door.)
 O my good goblins, we are late, all late!
 O now who wonders that the night had signs,
 That there was bitter frost in fairy land
 Which never happened in all time before
 And fairy souls from streams and flowers fled
 Wherefore upon the steeps the fountains rest
 And 'fore the sun the flowers' lips are closed?
 I now remember how an old grey man
 A world-worn pedlar with a bag and scythe
 Told me how I in after life would meet
 A great queen whom I'd slay with mine own hand
 O[r] scarce survive her for a minute's space.[14]   [SB23(3p191)]
 The streams shall never hear my harp again.
 O woe! There is a frost in fairy land
 And on the steeps the fountains rest.
      Oh Asphodel!
  (Dies.)
Mirror (laughs).

---

14. *O scarce* See discussion above (p. 16) of "Or scarce" as probably intended.

SCENE 3

A dark grove. Enter Asphodel. No light on the stage or audience. Light only on Asphodel.

Asphodel. O what a strange long sleep I've had! How long?[15]
    And stranger dreams I've dreamt in sleep,
    Of how a queen once loved me—loved—yes, loved!
    And hated then more than she loved at first.
    All vivid was as though it had been life:
    How in those strange dark quiet days that flowed
    In the short compass of one dream I found   [SB23(3p192)]
    Young Clarin whom I seemed to love.
    Now all is fading and I feel[16] alone,
    My whole soul bitterly athirst for peace.
    First Voice.

        Soon like us you'll find her
          And dwell with her above
        All mortal things and bind her
          If you neither hate or love.

    Second Voice.

        But quench, O thing of dust,
          Those awful flames that dart
        And gleam beneath the crust
          Of thy all-throbbing heart.

    Asphodel.   When shall I find peace, oh fairy voices?
    First Voice.

        When tall trees are crashing
        And lightning is flashing
        When thunder doth toll   [SB23(3p193)]
        And wild waters roll

    Both Voices.

        Still peace dwells alone
        On her judgement throne

15. *had how long*
16. *fell*

Second Voice.

When the bolts of death rattle
'Mong the dying in battle
O broods silence profound
On the lone desert ground

Both Voices.

Still peace dwells alone
On her judgement throne.

Asphodel.   And Clarin—

First Voice.   Sister!

Second Voice.   Sister!

First Voice.   [SB23(3p194)]

Peace in the end you shall have
And your o'erworn heart shall have rest

Second Voice.

When the yew and the cypress wave
In the cold earth over your breast.
            (Exit Asphodel upon her wanderings.)

                    END

🌿 Themes, Images, and Form

Vivien and Time is significant not only because, as Yeats asserts, it is his "first play," but also because it informs us about his early reading, and because it contains important themes and symbols used in his later writings. We learn from the play that in this very early period he was exploiting Indo-European folk tales such as "Snow White" and folk beliefs such as that a horseshoe over the door keeps evil beings from entering. He already finds references to Homer and Troy strongly evocative, though he gives them a medieval flavor with "Duchess" Helen. Circe and Diana are other figures from classical myth that he makes use of. We learn further that Provence was a magical place to Yeats long before his interest in "Speaking to the Psaltery" and the still later influence of Ezra Pound. Clarin is a "Troubador," and the courtly love ideal controls his actions. The Arthurian cycle, a frequent referent in his later work, is the background standing behind this early work. The Judeo-Christian myth of Eden attracts Yeats here long before that myth has an occult significance for him[1] and "Things that were fair / As Eve's bright hair / To Adam of old" [SB23(3p175)] has all the nostalgia of "John Kinsella's Lament for Mrs. Mary Moore,"[2] published less than two months before his death.

We learn that he read and honored "the great Eliza's sages," particularly Shakespeare, and particularly *The Tempest.* In the Dedication [SB23(3pp163–65)] the figure of Laura Armstrong is seen "Among the maids of old," of whom Yeats mentions only two. One is "Miranda / For virgin beauty famed." We are not surprised that Yeats singles out a

---

1. See Virginia Moore, *The Unicorn: William Butler Yeats' Search for Reality* (New York; The Macmillan Company, 1954), pp. 208–9; but also George Mills Harper, *Yeats's Quest for Eden* (No. IX of the Dolmen Press Centenary Papers, 1965).

2. *Variorum Poems,* pp. 620–21; cf. *Poems,* pp. 342–43.

Shakespearean heroine and specifically the magician's daughter. But his allusion to the other maid, "Penthea," is startlingly informative.

Nowhere in Yeats's published utterances does he mention John Ford or his play *The Broken Heart,* in which Penthea, betrothed to one man and then forced to marry another, goes mad and dies and is avenged by her betrothed. On January 8, 1884, Yeats writes a passionate tribute to Ford's heroine (whose name means "complaint").

> Near by is Penthea
>   As she was fitly named—
> O most fair and sad was she
>   Of the fairest saddest pages
> Of all the burning dramas
>   Of the great Eliza's sages.
>   [SB23(3p164)]

Penthea's tragedy results from her loyalty to what Yeats later called "the old high way of love."[3] Penthea is forced to be untrue to her conception of herself, forced to violate the "high courtesy"[4] of the conventions of courtly love. As M. L. Wine comments, "Ford does not ask, 'Why does one act?' but rather 'How will one act?'"[5] Ford's heroines "self-consciously seek identity; and they succeed by gracefully adhering to a code of noble gestures that in effect becomes a principle enabling them to assert continually their personal reality. Where nothing is certain, the assertion of the ego's image in conscious poses is at least something to believe in. . . . The individual ego takes an absolute stand in a socially relative world."[6] How Yeatsian this sounds! One is reminded of Yeats's wish to prepare his daughter to meet the storm of future years: ". . . Let her think opinions are accurst," that "all hatred driven hence, / The soul recovers radical innocence / And learns at last that it is self-delighting, / Self-appeasing, self-affrighting. . . ."[7] Or of his tribute to the declining Lady Gregory:

3. *Ibid.,* p. 206; cf. *Poems,* p. 81.
4. *Ibid.,* p. 205; cf. *Poems,* p. 81.
5. Wine, p. 690.
6. *Ibid.,* p. 688.
7. *Variorum Poems,* p. 405; cf. *Poems,* p. 189.

Why should I be dismayed
Though flame had burned the whole
World, as it were a coal,
Now I have seen it weighed
Against a soul?[8]

For "the old high way of love" Yeats "strove" until "weary-hearted."[9] The song for Penthea's death ends, "Love's martyrs must be ever, ever dying."[10]

The fascination with magic and medievalism which Yeats shared with the Romantics and Pre-Raphaelites is shown in *Vivien and Time* not just on the surface—Vivien with her Gothic room of magic and Merlin's book—but also in the profoundly serious themes of unappeasable longing and possession by supernatural beings and the imagery that carries these themes. In *Vivien and Time* people who are possessed become haggard and pale. The images are reminiscent of Keats's "La Belle Dame Sans Merci." As Keats's "palely loitering" knight who has lost his fairy vision is "haggard and woebegone" like other "death-pale" warriors who have been bewitched by the enchantress, so Clarin is "haggard-eyed with his dear phantom flying" [SB23(3p186)] and the Page calls him "strange pale man!" [SB23(3p190)]. This use of paleness predates by many years its appearance in *The Wind Among the Reeds* as a sign of longing for the supernatural or possession by it. There, as Ellmann has noted, the beloved is always pale—with "cloud-pale eyelids," "pale brows," and a "pearl-pale hand"[11] and Niamh, in "The Hosting of the Sidhe," cries out "Our cheeks are pale."[12] In *On Baile's Strand* (1903) Aoife and her son have "a stone-pale cheek."[13]

The figure of the wandering poet or singer is an important one in almost every period of Yeats's work. Clarin, "That wild singer of wild songs" [SB23(3p177)] "with his harp of lyric teen," is the earliest manifestation of this figure. He is related to Aleel, the harp-player in *The Countess Cathleen,* Yeats's first published play, and to Forgael, the

8. *Ibid.,* p. 267; cf. *Poems,* p. 97.   9. *Ibid.,* p. 206; cf. *Poems,* p. 81.
10. Wine, p. 763.   11. Ellmann, *Identity,* p. 23.
12. *Variorum Poems,* p. 140; cf. *Poems,* p. 55.
13. *Variorum Plays,* p. 504.

harper in *The Shadowy Waters*. Like Aleel in *The Countess Cathleen*, Clarin acts as a foil to the stronger character of the Queen as Aleel is a foil to the Countess, and Clarin's main purpose in the plot is to clarify the Queen's conflict and thus reveal her character to the audience. Aleel is on the side of earthly love and the old gods that Countess Cathleen rejects. Clarin provokes Vivien's vengeance by refusing her love. The wandering singer who slights or insults the Queen is important in two much later plays—*A Full Moon in March* and *The King of the Great Clock Tower*. In the *Full Moon*, as in *Vivien and Time*, the emphasis is on the virgin Queen—beautiful, but proud, bloodthirsty and revengeful—who takes a terrible vengeance on the man who slights her.

Clarin is also an example of another, related, character,—the figure who is possessed and wanders from land to land without rest, seeking the fulfillment of his vision. Clarin and Asphodel are both led on to endless wanderings by supernatural voices, "Souls of unrest" [SB23(3p172)], that possess them. This theme of endless search is one of the most important in Yeats's work. It is found in such early works of the eighties and nineties as "The Man Who Dreamed of Fairyland," "The Hosting of the Sidhe," "The Song of Wandering Aengus," "The Stolen Child," "Cuchulain's Fight with the Sea," and "The Land of Heart's Desire."

In those works, however, the search appears in a specifically Irish form. In "The Song of Wandering Aengus" (1897), Aengus (like Clarin, who is pale, grows old before his time, and wanders "haggard eyed") has "grown old with wandering" in search of "a glimmering girl" and determines to "find out where she has gone, / And kiss her lips and take her hands."[14] Forgael in *The Shadowy Waters* (1900) wanders in search of an immortal love. From Bryan O'Looney's translation of Michael Comyn's eighteenth-century Gaelic poem "The Land of Youth," Yeats took symbols of such a quest: "a young man following a girl who has a golden apple" and "a hound with one red

14. *Variorum Poems*, p. 150; cf. *Poems*, p. 60.

ear following a deer with no horns."[15] He borrows these symbols of "the immortal desire of Immortals"[16] for *The Wanderings of Oisin*[17] and the hound and deer for "He Mourns for the Change That Has Come upon Him and His Beloved, and Longs for the End of the World,"[18] and for *The Shadowy Waters.*[19]

Long before these poems, and in its pre-Irish form, the theme of the man who wanders searching for a phantom love has appeared in *Vivien and Time:*

> *Clarin.* By day and night crying aloud her name
> On hills and in the sombre forest
> Where shuddereth eternal night I seek
> Where pensive streamlets muse forever
> Like children in a dream so still they are
> Ever I follow the flying shadow
> But yet it flies and I must seek, still seek.
> Yonder it is on the hillside glowing
> While I live I follow without ceasing.
> I come, I come, shadow of Asphodel!
>
> [SB23(3p181)]

If we need a source, we may look to Shelley's "Alastor," although in Shelley it is the vision's bright eyes, not her shadow, that haunt the youth. The phantoms in *The Wanderings of Oisin* are "shadows,"[20] and the "immortal, mild, proud shadows" of *The Shadowy Waters* that "come from Eden on flying feet."[21] Most relevant is "The Woman of the Sidhe herself," of *At the Hawk's Well:* "The mountain witch, the unappeasable shadow" who "is always flitting upon this mountain-side, / To allure or to destroy." Cuchulain falls subject to the curse, gazes in "her unmoistened eyes,"[22] pursues her vainly, and is told ". . . Never till you are lying in the earth / Can you know rest."[23] Similarly Asphodel is told:

---

15. *Ibid.,* p. 807; cf. *Poems,* p. 593.   16. *Ibid.,* pp. 47, 807; cf. *Poems,* p. 593.

17. *Ibid.,* pp. 11–12, 29, 47; cf. *Poems,* pp. 359, 367, 374.

18. *Ibid.,* p. 153; cf. *Poems,* p. 61.   19. *Ibid.,* p. 764.

20. *Ibid.,* p. 29; cf. *Poems,* p. 367.   21. *Ibid.,* p. 217–18; cf. *Poems,* p. 405.

22. *Variorum Plays,* p. 407.   23. *Ibid.,* pp. 411–12.

> Peace in the end you shall have
> And your o'erworn heart shall have rest
> When the yew and the cypress wave
> In the cold earth over your breast.
>
> [SB23(3p194)]

Clarin's and Asphodel's "unrest" is partly a result of their separation. They are an example of yet another theme, the lovers who desire a perfect union but can never come together. The lovers in *The Dreaming of the Bones* are another example, as are Cuchulain and Fand in *The Only Jealousy of Emer*. Later lovers like Crazy Jane are not content with a mere physical union, remaining restless and unsatisfied because the two souls are not truly united. This theme of unsatisfied love is connected with Yeats's theory of the longing of the self and anti-self and their search for each other.

Certain of Yeats's central images appear first in *Vivien and Time*. In "A Prayer for my Daughter" (1919) Yeats prays that his daughter may flourish like a laurel tree, and the laurel has in that poem all its traditional associations with aesthetic achievement. He prays that her thoughts may be like linnets and she like a tree with "no business but dispensing round / Their magnanimities of sound."[24] The opening scene of *Vivien and Time* takes place in a whole grove of laurels among which the poet Clarin hears his beloved's name in wind, in bird-call, and in the notes of his "zittar." All these "magnanimities of sound" are dispensed around by the symbolic laurels: "The enamoured nightingale hath stolen / For a chorus thy name, my disturber, / And the laurel fondles the sound in joy" [SB23(3p166)].

Butterflies often symbolize the soul in Yeats, as in much ancient and modern symbolism. Etain is changed to "a silver fly" in the first published version of *The Shadowy Waters* (1900), and Aengus makes his magic harp "That she among her winds might know he wept."[25] In *The Hour Glass* (1914) the Wise Man's soul, after his death, takes the form of a butterfly released by an angel. The Fool explains:

24. *Variorum Poems*, p. 404; cf. *Poems*, p. 189.
25. *Ibid.*, p. 220; cf. *Poems*, p. 407.

O, look what has come from his mouth! O, look what has come from his mouth—the white butterfly! He is dead, and I have taken his soul in my hands; but I know why you open the lid of that golden box. I must give it to you. There then [*he puts butterfly in casket*], he has gone through his pains, and you will open the lid in the Garden of Paradise.[26]

"... Wisdom is a butterfly" we are told by "Tom O'Roughley,"[27] and Yeats notes that the butterfly symbolizes "the crooked road of intuition."[28] The "great purple butterfly" in "Another Song of a Fool" was once "a schoolmaster" like the Wise Man of *The Hour Glass* and has "learning in his eye...."[29] The butterflies of "Blood and the Moon"[30] "come in through the loopholes and die against the window-panes" of the tower,[31] seeming to "cling upon the moonlit skies" like souls trying to rise toward "the purity of the unclouded moon."[32]

These uses of the butterfly-soul symbolism are prefigured in *Vivien and Time:*

> (*A Page appears at the door to R., carefully enclosing something in both his hands.*)
>
> Page. Look, look you here!
> Vivien. What have you there, my child?
> (*The Page shows a large tropic butterfly. The Queen lays it on the table.*)
>   'Tis dead—you should not slay these sunny things;
>   They say they're souls of long dead fairies.
>
> [SB23(3p171)]

(Since fairyland is the setting of *Vivien and Time,* and she herself is a fairy queen, she is not making a distinction between the souls of fairies and those of humans. The butterfly is a dead person's soul.) Later, when Vivien, through the agency of the Page, has cast a fatal spell on Clarin and Asphodel, she addresses these unlucky souls as butterflies:

---

26. *Variorum Plays,* p. 639.
27. *Variorum Poems,* p. 338; cf. *Poems,* p. 141.
28. *Ibid.,* p. 827; cf. *Poems,* p. 599.   29. *Ibid.,* p. 381; cf. *Poems,* p. 170.
30. *Ibid.,* p. 482; cf. *Poems,* p. 238.   31. *Ibid.,* p. 831; cf. *Poems,* p. 600.
32. *Ibid.,* p. 482; cf. *Poems,* p. 238.

O butterflies, butterflies ruined by a child,
What did the laughter of thy wings for thee?
What did the people's favour do for thee,
Or all the fancies of thine idle harp?

[SB23(3p175)]

Swans, a major symbol in Yeats, also stand for the "solitary soul," as in "Nineteen Hundred and Nineteen" (1921):

Some moralist or mythological poet
Compares the solitary soul to a swan;
I am satisfied with that,
Satisfied if a troubled mirror show it,
Before that brief gleam of its life be gone,
An image of its state;
The wings half spread for flight,
The breast thrust out in pride
Whether to play, or to ride
Those winds that clamour of approaching night.[33]

There are also striking images of swans in "The Wild Swans at Coole," "The Tower," "Leda and the Swan," "Coole and Ballylee, 1931," and elsewhere. Maud Gonne, with her "Ledaean body," is one of the "daughters of the swan" in "Among School Children,"[34] but Vivien is the first of those daughters in Yeats's work.

The swan as incorporating a spirit goes back to the Leda myth. Irish stories about human swans include "The Children of Lir"[35] and "The Dream of Angus Og."[36] But Yeats could have found a similar tale in "The Six Swans" in *Grimm's Fairy Tales*, and with an attractive illustration by Walter Crane. There is no human being turned swan in *Vivien and Time*, but a swan is a sort of totem for Vivien and indeed shows "an image of [her] state":

33. *Ibid.*, pp. 430–31; cf. *Poems*, p. 208.
34. *Ibid.*, p. 444; cf. *Poems*, p. 216.
35. P. W. Joyce, *Old Celtic Romances: Tales from Irish Mythology* (New York: The Devin-Adair Company, 1962; first published 1879), pp. 1–26.
36. Lady Gregory, *Cuchulain of Muirthemne* (London: John Murray; fourth edition, October 1911; reprinted April 1926), pp. 143–47.

Men saw in the heaven when I was born
When a wild swan passed in the blinding blue
Great was the might and the mirth of his wings
Down 'fore their feet fell he dead in the way.
Then wan-faced augured the gray sign-tellers
That my life should have might like that wild wing
That had for a soul the powers of night
For 'twas no common bird, those old men said,
But that lame-footed fate would o'ertake me
When the tide of my strength was full.
So evil augured the grey sign-tellers. . . .   [SB23(3pp176–77)]

She defies this prophecy, believing she will triumph over her rival, Asphodel, in spite of Clarin's opposition, and in her confidence cries out, "The wild swan soars" [SB23(3p181)].

Later, having put Asphodel in a trance, she is "glad with triumphing" and sings a mysterious song ending hauntingly, "Now where is the wild swan's fellow?" [SB23(3p186)], echoed over thirty years later by an equally haunting line in *Calvary*, "What can a swan need but a swan?"[37] and by the image of the swans paddling "lover by lover" in "The Wild Swans at Coole."[38]

Another of Yeats's major symbols is the fountain, perhaps derived quite early on from Shelley,[39] though it is not until his essay, "The Philosophy of Shelley's Poetry" (1900), that Yeats speaks of Shelley's reading Porphyry on "intellectual fountains" and on "fountains and rivers [that] symbolise generation."[40] In "The Poetry of Sir Samuel Ferguson—I" (1886) the fountain is a symbol of the "living waters" of the "Irish cycle,"[41] as it is again in "The Celtic Element in Literature" (1897): ". . . And now a new fountain of legends, and, as I think, a more abundant fountain than any in Europe, is being opened, the fountain of Gaelic legends. . . ."[42] In "At Stratford on Avon" (1901), Yeats uses the figure of the fountain in preferring Richard II to that "natural force," Henry V. He praises "that lyricism which rose out of Richard's

37. *Variorum Plays*, p. 788.
38. *Variorum Poems*, p. 323; cf. *Poems*, p. 131.
39. *Essays and Introductions*, p. 81.   40. *Ibid.*, p. 83.
41. *Uncollected Prose*, I, 82.   42. *Essays and Introductions*, p. 186.

mind like the jet of a fountain to fall again where it had risen."[43] In "Discoveries" (1906) "Art . . . shrinks . . . from all that is of the brain only, from all that is not a fountain jetting from the entire hopes, memories, and sensations of the body."[44] The "abounding glittering jet" of the fountain of life rises in the rich man's garden in "Ancestral Houses"[45] and leaps high up on the mountain-side where "upstanding men / . . . / Drop their cast at the side / Of dripping stone" in "The Tower."[46]

In *Vivien and Time* life's fountains are part not only of the imagery but of the action. Vivien cannot die "Until the fountains on the steeps have rest" [SB23(3p175)], which, she thinks, can never happen, because it never has. But it does happen. Just after her death Clarin explains that

> there was bitter frost in fairy land
> Which never happened in all time before
> And fairy souls from streams and flowers fled
> Wherefore upon the steeps the fountains rest. . . .
>   [SB23(3p190)]

In *Time and the Witch Vivien* Yeats sets the scene of Vivien's contest with Time and her resulting death in "a marble-flagged, pillared room" which has "a fountain in the centre."[47] Just before the end Yeats makes sure that we recall this symbol of life: Vivien says, "I hear the carp go splash, / And now and then a bubble rise."[48] Immediately afterwards she loses the chess game and dies. It is of interest that, in the Merlin romances, a fountain in the forest of Briosque is a favorite haunt of Niniane's and that there she keeps tryst with Merlin.[49]

Vivien and Time begins cheerfully in a classical laurel grove, but ends in a Dantesque "dark grove," which also is a symbol that Yeats was to use in his later poetry. In the final scene Asphodel passes through "A dark grove" [SB23(3p191)]. She is "alone," her "whole soul bitterly

43. *Ibid.*, p. 108.   44. *Ibid.*, p. 292.
45. *Variorum Poems*, p. 417; cf. *Poems*, p. 200.
46. *Ibid.*, p. 414; cf. *Poems*, p. 198.   47. *Ibid.*, p. 720; cf. *Poems*, p. 517.
48. *Ibid.*, p. 722; cf. *Poems*, p. 520.   49. Paton, p. 205.

athirst for peace." She is told by fairy voices that she can dwell with peace "above / All mortal things" if she neither hates nor loves. They warn her

> But quench, O thing of dust,
>   Those awful flames that dart
> And gleam beneath the crust
>   Of thy all-throbbing heart.
>
> [SB23(3p192)]

More than forty years later, in "Blood and the Moon" (1928), Yeats has Jonathan Swift lament that "the heart in his blood-sodden breast had dragged him down into mankind."[50] In *The Words upon the Window-pane* (1934) Yeats shows a fascination with Swift's epitaph: "He has gone where fierce indignation can lacerate his heart no more."[51] In "Parnell's Funeral" Parnell is another solitary who has passed "Through Jonathan Swift's dark grove . . . and there / Plucked bitter wisdom that enriched his blood."[52] Yeats had no doubt long forgotten that in *Vivien and Time* Asphodel, too, passes "alone" through a "dark grove" seeking peace "above . . . mortal things" but escaping the "all-throbbing heart" only in death.

Vivien and Time is full of floral imagery. It runs from the beginning of the action in a laurel grove, through a profusion of flower imagery as Vivien's power rises, to the death of the flowers along with the death of Vivien and Clarin, and to the awakening of Asphodel in the dark grove of cypress and yew. Unlike the other images we have traced, however, flowers are few and far between in the later Yeats.

A glance at the concordance to Yeats's poems[53] shows that the word "flower" appears eighteen times before 1900 (arbitrarily using that date to distinguish early from late poetry) but only three times after, the plural "flowers" nineteen times before 1900 and ten times after. Of specific flowers, the rose, which is omnipresent before 1900, appears

---

50. *Variorum Poems*, p. 481; cf. *Poems*, p. 237.

51. *Variorum Plays*, p. 942.

52. *Variorum Poems*, p. 543; cf. *Poems*, p. 280.

53. *A Concordance to the Poems of W. B. Yeats*, ed. Stephen Maxfield Parrish, pro-grammed by James Allan Painter (Ithaca, New York: Cornell University Press, 1963).

afterwards only in "The Song of a Fool," "The Rose Tree," "My House," and "The Three Bushes." The lily appears in six poems before 1900, but later only in "The Gift of Harun Al-Rashid." The setting of *The Island of Statues* is an enchanted garden, and an enchanted flower is central to the plot. In that work there are references to many flowers that are seldom or never mentioned again in Yeats's poetry: pansies, anemones, monks-hood, foxglove, laburnum. Daffodils appear there and in two other very early poems. Violets are found only in "How Ferencz Renyi Kept Silent." The poppy appears in five pre-1900 poems; only in "Shepherd and Goatherd" after. Laurel, on the other hand, appears only in *The Wanderings of Oisin* before 1900 but in three later poems: "A Prayer for My Daughter," "Coole Park, 1929," and "News for the Delphic Oracle." However, the pre-1900 appearance is without symbolic overtones, while the post-1900 appearances are symbolical. "Blossoms" are found only before 1900. "Blossom" and "blossoming" prosper later, but often in a general sense and as verb or verbal.

"Why can't you English poets keep flowers out of your poetry," Yeats asked Dorothy Wellesley.[54] Cutting observation of flowers out of

54. *Letters on Poetry,* p. 173. Yeats's question provoked Lady Dorothy to several questionable assertions: that Yeats strongly disliked flowers; that he had a "lack of interest in natural beauty for its own sake"; that "most of the Celtic poets are not concerned with Nature at all"; that Yeats did not draw inspiration from details of nature but only from the massed effects a painter sees; that "his lack of observation concerning natural beauty was almost an active obsession" which dims "most poems of his concerned with Nature"; and that his poor sight made this "racial characteristic" more serious. Any of these assertions that are not simply incorrect are non sequiturs because Yeats was talking about flowers in poetry, not flowers in life. And flowers in poetry must have a meaning beyond their being just flowers. The symbolic rose gets into Yeats's poetry, early and late, because it is symbolic. It may be an actual rose, but actual roses that are not symbolic have, he felt, no place in verse. In the early manuscripts of *The Shadowy Waters,* for example, there are enough roses to satisfy even Dorothy Wellesley, yet they are all symbolic. Forgael throws himself on heaps of roses to get inspiration from their scent. They are "Danaan roses," roses of the Children of Dana, the Sidhe (*Druid Craft,* p. 169). In some versions heaps of apple-blossoms replace the roses (*ibid.,* pp. 87–88). These too are presumably supernatural and related to the dream life, though suggested by Maud Gonne's apple-blossom complex-

his poetry was one way in which Yeats cured himself of superficial imitation of the English tradition. *Vivien and Time,* however, like *The Island of Statues* (written later in 1884), is still very imitative of that tradition. Yeats's inability to keep flowers out of his 1883–84 poetry is simply a sign of his times. The reader will immediately think of the garden in Tennyson's *Maud* where Maud is "Queen Rose of the rose-bud garden of girls" and of the poppies in Swinburne's "Garden of Proserpine." The poems, like the paintings of Rossetti—and Pre-Raphaelite and symbolist painting generally—are full of the flower symbolism that crowds into *The Island of Statues* and *Vivien and Time.*

The marble statues in the "Dedication" are "Like unto hawthorn white," and the person to whom the poem is dedicated has bright eyes and black hair like "the peeping pansy's face" [SB23(3p164)]. The play opens in a laurel grove. The heroine is a flower of the otherworld, "Asphodel." Vivien contrasts herself with Asphodel as rosemary and rue [SB23(3p171)]. The magic mirror tells Vivien that her power will last until the flowers are frozen, which she believes can never happen. Flowers accompany the prime of Vivien's power. In act I, scene 3, Yeats has her *"arranging flowers in a large antique vase"* [SB23(3p176)]. She interrupts her soliloquy, which tells us her plots, with asides to the flowers: "lie there / Among thy sister mummers of the year / O pale Narcissus" [SB23(3p177)]. When the Page comes in she *"takes flowers from the vase and begins arranging them in his dress"* [SB23(3p179)]. Countering Vivien's colorful bouquet with a hint of frost, the Page carries a wreath of "snowy blossoms" [SB23(3p179)] which he will hang on a column set up to the memory of the supposedly dead Asphodel; the Page also carries a letter which brings Vivien the bitter news that Asphodel is not dead after all. For Vivien the death of

---

ion. "Her complexion was luminous, like that of apple-blossom through which the light falls, and I remember her standing that first day by a great heap of such blossoms in the window." *Autobiographies,* p. 123. That Yeats used the massed effects a painter sees, that "lack of observation concerning natural beauty was almost an active obsession," if true, show that he wanted to use nature for the purposes of art. "Art is art because it is not nature," he quotes Goethe (*Explorations,* p. 88).

Asphodel, flower of the otherworld, would be the death of death. But the "snowy blossoms" will triumph.

When Vivien, disguised as a gypsy, puts Asphodel into a trance, she does it not with a poisoned apple, as in "Snow White," but with a poisoned flower, perhaps borrowed from the "poison'd rose" of Tennyson's "Merlin and Vivien."[55] Asphodel recognizes too late that something is wrong when Vivien presents her autumn flower in springtime. Vivien triumphs over the fallen Asphodel by singing

> Every flower bows his head
> Passion worn and passion fed
> Green and gold and lustrous yellow
> Glutted with excess of sun
> All the flowers quire as one
> Now where is the wild swan's fellow?
> [SB23(3p186)]

Act II, scene 1, returns us to the laurel copse, in which Clarin plots Vivien's death. In act II, scene 2, Vivien rejoices that "The lily wristed Asphodel has slept / These summers three" [SB22(3p65)] and again that she herself "shall not bend / Until upon the steeps the fountains rest / And 'fore the sun the flowers' lips are closed" [SB22(3p66)]. In that scene as revised for *Time and the Witch Vivien,* the only reference to flowers is to Vivien's own "roseate fingers."[56]

In the next scene of *Vivien and Time* we learn "That there was bitter frost in fairy land" and that "'fore the sun the flowers' lips are closed" [SB23(3p190)]. As the prime of Vivien's power is marked by a choiring of flowers glutted with sun, her fall is marked by the death of flowers. Act II, scene 3, gives us a glimmering Asphodel: *"Light only on Asphodel"* in a *"dark grove"* [SB23(3p191)]. She is the only flower left, and that flower too is to be extinguished.

First voice.
> Peace in the end you shall have
> And your o'erworn heart shall have rest

55. Tennyson, pp. 373–88, esp. p. 382.
56. *Variorum Poems,* p. 720; cf. *Poems,* p. 517.

Second voice.
    When the yew and the cypress wave
    In the cold earth over your breast.
        (*Exit Asphodel upon her wanderings.*)
                    [SB23(3p194)]

So the play moves from a laurel grove and a profusion of flowers to a dark grove, the yew, and the cypress.

Returning to the foreshadowing in *Vivien and Time* of Yeats's later work, we note here devices of his dance plays. In his middle years, having led the Irish theatre to great achievement and having achieved distinguished stage plays of his own, Yeats withdrew to cultivate a new, private kind of drama. He urged the "Popular Theatre" to "grow always more objective" but announced that in his own work he would seek "not a theatre but the theatre's anti-self,"[57] "a mysterious art, always reminding and half-reminding those who understand it of dearly loved things, doing its work by suggestion, not by direct statement, a complexity of rhythm, colour, gesture, not space-pervading like the intellect, but a memory and a prophecy: a mode of drama Shelley and Keats could have used without ceasing to be themselves, and for which even Blake in the mood of *The Book of Thel* might not have been too obscure." He wished a hostess, "an audience of fifty, a room worthy of it (some great dining-room or drawing-room), half a dozen young men and women who can dance and speak verse or play drum and flute and zither"[58] (One thinks of Clarin's "zittar").

There was to be "no scenery."[59] His model was to be the Noh drama of Japan where "speech, music, song, and dance created an image of nobility and strange beauty."[60] He substituted masks for make-up "to bring the audience close enough to the play to hear every inflection of the voice."[61] He decided that "the most effective lighting is the lighting we are most accustomed to in our rooms."[62] He regrets that he did not

57. *Explorations*, p. 257.   58. *Ibid.*, p. 255.
59. *Essays and Introductions*, p. 221.   60. *Ibid.*, p. 229.
61. *Ibid.*, p. 226.   62. *Variorum Plays*, pp. 398–99.

discover in his youth that his "theatre must be the ancient theatre that can be made by unrolling a carpet or marking out a place with a stick, or setting a screen against the wall."[63]

Could Yeats's interest in returning to drawing-room drama have been a nostalgia for the occasion in his youth when he and a group of young friends presented *Vivien and Time* at the home of Judge Wright at Howth?[64] There are hints in this early play of the direction to come. There is little indication of scenery, although necessary props—an oak chair, the magic mirror, the horseshoe over a door, Merlin's book, magical instruments, etc.—are mentioned. No curtain is mentioned. The play opens in a laurel grove (at Howth this scene could have been presented outside, with rhododendrons for laurels).

The "Voices" at the end are like Yeats's later "Chorus of Musicians," and music is important in the play. Vivien both plays and sings when, disguised as a gypsy, she casts a spell on Asphodel. Later she sings again to celebrate her triumph. We are sure that, were it not for a misfortune of casting, the play would have opened with music and that Clarin would have *sung* the ominous song about the fate of the rosemary (Asphodel) and the rue (Vivien). Clarin's role begs for an actor who can play and sing. Vivien speaks of "the wild soul of his zittar" and calls him "the wild singer of wild songs" [SB23(3p177)]. But Yeats, who obviously played Clarin, was then (and always) almost entirely unmusical. Therefore Clarin holds the zittar unplayed in his hand and merely reads his ballad.

Masks figure in the action. When the two women first enter, Vivien holds a mask in her hand and Asphodel is masked. Asphodel's unmasking startles Clarin into his untactful praise of her beauty and causes Vivien's jealousy. Vivien continues to hold her mask in her hand when she enters in act I, scene 2, to consult her magic mirror.

Vivien and Time is clearly not a dance play, as there is no dance performed before the audience. Yet the dance is present as an idea and is important in the action. Vivien and Asphodel leave the masquerade

63. *Ibid.,* p. 415.
64. Ellmann, *Man and Masks,* p. 35.

FIGURE 1. J. B. Yeats, Illustration for "King Goll. An Irish Legend," by W. B. Yeats (*From* The Leisure Hour, *London, September 1887; by permission of the British Library*)

ball to get Clarin to tell them a tale: "I am weary with the dance," says Vivien. When she objects to the ballad he has bought "From a lean pedlar with a bag and scythe" [SB23(3p167)], Clarin responds with a reference to the dance she has left: "If mirth you need, why sought you the laurel? / The flood tide of joy is full in the hall" [SB23(3p168)]. Immediately after declaring Asphodel more beautiful than Vivien, Clarin asks her to dance: "Hear you! Again they dance! / So, Countess Asphodel, a measure, pray!" [SB23(3p169)]. Their departure to dance together leaves Vivien alone on the stage to tell us that her love for them has changed to hate and that she will avenge herself for the slight.

The play is episodic rather than concentrated and intense. Yet it perhaps presaged the dance plays to come. And like the Noh of Spirits, and like Yeats's own dance plays, the central scene is the manifestation of a spirit, or at least of an abstraction—Vivien's confrontation with Time.

❧ Yeats and the Arthurian Tradition

Y
EATS'S IMAGES, even as early as *Vivien and Time,* have
"the precision of symbols," as he said of Shelley.[1] And as
with Shelley, this precision arose from both meditation and
a fascinated consciousness of tradition.[2] The tradition that
gives backbone to *Vivien and Time* is the Arthurian legend.
When Yeats wrote the play, sometime between the fall of 1882 and
January 1884, the Arthurian tradition was still very popular in literature and, of course, had been popular for much of the century. Let us
recall certain highlights. In 1832 Tennyson published *The Lady of
Shalott* and planned to write "an epic or a drama of King Arthur,"
which he thought would take him twenty years and which took him
over twice that.[3] Besides Malory's *Morte d'Arthur,* Lady Charlotte
Guest's 1838 translation of the *Mabinogion* was grist for Tennyson's
mill. In 1842 appeared Tennyson's "Morte d'Arthur" (written about
1835) and the lyric poems "Sir Launcelot and Queen Guinevere" and
"Sir Galahad." Wagner's *Lohengrin* was first performed in 1850. In
1852 Matthew Arnold published his "Tristram and Iseult," containing
the story of Vivien and Merlin in its final section, "Iseult of Britanny."[4]

About 1854 Dante Gabriel Rossetti discovered Malory and began
using Arthurian subjects in his painting.[5] In 1856 Robert Southey's
edition of the *Morte d'Arthur* appeared and was discovered by the
youthful Edward Burne-Jones and William Morris. ". . . So great did
their love and veneration for this book become that [they] were almost

1. *Essays and Introductions,* p. 80.
2. *Ibid.,* pp. 78–86.
3. *The Poetical Works of Alfred Lord Tennyson,* intro. Eugene Parsons (New York:
Thomas Y. Crowell & Co., c. 1900), p. 705.
4. In *Empedocles on Etna and Other Poems.*
5. William Gaunt, *The Restless Century: Painting in Britain 1800–1900* (Oxford: Phai-
don, 1978), p. 235.

too shy to speak of it, even among their intimate friends. It was not till a year later, when they heard Rossetti say that the two greatest books in the world were the Bible and the *Morte d'Arthur* that their tongues were unloosed."[6] In 1857 Rossetti, Morris, Burne-Jones, and others joined to decorate the new Union Society at Oxford with scenes from the *Morte d'Arthur*. Burne-Jones did a *Nimuë Luring Merlin,* which, like all these paintings, later deteriorated.[7]

In 1858 Morris expressed his passionate love of the legends in his *Defence of Guenevere*. This is also the date of his one surviving oil painting, *Queen Guenevere*. Tennyson's "Nimuë," privately printed in *Enid and Nimuë: The True and the False* (1857) was revised as "Vivien" and included in the first series of *Idylls of the King* (1859), which sold 10,000 copies in a month and continued thereafter to sustain Tennyson as the most popular of English poets. In 1862 G. F. Watts painted his well-known *Sir Galahad*. And 1856 is the date of the first performance of Wagner's *Tristan und Isolde*.

Tennyson's "The Coming of Arthur," "The Holy Grail" and "Pelleas and Ettare" appeared in 1869, "The Last Tournament" in 1871, and "Gareth and Lynette" in 1872. In 1874 Tennyson expanded "Vivien" greatly. To this same year belongs Burne-Jones's well-known *The Beguiling of Merlin,* which seems to use objects from both Tennyson's version (Merlin's book) and Arnold's (the flowering thorn trees, which, however, may have come directly from the French medieval *Romance of Merlin*). This painting was part of Burne-Jones's first success, at his 1877 Grosvenor Gallery exhibition.

In 1882, not long before Yeats wrote *Vivien and Time,* appeared Algernon Charles Swinburne's *Tristram of Lyonesse*. In this year also Wagner's *Parsifal* was performed. In 1885, two years after the date of *Vivien and Time,* appeared "Balin and Balan," the last of Tennyson's *Idylls*.

All the writers and artists we have mentioned influenced Yeats, and

6. Henderson, p. 29.
7. *Ibid.,* pp. 43–45.

had not John O'Leary pointed him toward Ireland, *The Wanderings of Oisin* of 1889 might well have been a new treatment of Arthurian romance, the story not of Niamh but of her possible namesake Niniane. For Lucy A. Paton finds in Yeats's source, *The Lay of Oisin in the Land of Youth,* "the same theme that forms the kernel of the story told of Niniane, that of a mortal's retention by a fay in an enchanted dwelling"[8] and recognizes the name "Niamh" as the "possible original of *Niniane.*"[9] Fortunately for Ireland, Yeats strove instead, in his Fenian and Red Branch tales, for what he thought he saw at last realized in Lady Gregory's *Cuchulain of Muirthemne* (1902), "a book to set beside the *Morte d'Arthur* and the *Mabinogion.*"[10] Because of this new direction, we find little of Arthurian subject matter in Yeats's mature poetry and drama.

We cannot prove that Yeats, like his fictional counterpart Michael Hearne in *The Speckled Bird,* had, at an early age, read of "Merlin under the stone" in Malory's *Morte d'Arthur.*[11] It does seem probable, however. It seems likely, too, that he had read some Spenser. *Vivien and Time* may well be one of the works referred to when he says, "I had begun to write poetry in imitation of Shelley and . . . Spenser, play after play." Yeats's admission, in this same passage, that his "lines but seldom scanned" because he "spoke them slowly as [he] wrote"[12] sounds much like John Butler Yeats's description of the same process in his January 7, 1884, letter to Dowden, cited above. Although Yeats confesses in the introduction to his 1906 edition of *Poems of Spenser* that "Until quite lately I knew nothing of Spenser but the parts I had read as a boy," those parts did include "the enchanted persecution [or "procession"] of Amoret,"[13] i.e. Book III, Canto XII. If he had read Canto XII, he may

---

8. Paton, p. 244.   9. *Ibid.,* p. 242.
10. *Essays and Introductions,* p. 188.   11. *Speckled Bird,* p. 9.
12. *Autobiographies,* pp. 66–67.

13. *Essays and Introductions,* pp. 382–83. This edition gives "enchanted procession" where all earlier texts give "enchanted persecution." Although Yeats places this "persecu-

also have read "as a boy" Canto III, which tells of Merlin and his cave
and of the Ladie of the Lake.

Yeats may even have read a translation of Ariosto, whose Bradamant, like Spenser's Britomart, visits Merlin's cave, in *Orlando Furioso,*
Canto III. At seventeen Yeats loved "beyond other portraits" Titian's
Ariosto because of "its grave look, as if waiting for some perfect final
event."[14] How could he have failed to find out about Ariosto himself
and to dip into his book?

John Eglinton has recorded that in 1883, while still at Erasmus
Smith High School, Yeats was an admirer of Matthew Arnold's current essays. "Yeats told us that no one could write an essay now except
Herbert Spencer and Matthew Arnold."[15] It seems likely that Yeats
would have known Arnold's poems as well, perhaps including the
story of Merlin and Vivien from Arnold's "Iseult of Brittany." We do
know that he "had read as a boy," in a book belonging to his father,
Morris's *The Defence of Guenevere* (1858), which he had liked less than
The Earthly Paradise (1868–70).[16]

One can assume Yeats's knowledge of Tennyson at an early age. At
the High School Yeats had been required "to write an essay on 'Men
may rise on stepping-stones of their dead selves to higher things,' "[17]
lines from *In Memoriam.* Of the Metropolitan School of Art, which he
entered in May 1884,[18] four months after the date he placed on *Vivien
and Time,* Yeats writes, "Of England I alone knew anything. Our
ablest student . . . had never heard of Tennyson or Browning, and it

---

tion [or procession] of Amoret" in "the Fourth Book of *The Faerie Queene,*" he must mean
the "maske of Cupid" in III, xii.

14. *Autobiographies,* p. 116. The portrait that Yeats knew as "Ariosto" is now called
"Portrait of a Man" (National Gallery, London).

15. John Eglinton, "Dublin Letter," *The Dial,* 72 (March, 1922), 300; quoted in Dume,
p. 217.

16. *Autobiographies,* p. 141.

17. *Ibid.,* p. 58.

18. Ellmann, *Man and Masks,* p. 31. The records for 1884 of the School of Art, now the
National College of Art, show that Susan M. Yeats, Elizabeth C. Yeats, and Wm. B. Yeats,
all "Artisans," and all of 10 Ashfield Terrace, Harolds Cross, each paid a fee of £1. 2. 6 first
in May 1884. Courtesy of Richard Weber, National College of Art, Dublin.

was I who carried into the school some knowledge of English poetry. . . ."[19]

As we have said, Tennyson's "Merlin and Vivien"[20] was probably
the direct source of Yeats's *Vivien and Time,* in which the beguiler is
beguiled. Yeats's poem is almost a sequel to Tennyson's. In "Merlin and
Vivien" a young witch overcomes an old wizard, gaining the secret of
his magic book. In *Vivien and Time* the same young witch attempts to
win his hour-glass from another old wizard, Time (a "fierce magician"
in *Time and the Witch Vivien*[21]), and forfeits her life. Yeats's spelling of
the name is the same as Tennyson's, whereas Arnold had spelled it
"Vivian."

Vivien exhibits the same deplorable lack of respect for age in both
Tennyson and Yeats. Tennyson describes her triumph:

> Then crying "I have made his glory mine,"
> And shrieking out "O fool!" the harlot leapt
> Adown the forest, and the thicket closed
> Behind her, and the forest echo'd "fool."[22]

In *Time and the Witch Vivien* Vivien calls Time "a little, light old man,"
greets him "Ha, ha! ha, ha, ha! / The wrinkled squanderer of human
wealth,"[23] and mocks him with her triumph over Merlin, ". . . Young
girls' wits are better / Than old men's any day, as Merlin found,"[24] and
ascribes his victory at dice to "Chance, and not skill. . . ."[25]

Yeats's Vivien is a nicer person than Tennyson's, who is essentially
evil, a lamia—serpentine, and with a death's head showing through
her beauty: "How from the rosy lips of life and love, / Flash'd the bare-
grinning skeleton of death!"[26] In Tennyson, Vivien's pride craves
honor from Lancelot and Guinevere even if she has to win it through
blackmail:

19. *Autobiographies,* p. 81.
20. Tennyson, pp. 373–88.
21. *Variorum Poems,* p. 720; cf. *Poems,* p. 517.
22. Tennyson, p. 388.
23. *Variorum Poems,* p. 720; cf. *Poems,* p. 518.
24. *Ibid.,* p. 721; cf. *Poems,* p. 519.
25. *Ibid.,* p. 722; cf. *Poems,* p. 520.
26. Tennyson, p. 386.

". . . Ah little rat that borest in the dyke
Thy hole by night to let the boundless deep
Down upon far-off cities while they dance—
Or dream—of thee they dream'd not—nor of me
These—ay, but each of either: ride, and dream
The mortal dream that never yet was mine—
Ride, ride and dream until ye wake—to me!
Then, narrow court and lubber King, farewell!
For Lancelot will be gracious to the rat,
And our wise Queen, if knowing that I know,
Will hate, loathe, fear—but honor me the more."[27]

Although Vivien does not need a motive to do evil, she gains one in Arthur's rejection of her advances and in the Camelot gossip about her resulting embarrassment.[28]

Being jealous and murderous herself, Tennyson's Vivien assumes these motives in others. When Merlin describes a chaste lady whose eyes "Waged . . . unwilling tho' successful war / On all the youth,"[29] Vivien replies,

". . . Thy tongue has tript a little: ask thyself.
The lady never made *unwilling* war
With those fine eyes: she had her pleasure in it,
And made her good man jealous with good cause.
And lived there neither dame nor damsel then
Wroth at a lover's loss? were all as tame,
I mean, as noble, as their Queen was fair?
Not one to flirt a venom at her eyes,
Or pinch a murderous dust into her drink,
Or make her paler with a poison'd rose?"[30]

That poisoned rose is like the autumn flower with which Yeats's Vivien puts Asphodel into a trance. We have seen that both Yeats's Vivien and his Margaret Leland are jealous and even murderous creatures (latently in Margaret's case). In this they are like Tennyson's Vivien. Yet, as one nineteenth-century critic put it, Tennyson had

27. *Ibid.*, pp. 374–75.   28. *Ibid.*, p. 375.
29. *Ibid.*, p. 381.   30. *Ibid.*, p. 382.

"invented a Vivienne unknown to any previous writer, the creature and invention of his own brain."[31] None of the various tales of Vivien and Merlin that Paton summarizes have a Vivien as accomplished in evil as is Tennyson's or even Yeats's.[32] Arnold's Vivian is a "false fay,"[33] but no example of her falseness is given except her betrayal of Merlin. Swinburne's Nimue, only briefly mentioned, is a saint, and in any case Yeats probably did not read in *Tristram of Lyonesse* (1882) how "The heavenly hands of holier Nimue ... Should shut [Merlin] in with sleep as kind as death"[34] until the summer of 1887, when he writes to Katharine Tynan of having read the book "lately."[35] Surely Yeats's Vivien got her bad nature from Tennyson's Vivien.

A common motif between "Merlin and Vivien" and *Vivien and Time* is Merlin's magic book. The book is not mentioned in Malory, nor in Spenser, where the sage is busily "writing strange characters in the ground" like "Ille" in Yeats's "Ego Dominus Tuus."[36] There is a "triple claspèd book" which the wise Melissa consults before showing Bradamant the future in Harrington's Ariosto,[37] but Merlin himself consults no book.[38] There is no book in Arnold, nor in Swinburne.

Yeats may simply have associated magic book and magician since his father read Scott's *The Lay of the Last Minstrel* to him when he was a child.[39] (The book of the magician Michael Scott figures largely in the action.) And in Burne-Jones's *The Beguiling of Merlin*, probably based on the Early English Text Society translation of the French medieval *Romance of Merlin*,[40] Nimuë consults a book. Nevertheless the promi-

31. S. Humphreys Gurteen, *The Arthurian Epic* (New York and London: G. P. Putnam's Sons, 1895), p. 184.

32. Paton, pp. 204–27.

33. "Iseult of Brittany," l.161, Arnold, p. 105.

34. Swinburne, pp. 30–31.

35. *Letters to Katharine Tynan*, p. 34; cf. *CL1*, p. 29.

36. *The Faerie Queene*, III, iii, 14; *Variorum Poems*, pp. 370–71; cf. *Poems*, p. 162.

37. Ariosto, p. 74.

38. *Ibid.*, pp. 73–74.

39. *Autobiographies*, p. 46.

40. *Burne-Jones*, p. 51.

nence of a magic book in both Tennyson's poem and Yeats's is a definite link. Tennyson's book is most impressive:

> "Thou read the book, my pretty Vivien!
> O ay, it is but twenty pages long,
> But every page having an ample marge,
> And every marge enclosing in the midst
> A square of text that looks a little blot,
> The text no larger than the limbs of fleas;
> And every square of text an awful charm,
> Writ in a language that has long gone by.
> So long, that mountains have arisen since
> With cities on their flanks—thou read the book!
> And every margin scribbled, crost, and cramm'd
> With comment, densest condensation, hard
> To mind and eye; but the long sleepless nights
> Of my long life have made it easy to me.
> And none can read the text, not even I;
> And none can read the comment but myself;
> And in the comment did I find the charm.
> O, the results are simple; a mere child
> Might use it to the harm of any one,
> And never could undo it. . . ."[41]

In *Vivien and Time* it is indeed a "mere child" who recites the spell from the book—now an enormous volume that becomes fiery hot when the spell is read. Vivien's Page does not know the evil he is doing and cannot reverse it once the spell is spoken.

Another bit of evidence that Yeats is thinking principally of Tennyson's "Merlin and Vivien" is that he, like Tennyson, has Vivien imprison Merlin in an oak, rather than in a hawthorn, as do Arnold, Burne-Jones, and Swinburne. "No taste have I for slumber 'neath an oak," says Time in *Time and the Witch Vivien*.[42] This seems a direct allusion to Tennyson's poem.

---

41. Tennyson, p. 383.
42. *Variorum Poems*, p. 721; cf. *Poems*, p. 518.

Vivien and Time and *Time and the Witch Vivien* have such clearly vi-
sualized situations that our text begs for illustrations. Pictures abound
of the kinds Yeats must have known, whether or not he knew the exact
ones we point to. Yeats would have been aware of—and would have
seen if he could—symbolist and Pre-Raphaelite artists' representations
of the subject of his play.

It has been noted above that after Rossetti discovered Malory in 1854
the Pre-Raphaelites and their followers frequently treated Arthurian
material. Yeats says that when he was seventeen (1882–83) he "was
already an old-fashioned brass cannon full of shot,"[43] and it is well
to remember that Pre-Raphaelitism and symbolism were a considerable part of what he was loaded with. He was "in all things Pre-
Raphaelite." His father had told him about Rossetti and Blake when he
was fifteen or sixteen, and Rossetti's *Dante's Dream* at Liverpool fascinated him at about the same time.[44] His father's friends during the
family's first stay at Bedford Park (1879–81) "were painters who had
been influenced by the Pre-Raphaelite movement."[45] Therefore we
may be sure that when he created the enchantress who is the heroine
of *Vivien and Time* and *Time and the Witch Vivien* he had very much
in mind the enchantresses painted by Pre-Raphaelite and symbolist
painters. We may begin with a "portrait" of Vivien herself.

In 1863 Frederick Sandys painted a *Vivien,* a head proudly lifted
against a background of peacock plumes. She wears a rich necklace
and a gown patterned with interlocking forms. Her right hand holds a
sprig of flowers and leaves, and her left hand relinquishes (or reaches
toward) a fruit.[46] The same model (probably Keomy, a gypsy girl who
was Sandys's mistress for a time) posed for his *Morgan le Fay* (1862–63),
in which the witch is making incantations in a corner full of "*Magical
instruments*" (P 514) like those in *Time and the Witch Vivien*.[47] It is not

43. *Autobiographies*, p. 116.   44. *Ibid.*, pp. 114–15.

45. *Ibid.*, p. 44.

46. *Vivien*, oil on canvas, 25″ × 20½″, dated 1863, Manchester, City Art Gallery. Cf.
Sandys, cat. no. 63.

47. *Morgan le Fay*, 1862–63, oil on panel, 24¾″ × 17½″, City Museum and Art Gallery,
Birmingham. *Sandys*, cat. no. 58.

FIGURE 2. Frederick Sandys, *Vivien,* 1863. Oil on canvas, 25″ × 20½″. (© *Manchester City Art Galleries*)

FIGURE 3. Frederick Sandys, *Morgan le Fay*, 1862–63. Oil on panel, 24¾" × 17½". (*Published by permission of the Birmingham Museum and Art Gallery*)

hard to imagine this as a picture of Vivien herself conjuring, especially as the model of Sandys's *Vivien* was used: the leopard skin Sandys's Morgan le Fay wears hangs over the back of a chair in act I, scene 1, of *Vivien and Time* [SB23(3p166)]. Yeats's father visited Sandys's studio in June 1868, showed him his pictures, and received his praise and encouragement as well as an invitation for further visits, so that there would have been a family acquaintance with Sandys's work.[48] A drawing by Sandys, *Morgan le Fay*, appeared as a supplement to *The British Architect* in October 1879, four years before we believe Yeats to have been writing his play.[49] Burne-Jones, too, did a *Morgan le Fay*, a gouache of 1862, very cool and beautiful, though much touched-up since the original date. Morgan le Fay, like Vivien in Yeats's play, is surrounded by magical flowers.[50]

In Yeats's play Vivien sees herself as a successor to Circe: "Great Circe, Circe, now thy fame is fled / Since mine was born . . ." [SB23(3p175)]. And Circe is another enchantress painted by the Pre-Raphaelites. Yeats could certainly have known, or at least known about, Burne-Jones's *The Wine of Circe* (1863–69), exhibited at the Old Water-colour Society in 1869 and then attacked in the *Art Journal*, though one of the best works of the period and the inspiration of a poem by Rossetti. The room in which Circe bends to poison the bright wine for her "charmèd cup" [SB23(3p165)] was originally as Gothic as that in Sandys's *Morgan le Fay* but in the end became classical. "The ships had been moved back, light flooded the room, and the design was controlled less by the need to create atmosphere than by carefully balanced linear rhythms."[51] Yeats, interestingly enough, also chooses a

48. Murphy, pp. 57, and 556 note 13.

49. William E. Fredeman, *Pre-Raphaelitism: A Bibliocritical Study* (Cambridge: Harvard University Press, 1965), p. 297. Another striking enchantress is Sandys' *Medea*, oil on panel, 24½″ × 18¼″, 1868, City Museum and Art Gallery, Birmingham. This had been reproduced photographically as the frontispiece to Col. A. B. Richardson's poem "Medea" in 1869. *Sandys*, cat. no. 72.

50. *Morgan le Fay*, 1862, gouache, 86.5 × 48 cm., London, Borough of Hammersmith Public Libraries. Cf. Johnson, Plate 7.

51. *The Wine of Circe*, gouache, 70 × 101.5 cm., signed E. Burne-Jones, 1863–69, private

classical scene for his play, even though his characters and certain appurtenances are indeed medieval. His "Dedication" sings of a palace built of "dreamland marble" [SB23(3p161)] with pillars and statues. Vivien arranges flowers *"in a large antique vase"* [SB23(3p176)]. The scene of *Time and the Witch Vivien* is *"A marble-flagged, pillared room."* Though *"Magical instruments"* are collected *"in one corner,"* there is *"A fountain in the centre."* Such a scene recalls classical interiors painted at about the date of Yeats's play by Lord Leighton, by Sir Lawrence Alma-Tadema, and by Sir Edward J. Poynter. Walter Crane's frontispiece to Mary A. De Morgan's *The Necklace of Princess Fiorimonde,*[52] though not an interior, shows us a lady like Vivien whose "image" and "beautiful . . . roseate fingers" are reflected, along with "the little golden greedy carp,"[53] in a marble fountain. Marble statues, like those that figure in the "Dedication," line the walk, and a pillared temple is in the distance. These pictures are mentioned here, not as influences, but to show how representative of their time *Vivien and Time* and *Time and the Witch Vivien* were.

One year before Yeats wrote *Vivien and Time* several of the motifs he was to borrow from "Snow White" and "Sleeping Beauty" appeared in illustrations by Walter Crane to *Household Stories, from the collection of the Brothers Grimm,*[54] translated by Lucy Crane: a frontispiece of the sleeping Briar Rose being discovered by the Prince; a full-page picture of the evil Queen giving Snow White the poisoned apple, a head-piece of Snow White in a trance, and a tail-piece of the Queen looking proudly and cruelly into her magic mirror. Yeats had read both Grimm and Anderson as a boy in Sligo[55] but he would have been interested in these illustrations by a follower of the Pre-Raphaelites for a book from

---

collection. *Burne-Jones,* cat. no. 105. Reproduced in black and white in *Sir Edward Burne Jones* (London: George Newnes; New York: Frederick Warne & Co., n.d.; Newnes' Art Library), Plate 42.

52. (London: Macmillan, 1880).
53. *Variorum Poems,* p. 720; cf. *Poems,* p. 517.
54. (London: Macmillan & Co., 1882).
55. *Autobiographies,* p. 47.

FIGURE 4. Walter Crane, Frontispiece to *The Necklace of Princess Fiorimonde*. (*From Mary Augusta De Morgan*, The Necklace of Princess Fiorimonde [*London: Macmillan*, *1880*])

which he was constantly borrowing themes for his play. Yeats later met Crane "constantly"[56] at William Morris's suppers.

The Sleeping Beauty was, of course, one of Burne-Jones's favorite themes. In the early 1860s he had designed a set of tales illustrating Perrault's story. A "small *Briar Rose* series" was done between 1870–73. And in 1873 he began a series of four larger canvases finished only in 1890. Another of his favorite themes was Merlin and Nimuë. He chose "Merlin imprisoned beneath a stone by the Damsel of the Lake" as subject for his mural in the ill-fated Oxford Union series of 1857.[57] In 1861 he did a gouache, *Merlin and Nimuë*, in which the two stand near the open tomb. This is the most dramatic of Burne-Jones's handlings of the theme; the crisis is at its climax—Merlin is not yet defeated. Nimuë, her back to him, holds the magic book and glances back at him while he, gripped with sudden tension, realizes too late that she will take advantage of his trust. Dark hills and glimmering water and sky frame the lonely scene.[58]

The well-known oil *The Beguiling of Merlin* is dated 1874, though finished and first exhibited in 1877.[59] The grey-haired Merlin sinks down, falling into his last sleep but fixing glazing eyes on Vivien, who stands erect among triumphant blossoms, her back to Merlin as she holds the book of power safely out of his reach, her head turned toward him as she observes, with a basilisk stare, the effect of her magic. Her right knee is bent and she will hurry away when satisfied that he is helpless. Merlin sinks like a corpse among flowers as the ancient hawthorn tree overwhelms the scene with fresh blossoms. Its

56. *Ibid.,* p. 140.

57. Harrison and Waters, p. 35.

58. *Merlin and Nimuë,* gouache, 64 × 50.8 cm., signed and dated EBJ 1861, in the Victoria and Albert Museum. *Burne-Jones,* cat. no. 27. This watercolor was owned by the Newcastle industrialist James Leathart. It had been exhibited by the Old Water-colour Society in the year of Yeats's birth.

59. *The Beguiling of Merlin,* oil, 186 × 111 cm., signed and dated: E. BURNE JONES MDCCCLXXIV, Lady Lever Art Gallery, Port Sunlight, Cheshire. *Burne-Jones,* cat. no. 129; color reproduction between pages 8 and 9. Owned by Frederick Leyland; exhibited in the Grosvenor Gallery, 1877; and in the Exposition Universelle, Paris, 1878. Burne-Jones shows Merlin in a hawthorn tree; Yeats, like Tennyson, places him in an oak tree.

FIGURE 5. Sir Edward Burne-Jones, *The Beguiling of Merlin*, 1874. Oil, 72½″ × 43¼″. (*The Board of Trustees of the National Museums and Galleries on Merseyside [Walker Art Gallery, Liverpool]*)

serpentine branches, mediating between the tree and the blossoms, seem the struggles between the sexes and between age and youth. Ironically, the figure of the erect young woman is doubled in the bole of the old tree, while declining branches of flowers double the fall of Merlin, easing him gently down. Merlin's left index finger points, unconsciously, toward a blue-white iris springing up in the foreground and perhaps announcing a resolution of the two principles. The iris counters Merlin's declining age with erect new growth. Its simple thrusting up out of the ground counters also the twisted poses of Nimuë and the tree. Nimuë's head is bent like the tree's crown as she turns toward Merlin. As we have said above, the story of *Vivien and Time*, like the story of Tennyson's "Merlin and Vivien," shows the struggle of youth and age. The flowers and youth win in Burne-Jones's representation of the latter; the flowers are frozen and Time triumphant in Yeats's play.[60]

Around 1873 Burne-Jones had made a study for the head of Nimuë which he thought better done than that in the finished painting. There are no Medusa-like cords binding her hair, her brow is less tense (or less overhung by her hair), her eyes more frankly observant, and her lips more sensuously parted.[61]

In 1882 Burne-Jones started a group of "water-colour designs for a flower book based on the visual images inspired by flowers."[62] *Witch's Tree* again shows an erect Vivien and a reclining Merlin in the hawthorn tree. Vivien, crowned, stands at the left holding a stringed instrument with which, rather than a book, she has put Merlin to sleep. Merlin is much older than in the earlier conceptions, white-bearded and in a black robe. He is motionless, sound asleep, and his mouth is open, suggesting a gentle snore. Vivien, in autumnal brown, is facing

60. See the interpretation in Harrison and Waters, pp. 110–13, much elaborated upon here.

61. Study for the head of Nimuë in *The Beguiling of Merlin,* gouache, 76.2 × 50.8 cm., c. 1873, in the Samuel and Mary R. Bancroft Collection, Delaware Art Museum, Wilmington. *Burne-Jones,* cat. no. 130.

62. See Johnson, plates 39 (*Ladder of Heaven*), 40 (*Wake Dearest*), 41 (*Golden Shower*), 42 (*Adder's Tongue*), 43 (*White Garden*), 44 (*Traveler's Joy*), 45 (*Witch's Tree*), and 46 (*Fire Tree*). All are watercolors 16.5 cm. in diameter done 1882–98, now in the British Museum.

Merlin, bending toward him quietly like a mother toward a sleeping child before she tiptoes from the nursery. Although there is ambiguity—she may be waiting to see whether her poison has worked—there is none of the tension of *The Beguiling of Merlin*. The serpentine branches only rise to support the unthreatening old man. The hawthorn blossoms actually have begun to cover his robe. Moreover they are growing between us and Vivien's back, binding her in with her ancient lover. She will have to push them aside if she leaves, which she as yet has made no motion to do. The design is altogether more gentle and restful than that of *The Beguiling of Merlin*. One could do worse than sleep forever in that bower as the music dies away and the hawthorn blossoms mount everywhere. There is little likelihood that Yeats could have seen this series, done 1882–1898, before finishing his play. But it is interesting that so near to the same date the poet and the painter were surrounding the Vivien story with symbolic flowers.

Burne-Jones's are beautiful representations of how the youthful Vivien traps wise old Merlin in his own snares. Yeats would later see his enchantress as the *Leanhaun Shee* (fairy mistress) of Celtic literature. She is Niamh of *The Wanderings of Oisin,* the perpetually young fairy with whom Oisin lives for 300 years. On leaving her and touching the soil of Ireland he becomes an ancient man exiled in mortality. Or Yeats would see her as the Woman of the Sidhe of *The Only Jealousy of Emer* who wished to carry off the aging Cuchulain. But the subject of our present play is not the story of "Merlin and Vivien" but of *Vivien and Time.* Instead of the beguiling of aged wisdom by youthful beauty we get the sequel to that story in which an aged figure—Time—swiftly defeats all the youthful beauty's plots and overcomes her. In *Vivien and Time* Yeats combines two archetypal plots. He ends the story of the enchantress with the story of Death and the Maiden.

Somewhere there must be the perfect illustration for the climax of Yeats's play. The scene of the young woman's playing a game of chance or skill with hoary Time is immediately recognizable and visually evocative. We envision it, and we have seen it before. But where? It is related certainly to the Death and the Maiden motif. One thinks of

Schubert's song and of late medieval and Renaissance pictures of women being accosted by grisly skeletons. Often the women primp before a mirror, like Vivien. And often the skeletons carry Time's hour-glass.[63]

Missing in all these pictures is the theme of trying to defeat the holder of the hour-glass in a game of chance or skill. However, Jean Wirth shows a fifteenth-century copper plate engraving of a premonitory skeleton playing chess with an old king while a court of secular and clerical figures watch and the Angel of Death, holding an hour-glass, presides. The king turns away from the board as Death is about to make the winning move.[64]

Yeats may have known some treatment of this motif such as the drawing *Die Schachspiele* by Moritz Retzsch described by George Eliot in *Daniel Deronda* (1876): "Most of us remember Retzsch's drawing of destiny in the shape of Mephistopheles playing at chess with man for his soul, a game in which we may imagine the clever adversary making

63. Jean Wirth, *La Jeune Fille et la Mort: Recherches sur les thèmes macabres dans l'art germanique de la Renaissance* (Genève: Librairie Droz, 1979), especially figs. 8, 42, 44, 55, 62, 63, 64, 65, 66, 67, 69, 70, 72, 73, 76, 129, 131, 140, 142, 143, 144. Wirth (pp. 2–3, 87–93) traces the descent of the poem by Matthias Claudius which Schubert set to music as "Der Tod und das Mädchen" back through an old ballad called "Lenore," popularized by Bürger, of which Scott did a version called "William and Mary," echoed in *The Rime of the Ancient Mariner*. J. B. Beer, *Coleridge the Visionary* (New York: Collier Books, 1962), pp. 155–56. The late medieval source Wirth finds in graphic artists such as Hans Baldung Grien who treated the theme about 1515. Wirth also cites sixteenth-century German plays on the subject (p. 91). The Death and the Maiden theme persists in the nineteenth century and is well enough known in 1819 to get into George Cruikshank's political cartoon of a skeleton "Radical Reform" raping the maiden Britannia. *Graphic Works of George Cruikshank*, sel. and ed. Richard A. Vogler (New York: Dover Publications, 1979), fig. 17.

64. Wirth, fig. 14; Maître B R à l'Ancre, *Partie d'échecs avec la mort* (cuivre). See also p. 32. This theme persists in our own time in Ingmar Bergman's film *The Seventh Seal* in which the central situation is a game of chess between Death and the knight who is protagonist. Bergman, a minister's son, derived the situation from old church paintings. Jörn Donner, *The Films of Ingmar Bergman* (New York: Dover Publications, 1972), p. 138. The knight says that he knows from pictures that Death plays chess. One such picture is a wall painting by Albertus Pictor in Taby Church, Uppland, Sweden. (Thanks to Professor John Friedman for this information.)

a feint of unintended moves so as to set the beguiled mortal on carrying
his defensive pieces away from the true point of attack."[65]

The nearest pre-1884 analogue we have so far been able to find for
the situation in *Time and the Witch Vivien* in which a woman plays dice
or chess with Time or Death is section III of *The Rime of the Ancient
Mariner,* and there the female Life-in-Death plays dice with Death, not
for her own life, but for the Mariner's. What is more, she wins!

> And is that Woman all her crew?
> Is that a DEATH? and are there two?
> Is DEATH that woman's mate?
>
> *Her* lips were red, *her* looks were free,
> Her locks were yellow as gold:
> Her skin was as white as leprosy,
> The Night-mare LIFE-IN-DEATH was she,
> Who thicks man's blood with cold.
>
> The naked hulk alongside came,
> And the twain were casting dice;
> The game is done! I've won! I've won!
> Quoth she, and whistles thrice.[66]

Yeats's Vivien does not win the dice-throw, nor is she supernatural. Yet
she is a witch, and she indeed provides a life-in-death for her victims,
making them wander forever in search of a phantom.

Although in *The Road to Xanadu* John Livingston Lowes cites
Gothic horror stories in general, the only specific source he gives for
Coleridge's incident is the tale "of one Falkenberg, who, for murder
done, is doomed to wander forever on the sea, accompanied by two
spectral forms, one white, one black. . . . And in a ship with all sails set,
the two forms play at dice for the wanderer's soul."[67] This is not at all
the situation in Yeats's play, but that situation could have been sug-

65. George Eliot, *Daniel Deronda* (Chicago and New York: Belford, Clarke, & Co.,
1885), chap. 37, p. 421.
66. *The Best of Coleridge,* ed. Earl Leslie Griggs (New York: The Ronald Press
Company, 1947), p. 47.
67. John Livingstone Lowes, *The Road to Xanadu: A Study in the Ways of the Imagination*
(Boston and New York: Houghton Mifflin Company, 1927), p. 277.

gested by Coleridge's poem as remembered in an illustration. Illustrators inevitably leave out of the composition the Mariner for whose soul the dice game is played and concentrate on Death and the woman. Thus the situation in the illustrations looks closer than is the text to the Death and the Maiden pictures, with the added element of the dice game. Of seven illustrated editions published before 1884, one might point to that by J. Noel Paton, an associate of the Pre-Raphaelites.[68] The jubilance of Life-in-Death would be like that of Vivien had she won her wager with Time.

To conclude, we may look at two pictures that are superficially very much alike. The general theme of Time (or Death) and the Maiden is treated by Burne-Jones in an 1860 decoration on the panel of his upright piano. Seven maidens droop in melancholy poses listening to one of their number play a lute. Sunflowers, also in varying poses, stand behind them. At the doorway, pulling the bell-rope, stands a crowned and shrouded Death, a scythe over his arm.[69] We mention this to point up the contrast with the very beautiful *Death and the Maidens* (or *The Reaper*) of 1872 by Puvis de Chavannes, a painter for whom Yeats later expressed great admiration.[70] The point is not that Yeats knew either picture, but that Puvis has taken the youth-age alternation one step beyond the victory of Time. As Vivien defeats age in the Merlin and Vivien story, and is in turn defeated by Time in *Time and the Witch Vivien,* so Time in turn is defeated, at least momentarily, in Puvis's picture. Time or Death, the old man with the scythe, has indeed cut swathes of flowers, and the forest to the right of the picture is dark with shadow. But in the center six maidens move happily in the sun, and they have taken the flowers Time has cut down and are

68. *The Rime of the Ancient Mariner,* ill. David Scott (London and Edinburgh, 1837); ill. E. H. Wehnert, B. Foster, et al. (London, 1857); ill. J. Noel Paton (London, 1863); ill. W. Collins (Glasgow, 1875); ill. Gustave Doré (London, 1876); ill. [Vest Pocket Series] (Boston, 1876); ill. G. Doré, B. Foster, et al. (Boston, 1884).

69. Victoria and Albert Museum, London. Raymond Watkinson, *Pre-Raphaelite Art and Design* (Greenwich, Conn.: New York Graphic Society, 1970), fig. 67.

70. Oil; Sterling and Francine Clark Art Institute, Williamstown, Mass. Reproduced in color in Robert L. Delevoy, *Symbolists and Symbolism* (New York: Rizzoli, 1978), p. 117; cf. *Autobiographies,* p. 550.

admiring and playing with them. Time's havoc merely enriches the perpetual present in which—to quote Wallace Stevens—"maidens die, to the auroral / Celebration of a maiden's choral."[71] At their feet the grim reaper lies asleep—at least for the moment.

So much for *Vivien and Time*. John Butler Yeats's portrait of Yeats as "King Goll" was done almost four years after the date of Yeats's first play. And it illustrates a poem written after Yeats had decided to devote himself to Irish subjects. But since it shows the poet with harp in hand, it may serve to represent Clarin, the first of many portraits in Yeats's poetry of himself as bard. Unfortunately, he is ripping out the strings instead of playing them properly, but then Clarin in *Vivien and Time*, being acted by unmusical Yeats, can only hold, not play, the instrument and only speak, not sing, the words.

After writing *Vivien and Time* Yeats first mentions Arthurian matter in his published poems and plays in *The Island of Statues* (written after *Vivien and Time* in the summer of 1884; published in 1885). The third sleeper awakened from enchantment by Naschina asks, "Doth still the Man whom each stern rover fears, / The austere Arthur, rule from Uther's chair?"[72] Yeats liked this effect enough to use it in his 1906 revision of *The Shadowy Waters*. Aibric, falling under the enchantment of Forgael's harp, murmurs, "What name had that dead king? Arthur of Britain? / No, no—not Arthur."[73]

In the Summer 1887 letter to Katharine Tynan cited above, Yeats contrasts "the aristocratic young ladies in the 'Idylls of the King'" with Swinburne's Mary Tudor. Tennyson's heroines are "less heroic" than those of Swinburne, Morris, and Rossetti "and less passionate and splendid but realised, as far as they go, more completely, much more like actual, everyday people."[74] If Vivien may be thought of as a

71. "Peter Quince at the Clavier," *The Collected Poems of Wallace Stevens* (New York: Alfred A. Knopf, 1955), p. 92.

72. *Variorum Poems*, p. 678; cf. *Poems*, p. 481.

73. *Ibid.*, p. 242; cf. *Poems*, p. 424.

74. *Letters to Katharine Tynan*, p. 35; cf. *CL1*, p. 30.

heroine, this description includes her. In his 1892 review of Tennyson's last book, Yeats recalls that *The Idylls of the King* was a triumph.[75]

By 1893 it is clear that in Yeats's view Malory, along with Chaucer and the ballads, represented in English literature the stage of Homer in Greek literature, that all-important "period of narrative poetry"[76] out of which the periods of drama and of lyric poetry grew. This conception had developed but not changed when Yeats wrote in *A Vision* (1925), "The period from 1005 to 1180 is attributed in the diagram to the first two gyres of our millenium, and what interests me in this period, which corresponds to the Homeric period some two thousand years before, is the creation of the Arthurian Tales and Romanesque architecture."[77]

In 1895 Yeats deplores the present age of criticism, a literature of "wise comments," in which "Arthur and his Court are nothing, but the many-coloured lights that play about them are as beautiful as the lights from cathedral windows." Deploring the "criticism of life" in the Victorian treatments of the heroic stories, he hopes for an age of imagination or revelation like that of the ancients or the Elizabethans which "created beings who made the people of this world seem but shadows."[78]

From 1896 to 1902 or 1903 Yeats was actively engaged with his friends in creating Celtic mysteries based on the four sacred symbols of Celtic heathendom.[79] Yet this activity was a grail quest. "The Four Jewels . . . foreshadowed the Christian symbolism of the Saint Grail, whose legends Willie loved to trace to Ireland."[80]

The final version of *The Speckled Bird* (1902–3) gives fictional accounts based on Yeats's work on the mysteries with MacGregor Mathers. A convert draws

75. *Uncollected Prose*, I, 252.   76. *Ibid.*, I, 269–70.

77. *A Vision*, 1925, p. 198.   78. *Essays and Introductions*, pp. 196–97.

79. Lucy Shepard Kalogera, *Yeats's Celtic Mysteries* (1977 Florida State University dissertation; Ann Arbor, Michigan, and London, England; University Microfilms International, 1980), p. 9; *Speckled Bird*, p. xxv.

80. Maud Gonne, "Yeats and Ireland," *Scattering Branches*, ed. Stephen Gwynn (New York: The Macmillan Company, 1940), p. 23.

a series of diagrams representing the ascent of the soul above the slopes of a sacred mountain towards the castle of the Grail, the stages of [this] ascent corresponding to its ascent through earth and water and air, the castle itself being the divine fire.

Another day while they were elaborating a diagram of a symbolical wood where Arthur's knights were to hunt symbolical creatures, Michael thought he saw a faint flicker of fire on the ceiling, and then Maclagan saw the whole room become full of fire.[81]

"The poems of the Grail, that are so plentiful" lack "the rich life that one feels behind the great poems" because

the poets of the Grail have had no initiation behind them to fix the images of their poems and to so weave image to image that, when one is named, all float up in the mind and create so great a reverie about [the] dish and the[?] cup and about the more ancient images that are behind them and about the illusions and dangers of the quest that a common beauty would all but weave all the poems into one great epic.[82]

The mysteries were to create a new literature. "Young poets and painters" were to "come to this order of the Grail" whose myth "is as interwoven with the scenery and the history of England and Wales, as the myths of Greece were with the scenery and history of Greece." In the pictures or poems of the genius of this group "Men will see . . . , besides the charm that his genius gives him, the fanaticism of the saints or of those that fling themselves upon spears."[83]

No doubt William Morris was one of the "poets of the Grail" who failed to base his art on a religious initiation. In "The Happiest of the Poets" (1902), Yeats asserted that Morris

wrote indeed of nothing but of the quest of the Grail, but it was the Heathen Grail that gave every man his chosen food, and not the Grail of Malory or Wagner; and he came at last to praise, as other men have praised the martyrs of religion or of passion, men with lucky eyes and men whom all women love.[84]

81. *Speckled Bird*, p. 80.
82. *Ibid.*, p. 206.
83. *Ibid.*, p. 207.
84. *Essays and Introductions*, p. 55.

Spenser, too, had missed the Grail of Malory. In Yeats's 1902 introduction to his selection from Spenser, Yeats found that

Full of the spirit of the Renaissance, at once passionate and artificial, looking out upon the world now as craftsman, now as connoisseur, he was to found his art upon theirs rather than upon the more humane, the more noble, the less intellectual art of Malory and the Minstrels.[85]

The new Celtic movement was to be a resurgence of that Celtic fountain, which, "of all the fountains of the passions and beliefs of ancient times in Europe . . . alone has been for centuries close to the main river of European literature" and "has again and again brought 'the vivifying spirit' 'of excess' into the arts. . . ." Here in "The Celtic Element in Literature" (1897) Yeats declares that

the legends of Arthur and his Table, and of the Holy Grail, once, it seems, the cauldron of an Irish god, changed the literature of Europe, and, it may be, changed, as it were, the very roots of man's emotions by their influence on the spirit of chivalry and on the spirit of romance. . . .[86]

Only the Scandinavian tradition (in Wagner, Morris, and the early Ibsen) has rivalled in "passionate element" the "still unfaded legends of Arthur and of the Holy Grail; and now a new fountain of legends . . . is being opened, the fountain of Gaelic legends . . . ,"[87] which "comes at a time when the imagination of the world is as ready as it was at the coming of the tales of Arthur and of the Grail for a new intoxication. . . . The arts by brooding upon their own intensity have become religious, and are seeking, as I think Verhaeren has said, to create a sacred book."[88]

As part of the new "religious" movement based on old legends, particularly the Celtic, Yeats, in an April 1898 review, welcomed Ernest Rhys's *Welsh Ballads*. He quoted one poem which remembered "the world's great mystery,— / The grave of Arthur." He praised most another Arthurian translation: " 'The House of a Hendré,' which is

85. *Ibid.,* p. 356.
86. *Ibid.,* p. 185.
87. *Ibid.,* p. 186.
88. *Ibid.,* p. 187.

inspired by some legend of a poet who saw in a vision the seven heavens, and Merlin and Arthur there, and the heroes and the poets about them, and his own seat waiting, and so longed for death. . . ." This he thought "the best of the original poems" with "a melancholy, like that of curlews crying over some desolate marsh. . . ."[89]

When in the late 1890s Yeats first knew Lady Gregory "the *Morte d'Arthur* was her book of books,"[90] and undoubtedly she stimulated him to read Malory in the period 1899–1902.[91] In a 1902 postscript to "The Celtic Element in Literature" he claims to have found in her *Cuchulain of Muirthemne* "a book to set beside the *Morte d'Arthur* and the *Mabinogion*."[92]

These same books, the *Morte d'Arthur* and the *Mabinogion,* are the first that the boy Michael Hearne takes an interest in in the final version of *The Speckled Bird* (February 1902–May 1903). In them he seeks not amusement but belief. He has a more religious than literary interest, yet thinks "not indeed of devil or angel, God or saint, but[?] of Merlin under the stone."[93] God the Father in a certain religious picture looks to him like Merlin or Taliesin.[94] He delights most in "the story of the Grail and the stories of Merlin and of Morgan le Fay. . . ."[95]

Yeats himself had experience of "unintentionally" casting "a glamour, an enchantment," in other words a mild hypnosis, over friends. In "Magic" (1901) he based on this fact the belief "that men could cast intentionally a far stronger enchantment, a far stronger glamour, over the more sensitive people of ancient times, or that men can still do so where the old order of life remains unbroken. . . . Why should not enchanters like him in the *Morte d'Arthur* make troops of horse seem but grey stones?"[96] The "wizard that changed a troop of horses into grey stones" is one of the Arthurian images in *The Speckled Bird* which "expressed by . . . extravagance an energy or a magnificence or a mystery not in the sober images of life."[97] That Yeats did not get his

89. *Uncollected Prose,* II, 93, 94.

90. *Ibid.,* II, 467.

91. Dume, p. 266.

92. *Essays and Introductions,* p. 188.

93. *Speckled Bird,* p. 9.

94. *Ibid.,* p. 12.

95. *Ibid.,* p. 9.

96. *Essays and Introductions,* p. 42.

97. *Speckled Bird,* pp. 9–10.

wizard from the *Morte d'Arthur,* as he misremembered, but from Whitley Stokes's 1890 *Lives of the Saints, from The Book of Lismore,*[98] only shows how thoroughly Yeats had confounded the Irish and the Arthurian traditions.

"Under the Moon," first published June 15, 1901, seems a tour de force, an advertisement of Yeats's program for placing *Cuchulain of Muirthemne* beside the *Morte d'Arthur* and the *Mabinogion.* The evocative list of names juxtaposes people and places from Arthurian tales, from the *Mabinogion,* and from Irish myth and legend. The first images, however, are Arthurian:

> I have no happiness in dreaming of Brycelinde,
> Nor Avalon the grass-green hollow, nor Joyous Isle,
> Where one found Lancelot crazed and hid him for a while. . . .[99]

Brycelinde, the wood Broceliande in which Vivien beguiled Merlin, is thus the most prominent image in the poem, but Vivien is not named as one of the "women whose beauty was folded in dismay" that Yeats is trying, in the poem, not to think about.[100]

In "Speaking to the Psaltery" (1902) Yeats tells us that "Sir Ector's lamentations over the dead Lancelot out of the *Morte d'Arthur*" were among the verses spoken by Florence Farr as she "sat with a beautiful stringed instrument upon her knee, her fingers passing over the strings."[101] Yeats's preoccupation with "cantillation" at this period is another form of the fascination that Arthurian ballads on the lips of a troubador had for him from first to last. It ends only with the publication after his death of "The Statesman's Holiday," a parody of his "early sentimental poems."[102]

---

98. *Ibid.,* p. 10, note 15.

99. *Variorum Poems,* p. 209; cf. *Poems,* pp. 82–83, and p. 634, note to 86.2–3.

100. George Brandon Saul, *Prolegomena to the Study of Yeats's Poems* (Philadelphia: University of Pennsylvania Press, 1957), p. 80, notes that " 'Joyous Isle' (*idem*) may be found in the 'Agravain' portion of the Prose Vulgate *Lancelot:* Yeats's reference implies a confusion of the story of Lancelot and Pelles' daughter."

101. *Essays and Introductions,* p. 13.

102. *Explorations,* p. 452.

> Here's a Montenegrin lute,
> And its old sole string
> Makes me sweet music
> And I delight to sing:
> *Tall dames go walking in grass-green Avalon.*[103]

It begins with Clarin-Yeats who, in *Vivien and Time,* speaks the ballads he cannot sing.

Also in 1902 Yeats added to *The Celtic Twilight* a section on "Miraculous Creatures." These contemporary Irish phenomena in the "Enchanted Woods" are "of the race of the white stag that flits in and out of the tales of Arthur, and of the evil pig that slew Diarmuid where Ben Bulben mixes with the sea wind."[104] (Again Yeats has melded contemporary spiritualistic phenomena with both Irish and Arthurian myth.) Followed by a white bracket and a lady on a white palfrey, the stag bounds into the room at the wedding celebration of Arthur and Guinevere (Malory III, 5) and is the cause of numerous adventures, in one of which the lady is kidnapped and on her return proves to be Nimuë (Malory III, 14). The beguiling of Merlin by Nimuë takes place in the very next chapter (Malory IV, 1). The white stag was a male symbol in a dream Mrs. Yeats had one night in January 1919 when Yeats himself dreamed of a female symbol, the Glencar waterfall.[105] "Towards Break of Day" was the result:

> But she that beside me lay
> Had watched in bitterer sleep
> The marvellous stag of Arthur,
> That lofty white stag, leap
> From mountain steep to steep.[106]

Yeats's determination to graft the Irish onto the Arthurian comes out even in his formula, in 1905, for that most important mark of the Irish

---

103. *Variorum Poems,* p. 627; cf. *Poems,* p. 587.

104. *Mythologies,* p. 65.

105. A. Norman Jeffares, *W. B. Yeats: Man and Poet* (London: Routledge & Kegan Paul, 1962), p. 210 and pp. 325–26, note 69; John Unterecker, *A Reader's Guide to William Butler Yeats* (The Noonday Press; New York: Farrar, Straus & Giroux, 1959), p. 163.

106. *Variorum Poems,* p. 399; cf. *Poems,* p. 185.

Renaissance, the Anglo-Irish idiom as it appeared in the plays of Lady
Gregory and of John Synge—"the beautiful English which has grown
up in Irish-speaking districts, and takes its vocabulary from the time of
Malory and of the translators of the Bible, but its idiom and its vivid
metaphor from Irish."[107]

Yeats's quest for wisdom would always take the form of a quest for
love and his quest for love that of a quest for wisdom. In a note to *The
Wind among the Reeds* (1899), which came out the year before *The
Shadowy Waters* (1900), Yeats claims to have found in the *Encyclopaedia
Britannica* that "Tristram, in the oldest form of the tale of Tristram
and Iseult, drank wisdom, and madness the shadow of wisdom, and
not love, out of the magic cup."[108] This may explain why *The Shadowy
Waters*, which reminds us so much of Wagner's *Tristan and Isolde*,
nevertheless has, compared to the opera, much more emphasis on the
supersensual and less on the sensual.[109]

Nevertheless there is no asceticism in Yeats's play. A.E., preferring
the earlier end of *The Shadowy Waters*, commented, "Merely because . . . [love] changes from a mortal world into an immortal [it] does
not change from sexual to spiritual. It can only do so by sacrifice and
experience. . . ." But Yeats was finally and unashamedly seeking not a
merely spiritual love, but one which stands, immortally, "In all the
vigour of its blood," as he wrote in "Tom the Lunatic" (1932).[110]

As Yeats was glad to connect wisdom with the great lover Tristram,
so he was glad to connect love with the wise Merlin. Other than *Vivien
and Time*, Yeats's most interesting citation of the story of Merlin and
Vivien, or in this instance "Niniene," is of William Wells Newell's
King Arthur and the Table Round (1897). He alludes to it in 1914, 1925,

107. *Essays and Introductions*, p. 299.

108. *Variorum Poems*, p. 801; cf. *Poems*, p. 625, where Finneran notes Yeats's probable
source.

109. In 1898 Yeats wrote that ". . . Richard Wagner's dramas of 'The Ring,' are, together
with his mainly Celtic 'Parsifal' [*sic*] and 'Lohengrin,' and 'Tristan and Iseult,' the most
passionate influence in the arts of Europe." *Uncollected Prose*, II, 125.

110. *A Tower of Polished Black Stones: Early Versions of* The Shadowy Waters, ed. David
Ridgley Clark and George Mayhew (Dublin: Dolmen Editions XI, 1971), p. xi. *Variorum
Poems*, p. 529; cf. *Poems*, p. 269.

and 1935—always as from Chrétien de Troyes, although it is actually from the *Huth Merlin*.[111] A digression here may help us understand the importance of this citation. In early unpublished versions of *The Shadowy Waters* Yeats has his hero Forgael reject Dectora. He seeks an immortal love, and when he sees that Dectora is not an immortal he goes celibate to death and eternity.[112] In the published versions Forgael and Dectora seek the other world together. A.E. guesses that "when the poet came himself to love, the thought of that lonely journey to the Everliving grew alien to his mood."[113]

Yeats's meeting Maud Gonne may not, however, have had more effect than his becoming, in the early 90s, a member of the cabalistic society the Golden Dawn and a student of the work of William Blake. Yeats's thought in *The Shadowy Waters* is cabalistic: "The reunion of God and His *Shekhinah* constitutes the meaning of redemption. In this state, again seen in purely mythical terms, the masculine and feminine are carried back to their original unity, and in this uninterrupted union of the two the powers of generation will once again flow unimpeded through all the worlds."[114]

In the 1925 *A Vision* Yeats summarizes:

When Merlin in Cretien de Troyes loved Ninian he showed her a cavern adorned with gold mosaics and made by a prince for his beloved, and told her that those lovers died upon the same day and were laid "in the chamber where they found delight." He thereupon lifted a slab of red marble that his

111. Newell, II, 134–39. Yeats's mistake was easy to make. Most of the book *is* taken from Chretien, and the introductory chapters concentrate on him, leaving an impression in the reader's mind that all the stories are his. In a vaguely worded note at the end of the book, however, we learn of the "Merlin" episode, "The romance is edited by G. Paris and J. Ulrich, Paris, 1886." If one reads the whole note carefully, one can deduce that the "romance" is not by Chretien. The note ends, "The story recites, that . . . Arthur became the father of Mordred . . . This relation . . . was . . . created by minstrels in order to heighten the tragic situation, and foreign to the story as known to Crestien" (Newell, II, 258–59). Dume explains that the Gaston Paris book is an edition of the *Huth-Merlin,* not of a Chretien romance at all (Dume, 276, note 298).

112. *Druid Craft,* p. 72.

113. *Song and Its Fountains* (New York: The Macmillan Company, 1932), p. 11.

114. Gershom G. Scholem, *On the Kabbalah and Its Symbolism* (New York: Schocken Books, 1969), p. 108.

art alone could lift and showed them wrapped in winding sheets of white samite. The tomb remained open, for Ninian asked that she and Merlin might return to the cavern and spend their night near those dead lovers, but before night came Merlin grew sad and fell asleep, and she and her attendants took him "by head and foot" and laid him "in the tomb and replaced the stone," for Merlin had taught her the magic words, and "from that hour none beheld Merlin dead or alive."[115]

The chamber carved from the rock, the gold mosaics, the tomb covered with a red cloth embroidered with beasts worked in gold, are all described by Newell.[116]

"Swedenborg, Mediums, and the Desolate Places" (1914) contains Yeats's earliest allusion to this tale. Yeats is distinguishing Swedenborg, who "but half felt, half saw, half tasted the kingdom of heaven,"[117] from Blake. The "impulse towards what is definite and sensuous . . . went out of Swedenborg when he turned from vision . . . whereas Blake carried it to a passion and made it the foundation of his thought."[118] In Blake's work, although we find there "the peaceful Swedenborgian heaven," we achieve that heaven "by no obedience but by the energy that 'is eternal delight,' for 'the treasures of heaven are not negations of passion but realities of intellect from which the passions emanate uncurbed in their eternal glory.'"[119]

For Blake "those who have come to freedom" live "above good and evil, neither accused, nor yet accusing, . . . their senses sharpened by eternity." These souls are higher than those exalted by theology. "Merlin, who in the verses of Chrétien de Troyes was laid in the one tomb with dead lovers, is very near and the saints are far away."[120] Stirred by natural "as by human beauty, he saw all Merlin's people, spirits 'of vegetable nature' and faeries whom we 'call accident and chance.' He made possible a religious life to those who had seen the painters and poets of the romantic movement succeed to theology. . . ."[121]

Yeats's lengthiest reference to the tale of Merlin and Vivien (or

115. *A Vision*, 1925, p. 197.
117. *Explorations*, p. 42.
119. *Ibid.*, p. 44.
121. *Ibid.*, p. 45.

116. Newell, II, 137–39.
118. *Ibid.*, p. 43.
120. *Ibid.*

Ninian) is that in the 1925 *A Vision* quoted above. It appears in section four of "Dove or Swan," Yeats's account of the historical aspects of his "system," in the section "A.D. 1050 to the Present Day."[122]

Perhaps Yeats sees the Romantic movement as understanding at last "something [which] must have happened in the courts and castles . . . that could not find its full explanation for a thousand years."[123] Romance replaced theology. A Byzantine bishop saw in a certain female singer "a beauty that would be sanctified" while in another singer Harun Al-Raschid saw a beauty "which was its own sanctity, and it was this latter sanctity, come back from the first Crusade or up from Arabian Spain or half Asiatic Provence and Sicily, that created romance. What forgotten reverie, what initiation it may be, separated wisdom from the monastery and, creating Merlin, joined it to passion."[124]

The initiation and reverie that created Merlin and joined wisdom to passion were, Yeats thought, missing from modern poems of the Grail.[125] And we have seen that the purpose of the Celtic mysteries was to provide again that initiation and reverie.

Yeats reinforced the example of Merlin in the tomb of dead lovers with the example of Parsifal's replacing church ceremony with the love trance, and of his praying to his lady rather than to God or the Virgin when going into battle.[126]

In his essay on "The Mandukya Upanishad" (1925) Yeats has harmonized the love trance with Tantric worship, "where a man and woman, when in sexual union, transfigure each other's images into the masculine and feminine characters of God." He speaks of married people who practise, "a meditation, wherein the man seeks the divine

122. *A Vision*, 1925, pp. 196–215. Rewritten as section five in the 1937 *A Vision* without significant change in the passage about Merlin. *A Vision*, 1937, pp. 285–300.

123. *A Vision*, 1925, pp. 196–97.

124. *Ibid.*, p. 197.

125. *Speckled Bird*, p. 206.

126. *A Vision*, 1925, p. 198. Yeats refers on several occasions to Wolfram von Eschenbach's *Parsival: Explorations*, p. 113 (1903), pp. 214–15 (1906); *Autobiographies*, p. 151 (1922); *A Vision*, pp. 198–99 (1925); *Essays and Introductions*, p. 484 (1935). He read it in Jessie L. Weston's translation (1894) according to Dume, p. 337.

Self as present in his wife, the wife the divine Self as present in the man" and asks, "Did this worship, this meditation, establish among us romantic love, was it prevalent in Northern Europe during the twelfth century?"[127] The love trances of Gawain and Parsifal are here his primary examples of romantic love, with Merlin as a supporting example.

In the German epic *Parsifal* Gawain drives a dagger through his hand without knowing it during his love-trance, Parsifal falls into such a trance when a drop of blood upon snow recalls to his mind a tear upon his wife's cheek, and before he awakes overthrows many knights. When riding into battle he prays not to God but to his wife, and she, falling into trance, protects him. One thinks, too, of that mysterious poem by Chrétien de Troyes, wherein Vivien, having laid Merlin, personification of wisdom, by the side of dead lovers, closes their tomb.[128]

Vivien and Time, then, is an example of the fascination with the stories of Arthur—and particularly with the figure of the magician Merlin—which Yeats felt all his life. Merlin and Arthur are not necessary to the bare plot of Yeats's first play. They are brought in because of his early awareness of the need of myth to support the meaning of his story and because of his great and lasting interest in the Arthurian tradition. But *Vivien and Time* is unique in Arthurian literature. Everyone knows what happened to Merlin. But what, in the end, happened to Vivien? Only Yeats, so far as we know, adds this tale to the Arthurian cycle.

127. *Essays and Introductions,* p. 484.
128. *Ibid.*

PART TWO

Maturity: The Theatre of Desolate Reality

The Abbey Dramatist

🌿 "The struggle for intellectual or imaginative freedom"

EFORE TURNING from the Young Yeats to his development as a mature dramatist, we should say something about the dramatic movement of which he was a part. What better than to hear Yeats himself on *The Irish National Theatre* in a previously uncollected address to the fourth Congress of the Alessandro Volta Foundation, held in Rome, October 8–14, 1934?[1] Playwrights and people of the theatre from all over Europe attended.

The subject of Yeats's address is the theatre, not his own work, about which he says almost nothing. In his account, he is concerned with imaginative truth rather than literal. He makes mythic figures of Lady Gregory and John Synge and conceives as dramatic action this national theatre's battles with the nationalist press and nationalist audiences.

When he describes the 1899 founding of the Irish Literary Theatre, he remembers that he conceived it and that Lady Gregory helped to make it possible, but he forgets the considerable efforts of George Moore and Edward Martyn. They are part of the Theatre's history but because of a divergence of goals were not to be enshrined by Yeats as part of its myth. The name of Douglas Hyde, however, is evoked, though he was only peripheral to the founding of the Theatre. But, as founder of the Gaelic League, first president of the Irish Free State, and—most important of all, probably—author of *The Love Songs of Connacht,* he was a positive symbol.

Yeats does give credit to Frank and William Fay, leaders of the company of Irish actors with whom Yeats, Synge, and Lady Gregory founded the Irish National Theatre Society in 1903. But he gives credit to them as "our two best men actors" (see below, p. 113) and obscures

1. *Convegno di Lettere,* 8–14 Ottobre 1934–XII, Tema: Il Teatro Drammatico. Reale Accademia d'Italia, Fondazione Alessandro Volta, Atti dei Convegni, 4 (Roma: Reale Accademia d'Italia, 1935–XIII) pp. 386–92.

his wresting of control from them under the rubric "theatrical organisation" (p. 114). The Fay brothers, like the Allgood sisters, have their place in the myth. They all show the natural dramatic talent of the naïve Irish artisan when uncorrupted by the English theatre. They are positive symbols.

What kind of symbol was the "generous Englishwoman" (p. 115), Miss Annie Horniman? Perhaps not exactly the one Yeats would have chosen. The fact is, however, that she made possible the Abbey Theatre, which opened its doors on December 27, 1904. Yeats pays his debt to her in a warm paragraph. James Joyce is mentioned, not because of any connection with the Irish theatre, but because Yeats's audience would know the name.

Yeats's portrait of Synge, as elsewhere, is moving. Synge preoccupied Yeats's imagination. Moreover, in defending Synge, and evoking the pathos or tragedy of his martyrdom to disease, he defended his own aims in the theatre and, scorning his and Synge's enemies, made of the cancer victim a literary martyr triumphant in his posthumous fame and the fame of the theatre with which both their names are associated. Yeats romanticizes his meeting with Synge and no doubt confuses their first meeting in Paris on December 21, 1896, with later meetings. That he "sent him to the Aran Islands to study common life" (p. 110) like other such assertions elsewhere, "may reasonably be regarded as much as a comment upon what Synge did as an accurate memory of what [Yeats] told Synge to do."[2] And there are other inaccuracies.[3] But Yeats's portrait of Synge is powerful and appealing, and we need not quibble.

Yeats leaves us with some strong thoughts—that he, Synge, and Lady Gregory were "typical of an Ireland that was passing away . . .

2. Robin Skelton, *The Writings of J. M. Synge* (Indianapolis: Bobbs-Merrill, 1971) p. 24. See also the account in J. M. Synge, *The Well of the Saints,* ed. Nicholas Grene (Washington, DC: The Catholic University of America Press; Gerrards Cross, Bucks: Colin Smythe, 1982) pp. 1–2.

3. Yeats speaks of Synge's death "in his 35th year." Synge, born 16 April 1871, died on 24 March 1909. He would have been thirty-eight on his next birthday. Further on Yeats says Synge died in 1910.

'the Protestant Ascendancy' " and that they gave "to the new Catholic Ireland that was about to take its place a parting gift, the Irish National Theatre" (p. 112); that in this theatre Ireland, having won political freedom, might fight out upon the stage "the struggle for intellectual or imaginative freedom." As always, Yeats moves from the public struggle to the struggle in the deeps of the mind. The Irish must struggle "for an escape from the tyranny of the second-rate, whether it comes from the commercialised newspaper, or from the commercialised art of the contemporary stage, or from the nightmare in our own souls" (p. 116). The drama in our own souls is always the subject of Yeats's plays.

During the sixth session of the congress, the revolutionary stage-designer Edward Gordon Craig, friend and ally of Yeats in theatrical experimentation, called his colleagues' attention to the poet's presence:

Edward Gordon Craig: The remarkable fervour shown by most of the speakers who have insisted on the prime importance of the Dramatic Poet, the written word, the part which lives when all else is forgotten, urges me to remind the delegates and all present, that we have had in our midst for 3 to 4 days a great Dramatic Poet and no one has till now even mentioned his name. . . . I refer to W. B. Yeats, of Ireland.[4]

Yeats presided in the seventh, and spoke in the ninth, sessions. Maurice Maeterlinck was among those present, and Luigi Pirandello had suggested that Yeats take the chair. When he delivered his own address, Yeats followed Sergo Amaglobeli, head and artistic director of the State Academic Theatre "Maly" of Moscow. Amaglobeli spoke in Russian, and the French report of his closing remarks reads:

Le prolétariat victorieux de l'Union Soviétique a démontré, en effet, qu'il se considère comme l'héritier de tous les progrès de l'humanité dans le domaine de la culture et de l'art; qu'il sait conserver avec amour et avec tous les soins nécessaires les trésors de la civilisation et en fait jouir les millions de travailleurs; qu'il possède une énergie créatrice puissante et que de son sein sortent et sont déjà sortis des dramaturges, des régisseurs, des acteurs, des

---

4. *Convegno di Lettere*, p. 269.

peintres et des hommes de théâtre en général de grande valeur; qu'il crée un théâtre nouveau, inspiré aux idées de Marx-Lénine-Staline,—le théâtre de la société socialiste.[5]

Yeats responded, and his remarks were also reported in French, as follows:

William Butler Yeats est absolument opposé à la propagande par le théâtre, l'oeuvre d'art ne doit rechercher et exprimer que la sincérité et l'humanité les plus profondes. De même il n'est pas du tout partisan d'un théâtre qui s'adresse aux masses, ce qui ne veut pas dire au peuple, car le public le plus fidèle et le plus dévoué de son Théâtre national irlandais est justement celui qui occupe les places les plus modestes, ouvriers, employés de commerce, étudiants. Il faut s'adresser à quelques-uns, leur imposer ce qu'ils devront aimer et admirer, et n'étendre que peu à peu son rayon d'action.[6]

Yeats's address followed.

5. *Ibid.*, p. 380.
6. *Ibid.*, pp. 385–86.

The Irish National Theatre

BY W. B. YEATS

I am about to describe the rise and achievement of a small, dingy, impecunious theatre, known to Irishmen all over the world because of the fame of its dramatists and its actors, because of the riots that have accompanied certain of its performances, because of its effect upon the imagination of Ireland. But first I must speak of an historical event. Some forty years ago the national leader, Charles Stewart Parnell, stood at the height of his power. Then came the divorce case, he had been, it was discovered, for many years the lover of a married woman. The Irish people at a great meeting in Dublin and by the unanimous voice of its politicians proclaimed him still the national leader. Then the English Prime Minister declared in a notorious letter that if Parnell remained leader his own leadership of the English Liberal Party would "become a nullity." The majority of Irish politicians, believing that Ireland could not obtain a National Parliament without the English Liberal Party, turned against Parnell. He died in the midst of the turmoil, worn out with work and grief, and for nine years political Ireland gave itself up to the bitterest dispute in its history. Had Parnell been betrayed? Who had betrayed him? Families were divided, son against father, brother against brother.

In the midst of that disillusionment, of that bitterness, the Irish imaginative movement began. Everywhere men and women turned from politics in despair. Four or five years after the beginning of this movement I was sitting in a garden off the Galway coast talking to my friend Lady Gregory. I told of an old ambition to found an Irish National Theatre. Her friend Dr. Douglas Hyde had founded the Gaelic League which had for its object the substitution of Gaelic, the ancient language of the country, for the English in which we had all come to write and think, but that if it were indeed possible, would take many years. We must put Irish emotion into the English language if we were to reach our own generation. The people, after generations of politics, read nothing but the newspapers, but they could listen (to what interminable speeches had they listened) and they would listen to plays. I told Lady Gregory that I had given up the project because I saw no likelihood of finding the money. She offered to raise it among her friends, and at that moment our National Theatre was founded. Yet, when the Theatre had taken its final shape, it was not that money, which was never called for, but her own energy and her own dramatic and literary genius which neither I nor she foresaw that proved of the first importance. When we talked in that garden, she, a woman of forty-six or forty-seven, had written nothing. When she died three years ago in extreme old age she was of all Irishwomen the most famous. She belonged to an old Protestant Galway family, had spent most of her life in two Galway houses; the house where she was born, since burnt down in a year of trouble, the house into which she married; both surrounded by vast desmesnes and ancient trees. All about her lived a peasantry who told stories in a form of English which has much of its syntax from Gaelic, and it was she who discovered that this dialect, vivid, sonorous, novel to modern ears, was our most powerful dramatic vehicle. Her plays are constantly acted, not only in Dublin but by little companies in village halls. Their names are as familiar as old proverbs.

The second miracle of my life was that I found in a Paris Student's hotel John Synge and sent him to the Aran Islands to study common life. Two or three years later, moved by Lady Gregory's example, he put that life into those strange dialect plays, "The Well of the Saints" and "The Playboy of the Western World." I sent him to the Aran Islands because I had just been there. I landed from a fishing yawl, a little group of Islanders, who had gathered to watch a stranger's arrival, brought me to "the oldest man upon the island." He spoke but two sentences speaking them very slowly, "If any gentleman has done a crime we'll hide him. There was a gentlemen that killed his father and I had him in my house three months till he got away to America." It was a play founded on that old man's story Synge brought back with him, called "The Playboy of the Western World." A young man arrives at a little public house and tells the publican's daughter that he has murdered his father. He so tells it that he has all her sympathy, and every time he re-tells it, with new exaggerations and additions, he wins the sympathy of somebody or other, for it is the countryman's habit to be against the law. The countryman thinks the more terrible the crime the greater must the provocation have been. The young man himself, under the excitement of his own story, becomes gay, energetic and lucky. He prospers in love, comes in first at the local races, and bankrupts the roulette tables afterwards. Then the father arrives with his head bandaged but very lively, and the people turn upon the impostor. To win back their esteem he takes up a spade to kill his father in earnest, but horrified at the threat of what had sounded so well in the story, they bind him to hand over to the police. The father releases him and father and son walk off together, the son still buoyed up by his imagination announcing that he will be master henceforth. Picturesque, poetical, fantastical, a masterpiece of style and music, it roused the populace to fury. We played it under police protection, seventy policemen in the theatre the last night, and five hundred some newspaper said keeping order in the streets outside. It is never played before any Irish audience for the first time without something or other being flung at the players. In New York a currant cake and a watch were flung, the owner of the watch claiming it at the stage door afterwards. The Irish democratic party, a party of smooth rhetoricians, had made the virtues of the Irish peasant canonical, to mock those virtues was to mock Ireland herself.

The Dublin audience has however long since accepted the play. It has noticed I think that everyone upon the stage is somehow lovable and companiable, that Synge has described through an exaggerated symbolism a reality which he loved precisely because he loved all reality. The fall of Parnell had not turned Synge from politics; he had no politics. So far from being, as they had thought, a politician working in the interests of England, he was so little a politician that the world merely amused him and touched his pity.

But who was Synge himself? This man who had influenced Ireland so much before his death in a Dublin hospital in his 35th year. I had been told when I first met him in 1896 that I would find in an attic an Irishman much poorer than myself, and I was very poor. Like Lady Gregory he belonged to an old Irish Protestant family, a Dublin street is named after it, the Synge house in Dublin, now let as offices, is one of the show houses of Dublin; there were seven Bishops among his ancestors, one that Bishop who refused to ordain Oliver Goldsmith because Oliver Goldsmith wore red breeches. Sometimes, though a simple courteous man, he seemed to remember that past and became reserved and lonely. With just enough money to keep him from starvation and not always from half starvation, he had wandered about Europe, travelling third class or upon foot, playing his fiddle to poor men on the road or in their cottages. He was the man that we needed because he was the only man I have ever known incapable of a political thought or of a humanitarian purpose. He could walk the roadside all day with some poor man without any desire to do him good or for any reason except that he liked him. He was to do for Ireland, though more by his influence on other dramatists than by his direct influence, what Robert Burns did for Scotland. When Scotland thought herself gloomy and religious Providence restored her imaginative spontaneity by raising up Robert Burns to commend drink and the Devil.

During its first years our Theatre received its character from Lady Gregory's comedies, always gracious and indulgent in their attitude to life, from the bitter-sweet of Synge's tragic comedies, and from the work of a third writer who wrote in verse and chose his themes from ancient Irish legends. I was that third writer, and who am I, how shall I characterise myself? I also come of a Protestant family. My father was an artist, his work is in public galleries, but in his life he had little fame and a hard struggle to live. His small Kildare estate had vanished in the land war. Lady Gregory, John Synge and I were in some sense typical of an Ireland that was passing away. The Ireland of what the historians call "the Protestant Ascendancy," and it was right that we should give to the new Catholic Ireland that was about to take its place, a parting gift, the Irish National Theatre.

Our first players came from England, but presently we began our real work with a company of Irish amateurs. Somebody had asked me at a lecture "Where will you get your actors?" and I had said "I will go into some crowded room, put the name of everybody in it on a different piece of paper, put all those pieces of paper into a hat and draw the first twelve." I have often wondered at that prophecy, for though it was spoken probably to confound and confuse a questioner it was very nearly fulfilled. Our two best men actors were not indeed chosen by chance, for one was a stage-struck accountant's clerk, the other a working man who had toured Ireland in a theatrical company managed by a negro. I doubt if he had learned much in it, for its methods were rough and ready, the negro whitening his face when he played a whiteman, but, so strong is stage convention, blackening it when he played a black man. If a player had to open a letter on the stage I have no doubt that he struck it with the flat of his hand, as I have seen players do in my youth, a gesture that lost its meaning generations ago when blotting paper was substituted for sand. Both these men, Frank and William Fay, were men of remarkable character and talent. The first, the accountant's clerk, had studied the speaking of verse on the French and English stage in the Seventeenth and Eighteenth centuries and was an exquisite elocutionist, the other was a comedian of genius with a curious power of keeping a personal distinction in the midst of farce. We got our women, however, from a little political society which described its object as educating the children of the poor, or, according to its enemies, teaching them a catechism that began with this question: "What is the origin of evil," and the answer, "England." They came to us for patriotic reasons and acted from precisely the same impulse that had made them teach, and yet two of them proved players of genius, Miss Allgood and Miss "Maire O' Neill." They were sisters, one all simplicity, her mind shaped by folk song and folk story; the other sophisticated, lyrical and subtle. I do not know what their thoughts were as that strange new power awoke within them, but I think they must have suffered from a bad conscience, a feeling that the patriotic impulse had gone, that they had given themselves up to vanity or ambition. Yet I think that first misunderstanding of themselves made their peculiar genius possible, for had they come to us with theatrical ambitions they would have imitated some well-known English player and sighed for well known English plays. Nor would they have found their genius if we had not remained for a long time obscure like the bird within its shell, playing in little halls, generally in some shabby out of the way street. We could experiment and wait, with nothing to fear but political misunderstanding. We had little money and at first needed little, twentyfive pounds given by Lady Gregory, twenty pounds by myself and a few pounds picked up here and there. And our theatrical organisation was preposterous, players and authors all sitting together and settling by vote what play should be performed and who should play it. It took a series of disturbances, weeks of argument during which no performance could be given, before Lady Gregory, John Synge and I were put in control. And our relations with the public were even more disturbed. One play was violently attacked by the patriotic press because it described a married peasant woman who had a lover, and when we published the old Aran folktale upon which it was founded the press said the tale had reached Aran from some decadent author of pagan Rome. My verse plays were not long enough to fill an evening so Lady Gregory wrote her first comedy, a little play on a country love story in the dialect of her neighbourhood. A countryman returns from America with one hundred pounds and discovers his old sweetheart married to a bankrupt farmer. He plays cards with the farmer and by cheating against himself gives him the hundred pounds. The company refused to perform it because they said to admit an emigrant's return with a hundred pounds would encourage emigration. We produced evidence of returned emigrants with much larger sums but were told that only made the matter worse. Then, after interminable argument had worn us all out Lady Gregory agreed to reduce the sum to twenty and the actors gave way. That little play was conventional and sentimental, but her next discovered her genius.

Nobody reading today her "Seven Short Plays" can understand why one of them, now an Irish classic, "The Rising of the Moon," could not be performed for two years because of political hostility. A policeman discovers an escaped Fenian prisoner and lets him free because the prisoner has aroused with some old songs the policeman's half forgotten patriotism. The players would not perform it because they said it was an unpatriotic act to admit that a policeman was capable of patriotism. One well known leader of the mob wrote to me, "How can the Dublin mob be expected to fight the police if it looks upon them as capable of patriotism?" When performed at last the play was received with enthusiasm but only to get us into new trouble. The chief Unionist Dublin newspaper denounced us for slandering His Majesty's forces, and Dublin Castle denied to us a privilege we had shared with the other Dublin theatres of buying, for stage purposes, the cast off clothes of the police. Castle and Press alike knew that the police had frequently let off political prisoners but "that only made the matter worse." Every political party had the same desire to substitute for life, which never does the same thing twice, a bundle of reliable principles and assertions.

The little halls where we performed could hold a couple of hundred people at the most and our audience was often not more than twenty or thirty, and we performed but two or three times a month and during our periods of quarrelling not even that. But there was no lack of leading articles, we were, from the first, a recognised public danger. Then a generous Englishwoman gave us a theatre. After a particularly angry leading article I had come in front of the curtain and appealed to the hundred people of the audience for their support. When I came down from the stage an old friend, Miss Horniman, from whom I had been expecting a contribution of twenty pounds said, "I will find you a theatre." She found and altered for our purpose what is now the Abbey Theatre, Dublin, and gave us a small subsidy for a few years.

When Synge died in 1910 we were playing to an empty theatre, partly the result of the "Playboy" riots, partly because the country had a different mood. We had led it to the villages that never change and to the past of legend, the past that is a more living present, but it could follow us no longer. A generation had grown up that had spent its boyhood in the midst of the Parnellite dispute. It had no time for the past, no patience with the village. Ireland had failed, had shown herself ungrateful, self-seeking, ignoble, or so their fathers and mothers had said. Ireland must be shown as she actually was that she might be transformed. One man of that generation, not a dramatist, has sent his bitterness and his genius through Europe. James Joyce, the son of a small Parnellite organiser had begun to write though not yet to publish; he was an exile, at first in Zurich, then in Paris, in flight from the objects of his hatred, bearing in mind always in minute detail, even to the names over the shops, the Dublin that he hated but could never forget. This generation came into the theatre through a group of writers that we call the Cork Realists. They received their dramatic form from the first and no longer acted plays of the present manager of the Abbey Theatre, Mr Lennox Robinson. He has written many admirable plays of historical or psychological drama but has never returned to that first mood, but the form once created enabled a score of realists to attack every popular abuse, bribery in local affairs, subserviency to the English government. Comic figures were created, and of these one at any rate, a satire on Parliamentary politics, has given phrases to cabmen and to peasants. Just as that impulse was dying away, came the fantastic genius of Sean O' Casey; his "Juno and the Paycock," his "Plough and the Stars." Then came more and perhaps worse riots, for his mind, which combined the fantastic imagination of Synge with the precise purpose of the realists, attacked not the peasant, but, as it seemed, the methods of a triumphant rebellion. For a few years the theatre had a great prosperity, but now the tide has sunk again, and it must every two or three years tour the United States. It is a repertory theatre, changing its bill every week, and the repertory is now immense, but the whole repertory seems to rise or sink in popular favour according to that granted to or witheld from some one dramatist. I await with confidence our next popular dramatist. Ireland has won its political freedom; the struggle for intellectual or imaginative freedom, for an escape from the tyranny of the second-rate, whether it comes from the commercialised newspaper, or from the commercialised art of the contemporary stage, or from the nightmare in our own souls, must, in some measure, be fought out upon the stage.

The Drama of Passionate Perception

WE TURN NOW from Yeats's account of the Irish theatre to distinguish the nature of his own drama and to
plot the course of his development as a dramatist. All
the Rome talk tells us about his plays is that he "wrote
in verse and chose his themes from ancient Irish
legends." Yet the thought of the concluding sentence—that we must
struggle to escape "from the nightmare of our own souls"—strikes the
true Yeatsian note.

The Nature of Yeatsian Drama

From first to last Yeats's is a subjective drama. He was always in
revolt against modern realism. He felt that as great drama approached
its highest themes and its richest, most concentrated representation of
human action, it portrayed the self-conquest of a soul and used the
language of poetry. An age in which people derived their view of life
from science and commerce had produced a realistic and naturalistic
drama having the force of fact but lacking the imaginative power and
richness of traditional poetic drama. Ibsen, the greatest in this kind,
was dwarfed when placed beside Shakespeare and Sophocles, not
simply because of a difference in genius, but because of the limitations
of the realistic mode. "Is not the greatest play," Yeats asks, "not the
play that gives the sensation of an external reality but the play in which
there is the greatest abundance of life itself, of the reality that is in our
minds?"[1] He saw Ibsen's *Ghosts* in December 1904 and wondered
"What law had these people broken that they had to wander round
that narrow circle all their lives?" Yeats found the characters "less than

1. *Explorations*, p. 167.

117

life-size . . . ," and called them "little whimpering puppets." "Why did they not speak out with louder voices or move with freer gestures?" Perhaps the mob in the great cities, "where nobody is ever alone with his own strength," had "robbed those angelic persons of the energy of their souls."[2] Yeats would have applauded Francis Fergusson's diagnosis in *The Idea of a Theater:* The action of *Ghosts* "is not completed: Mrs. Alving is left screaming with the raw impact of the calamity. . . . The acceptance of the catastrophe, leading to the final vision or epiphany . . . is lacking." Fergusson concludes that "Ibsen could not find a way to represent the action of his protagonist, with all its moral and intellectual depth, within the terms of modern realism."[3]

Eric Bentley called Yeats "the only considerable verse playwright in English for several hundred years," not simply for creating "dramatic passages," but for having a truly "dramatic conception" and realizing it in a "dramatic whole."[4] T. S. Eliot, on the other hand, found Yeats's achievement to be that of solving the problem—which one must admit to be the chief one—of dramatic speech in verse. "A study of his development as a dramatist would show, I think, the great distance he went, and the triumph of his last plays. . . . It was only in his last play *Purgatory* that he solved his problem of speech in verse, and laid all his successors under obligation to him."[5]

In the writing of a play, the problems of style and of dramatic construction are, of course, subservient to the dramatist's fundamental intention. If Yeats ultimately succeeded in capturing, in both poetic speech and theatrical art, a truly dramatic vision of life, what was the nature of that vision?

To clarify the quality of Yeats's vision and to help me place Yeatsian drama in relation to the tradition, I use the formula of "the tragic rhythm" from Fergusson's *The Idea of a Theater.* Fergusson applies to a number of great plays Kenneth Burke's description of the tragic rhythm from purpose through passion to perception.[6] Sophocles' *Oedi-*

2. *Ibid.,* pp. 168–69.
3. Fergusson, pp. 156–57.
4. Bentley, p. 197.
5. Eliot, *Poetry and Drama,* pp. 22–23.
6. Kenneth Burke, *A Grammar of Motives* (New York: Prentice Hall, 1945), pp. 38–40.

pus Rex presents the full tragic rhythm and is therefore a "realist" drama, not in the sense of circumstantial realism, but in the sense that in it no aspect of this basic rhythm of experience is ignored. The action "starts with the reasoned purpose of finding Laius' slayer."

This attempt encounters unexpected difficulties, and the shaken characters "suffer the piteous and terrible sense of the mystery of the human situation. From this suffering or passion, with its shifting visions, a new perception of the situation emerges; and on that basis the purpose of the action is redefined, and a new movement starts." This tragic rhythm is, in *Oedipus Rex,* the form of the play as a whole, and the form of each episode in the play.[7] *Hamlet* also presents or contains the full tragic rhythm, using analagous action—the double plot, the several fathers (Hamlet's, Laertes', Fortinbras'), etc., to multiply what happens in a number of mirrors. Yeats called this effect "Emotion of Multitude."[8]

Racinian tragedy on the other hand is "idealist," as, in a different way, is Wagnerian opera. Neither presents the full tragic rhythm. Racine's *Berenice* dramatizes human action as purpose, Wagner's *Tristan und Isolde* as passion. Reason is the reality of Racine's world. If Oedipus were a Baroque hero, his "rationalization of his moral being, and of his duty as a monarch, would be fixed at the brink of his perpetually rejected passion of fear and anger."[9] And passion is the reality of Wagner's world. "The action of Tristan is related to that of the Sophoclean tragic rhythm . . . at the moment when passion breaks through the conflicts of the protagonists, with their individual beings and their reasoned platforms, and before this surge of feeling and imagery has assumed the form which the pious expectation of the Sophoclean chorus will give it."[10] Each of these "idealist" theatres produces plays that are "univocal" in form. The Racinian alexandrines demonstrate a rational syllogistic progression. Yeats had called French dramatic poetry rhetorical, "for what is rhetoric but the will trying to

7. Fergusson, p. 18.   8. *Essays and Introductions*, pp. 215–16.
9. Fergusson, p. 62.   10. *Ibid.,* p. 74.

do the work of the imagination?"[11] On the other hand, Wagner's images create a pattern of emotional association.

Ibsen's theatre of circumstantial realism, although it reproduces the tragic rhythm in a small figure (and is therefore not univocal or idealist) is, as we have seen, curtailed before the moment of vision or epiphany. In Yeats's drama, however, that vision is not curtailed (although almost everything else often is). Eric Bentley finds the tragic rhythm in a typical play by the later Yeats.[12] I find, however, that although Yeats's theatre contains implicitly the whole tragic rhythm, there is only one movement explicit and central in most of his plays—the movement from passion to perception. The plays are recognition scenes, showing heroic suffering becoming deep knowledge. They may be regarded as manifestations, "epiphanies," as Joyce called his recorded insights. They are a "showing forth" like Dante's vision of Paolo and Francesca. In many of the plays the character of manifestation extends to the most external surface aspects of the situation. We are asked to witness the phenomena of spiritualism. Whatever we think about such matters, we should not ignore the importance of the action Yeats is attempting to imitate; an apprehension of reality, beyond those granted by mere reason or passion, in a drama of perception. As *Berenice* represents the action and theatre of reason, so Yeats's plays represent the action and theatre of perception. Since the action of perception implies the protagonist's discovery and awareness of the total rhythm, the drama of perception will not be "idealist" or "univocal" in quite the same sense that the drama of reason or the drama of passion is. Both form and language must have a realism appropriate to the action of perception. They will not be limited to demonstrating reason or to expressing passion but will be marked by the microcosmic inclusiveness of seeing, discovering, recognizing the total rhythm.

11. *Essays and Introductions*, p. 215.
12. Bentley, p. 207.

Yeats's Development as a Dramatist

Yeats's development as a dramatist, through at least fifty-four years of play-writing (1884–1938), was guided by his attempt to achieve a dramatic form and a dramatic-poetic speech suitable to this action of perception. Most of the plays of his first period—*The Countess Kathleen* (published 1892), *The Land of Heart's Desire* (1894), *Cathleen ni Houlihan* (1902), *The Pot of Broth* (performed 1902), *Where There Is Nothing* (published 1902; later revised as *The Unicorn from the Stars*, performed 1907), *The Hour Glass* (1903)—show "real" folk characters, in whom we can believe, perceiving some sort of vision which gains an objective reality through our confidence in these witnesses. In this period Yeats attempted to adopt folk-material directly without tampering with its mythic grasp of the full tragic rhythm. He was at the same time attempting, under the tutelage of George Moore, to learn construction. The two attempts were not compatible. When, after learning what Moore had to teach him, he began to seek a unity less mechanical, more pervasive than Moore was capable of, he revised *The Countess Kathleen* according to idealist principles, improving construction (according to those principles) but abstracting away the primitive form and awareness. *The Countess Kathleen* (published 1892) is closer to a mythic grasp of reality than is *The Countess Cathleen* (1913), where all obeys standards of good construction and is assimilated to the poet's individual ideas, emotions, and autobiographical expression.

In his second period Yeats loses contact with the "real" Irish peasantry and retreats into the Celtic twilight, dissolving the old myths and remolding them about a single individual idea or emotion. Contingent reality disappears as *The Shadowy Waters* (published 1900), *On Baile's Strand* (published 1903), *The King's Threshold* (performed 1903), and *Deirdre* (performed 1906) develop an idealist, univocal construction in which everything is sacrificed to a tight dramatic logic inseparable from a poetry of controlled associationism. The form borrows both from the idealist theatre of reason and the idealist theatre of passion. Objective reality is not genuinely recognized in these plays. In each of them solipsistic passion is shown as the road to true knowledge. It is the knowledge, however, that makes the passion valuable.

In the dance plays written in imitation of the Japanese Noh of Spirits—*At the Hawk's Well* (performed 1916), *The Cat and the Moon* (dated 1917), *The Dreaming of the Bones* (published 1919), and *Calvary* (published 1921)—Yeats developed a form that eliminated scenery and used masks, the dance and a chorus of musicians. By sacrificing the last trace of realistic demonstration of purpose and expression of passion, he was able to give a concentrated representation of the moment of vision. These plays are the "anti-self" of circumstantial realism. At a time when the movement of naturalistic drama had the widest circumference of opinion turning with it, Yeats set up a counter movement at a little central point. For a time, he gave up the stage entirely, writing the dance plays to be acted in friends' drawing rooms, and abandoning every realistic illusion.

To abandon circumstantial realism entirely was somehow to approach again, distantly, that greater realism lost by both realistic and poetic dramatists of our time. Since scenery and movement were eliminated or completely stylized, they had to appear in the verse, in order to clarify what was going on. Thus the lyric softness of Yeats's earlier dramatic verse (though that too had been much revised towards naturalness and strength) was replaced gradually by a language often made masculine and objective by realistic reference to place and action. This change was of great significance for the dramatist in poetry.

The language of the dance plays, however, retained much of the metaphorical richness and associationism more effective in his second period dramas of passion. The prose plays that follow show Yeats attempting to purge his dialogue of poetic ornament. Yeats completed his prose farce *The Player Queen* (performed 1919), *The Cat and the Moon* (dated 1917), and *The Resurrection* (published 1927;[13] revised 1931); made his prose versions of *Sophocles' King Oedipus* (performed

---

13. In *The Resurrection,* although no dance is staged, much is made of the dancing offstage of the worshippers and of the wordless entrance of Christ, which occupies the position that the dance fills in other plays.

1926) and *Sophocles' Oedipus at Colonus* (performed 1927); rewrote *The Only Jealousy of Emer* in prose for a stage performance, entitling it *Fighting the Waves* (performed 1929); and wrote in prose and for the realistic stage *The Words upon the Window-pane* (performed 1930). In the latter play (in which the devices of modern realism—showing forth a supernatural event—are used to discredit the world-view they imply), Yeats lets a symbolic structure of place and action carry his meanings, eliminating metaphorical richness from the dialogue.

The King of the Great Clock Tower (1934) was written in prose with lyrics worked into the action. Then Yeats returned to poetry with a second version in verse (published 1935). This he revised into the more concentrated *A Full Moon in March* (published 1935),[14] also in verse, avoiding ornamentation and applying the technique, which he had learned in his prose plays, of laying bare the structure. In *The Herne's Egg* (published 1938) Yeats escapes at last from blank verse, experimenting with tetrameter and trimeter, rhymed and unrhymed, and occasionally resorting to sprung rhythm. The diction and idiom are inclusive, unpoetic, often using everyday or proverbial language.

The experiments of many years reach fruition in *Purgatory* (performed 1938) which, while eliminating the superficial dance-play paraphernalia of chorus, dance and mask, retains the essential structure of a spirit drama. The play is realist and analogical, showing a multitude of simultaneous objective and subjective actions. The style is bare, gaining great strength from the microcosmic structure. The verse—basically an unrhymed iambic tetrameter—represents a virtuoso performance in fusing speech and poetry, taking the greatest liberties with metrics without ever losing control.

The coda to Yeats's career is his *The Death of Cuchulain* (published 1939), in which again much of the dance play paraphernalia is dropped. Complicated analogical actions are skillfully fitted together into a brief play in which Cuchulain is faced, one after another, with the "opposites" of his struggles in war and love. The doctrines of

14. Cf. "Preface," *A Full Moon in March* (London: Macmillan, 1935), pp. v–vi; *Variorum Plays,* pp. 1310–11.

character as passion and of tragedy as the struggle of passion with passion, or of will with mask, are here given their climactic demonstration. Abandoning the use of actual masks, Yeats shows us characters who are themselves masks, symbolical representations of fundamental passions, and who, therefore, need to wear no painted wood nor papier mâché. In this play Yeats reviews his career and sees it as a "gay struggle without hope."[15] In death, this "great fighting-man"[16] perceives his soul to be a singing bird and finds the perception worth death and defeat.

In these last plays, although Yeats has not achieved a poetic drama to equal the greatest dramas of the past, he has succeeded in imitating action as perception. As we have seen, by abandoning circumstantial realism he has been able to develop a drama which, while imitating this culminating part of the tragic rhythm, conveys, in economical form, a sense of the total rhythm that is a part of the perception. The actions of these plays, like ritual or the games of children, are direct imitations of psychic action.[17] At the same time, Yeats developed, by necessity, a speech that is realist in its inclusion of the total rhythm. He came as close as one perhaps can in our time to fusing theatre and poetry.

Throughout the stages of this development, Yeats reveals a remarkable consistency in subject preference. Some sort of vision of the supernatural is important in almost every play. *The Countess Cathleen,* to which we now turn, is based on a folk story, and, appropriating the authority of the simple faith of the country people, ends in all versions with a vision, actually seen by characters and audience, of heavenly

15. *Yeats and Sturge Moore,* p. 154.

16. *Variorum Plays,* p. 1061.

17. "Yeats's dramatic art tends more and more towards the representation of myth on the stage not in the old way, by making any suitable mythological characters speak and act out his abstract themes, but by actually showing the myth as it happens. The abstractions are already within its substance. If we accept the theory that the myths of the world are descriptions of the rituals that preceded them, and not distorted accounts of historical events, Yeats was actually leading both myth and drama back to their common ritual cradle." Ure, *Towards a Mythology,* pp. 88–89.

spirits rescuing the soul of Cathleen. *Deirdre,* which I analyze after *The Countess Cathleen,* does not involve the showing forth of supernatural events. Although the essential action is recognition, it is not a Dante-like observer's vision of the supernatural. It is the central characters' realization of their fate, and the chorus of musicians' witness of the events of the famous story. It is awareness of tragedy and aesthetic contemplation which are important there. But in form the play represents the point Yeats had reached when he began his important middle and late experimentation. In it one may see what Yeats had achieved, may sense a new aim, and a dissatisfaction with his current methods. *Deirdre,* in its working together of will and feeling, demonstration and association, is like a beautifully woven cocoon which will release the middle and late dramas of perception.

The Countess Cathleen: Vision and Revision

W B. YEATS's *The Countess Cathleen* ends with a vision and is progressively revised towards a unity in which everything is subordinated to that vision. First the final scene—the showing forth of the Countess's salvation—is redone. Then the rest of the play is from time to time altered to support that scene. In the process, the quality of the original fable is much changed.

In the revisions of *The Countess Kathleen,*[1] Yeats's preoccupation with learning to write drama as it had already been written competed with his attempts to write his own particular kind of drama. To learn dramatic as distinguished from narrative plotting and to make his composition reflect the possibilities and limitations of staging—these were his first problems. If he had rewritten the play many years later, all of this practice work might have disappeared. There would have been one act, set where the devils are bargaining for souls, and centred on Cathleen's transformation. There would have been a moment when she, suffering damnation, has a clear, bitter, yet impenitent knowledge of what her sacrifice has been—that she has refused a heavenly mansion, raging in the dark: "It was not, nor is it now, more than a piece of tapestry. The Countess sells her soul, but she is not transformed. If I were to think out that scene to-day, she would, the moment her hand has signed, burst into loud laughter, mock at all she has held holy, horrify the peasants in the middle of their temptations."[2]

---

1. Spelt thus in the first edition of 1892 only. The principal revisions are in *Poems* (London: T. Fisher Unwin, 1895); *Poems,* 1899; *Poems,* 1901; *The Poetical Works of W. B. Yeats in Two Volumes,* Volume II, *Dramatical Poems* (New York, London: Macmillan, 1907); *The Countess Cathleen* (London: T. Fisher Unwin, 1912); and the "almost final" version, *A Selection from the Poetry of W. B. Yeats* (Leipzig: Bernhard Tauchnitz, 1913). (Cf. *Variorum Plays,* p. xiii.)

2. *Autobiographies,* p. 417.

Comparison of the various versions of *The Countess Cathleen* will show both Yeats's progress in dramatic construction and his attempts to represent more completely the unique nature of his vision. It does not show these two movements in complete harmony. A comparison of the final scene of the play in the first published version with a revised version of the same scene will show great advance in dramatic construction but a change, perhaps an at least temporary loss, in Yeats's ability to unite, in one representation, vision and the objective world.

The Countess Cathleen uses as its material the convergence of pagan and Christian Irish tradition. The original fable was included among traditional Irish stories about the devil in Yeats's *Fairy and Folk Tales of the Irish Peasantry.*[3] Demons bring plague and famine to Ireland and then offer the oppressed peasants gold for their souls. The Countess Cathleen O'Shea, who is so good she would be nobility in Heaven as on earth, in desperate pity redeems the other souls with the sale of her own. She dies broken-hearted, but Heaven cancels the bargain; her soul is saved and the demons disappear. Yeats remarks: "I have no doubt of the essential antiquity of what seems to me the most impressive form of one of the supreme parables of the world."

He finds "the sacrifice of Alcestis . . . less overwhelming, less apparently irremediable."[4]

This redoubtable claim will surprise us less if we reflect that the question, May a soul sacrifice itself for a good end?[5] was of central importance to Yeats. He sought "unity of being,"[6] and this search was

3. *Fairy and Folk Tales of the Irish Peasantry* (London: Walter Scott, 1888), pp. 211–14, 232–35. Yeats had found the story "in what professed to be a collection of Irish folklore in an Irish newspaper" (*Poems* [1901], p. 295; *Variorum Plays*, pp. 170, 177). By 1895 he had learned that the story was of recent introduction (*Poems* [1895], p. 282; *Variorum Plays*, p. 178). But not until 1901 was he able to note the source, *Les Matinées de Timothé Trimm* by Léo Lespès. Poems (1901), p. 295 (*Variorum Plays*, pp. 170, 177). Yeats never admitted the irony in the fact that his intensely national drama had cosmopolitanism to thank for its genesis.
4. *Poems* (1901), p. 295; *Variorum Plays*, pp. 170, 177.
5. *Autobiographies*, p. 468.
6. *Ibid.*, p. 190.

complicated by the division of his loyalties among art, patriotism, love, and religion.

Yeats had written in 1888: "To the greater poets everything they see has its relation to the national life, and through that to the universal and divine life: nothing is an isolated artistic moment; there is a unity everywhere. . . ."[7] Art, which is but a vision of reality, put this easy unity to the test in *The Countess Cathleen*.

In the preface to *Poems* (1901) Yeats discussed the poetic use of the Irish Christian cycle.

Christianity and the old nature faith have lain down side by side in the cottages, and I would proclaim that peace as loudly as I can among the kingdoms of poetry, where there is no peace that is not joyous, no battle that does not give life instead of death; I may even try to persuade others, in more sober prose, that there can be no language more worthy of poetry and of the meditation of the soul than that which has been made, or can be made, out of a subtlety of desire, an emotion of sacrifice, a delight in order, that are perhaps Christian, and myths and images that mirror the energies of woods and streams, and of their wild creatures. Has any part of that majestic heraldry of the poets had a very different fountain? Is it not the ritual of the marriage of heaven and earth?[8]

The convergence of Christianity and the old nature faith is used in this play to show the struggle of two universal ways of life—a spiritual and a materialistic—for control of a particular place—Ireland.

Universal spiritual values are represented by the Christian God and spirits, who are at home everywhere. They struggle with universal material values, represented by Satan and his demons, who, wherever they may go, are foreign exploiters. The plague-smitten land, the starving peasants, and the enslaved gods of ancient Ireland represent the Irish land and people, individual targets of temptation by material values. The land, the peasants, the fairies all fare ill under the domination of foreign demons. The fairies, though pre-Christian, serve the demons unwillingly, and feel gratitude to the kind Countess, who, loving Ireland as well as God, has done them service. The land itself

---

7. *Letters to the New Island*, p. 78.
8. *Variorum Plays*, p. 1290.

flourishes wherever the influence of the demons has not reached. Food will be purchased with the sale of Cathleen's castles, pastures, and forests. Men are still unspoiled on the mountains, to which the foreign influence has not penetrated. The Herdsman says:

> The vales are famine crazy—I'm right glad
> My home is on the mountain near to God.[9]

Aleel, the man of songs (Kevin in the 1892 version), is a bridge between the old gods and the people of the present. He sings the ancient Irish myths, but he has given his soul to the Christian Cathleen, and the devils cannot take it from her. Their ultimate defeat is hinted in their difficulty with this figure, who stands for an art both spiritual and national.

Cathleen is caught in an apparent quandary, forced to choose love and beauty, or patriotism, or God. But, since the lover Aleel is also a poet of Irish legend, her renouncing him for her country is really a gesture of love and a defense of aesthetic values. Again, she is forced to choose between serving her particular people and serving her universal God. She chooses to serve her people. We learn, however, that to serve her people is to serve her God. What would puzzle abstract thought and conventional morality, she knows through sympathetic intuition. The coming together of the spiritual values indigenous to Ireland with those of universal Christianity resolves the apparent conflict between duties.

The dilemma is to settle the relative claims of art, love, patriotism, and belief; to find a way of uniting these by fusing Irish paganism, traditional Christianity and an aesthetic faith in the occult symbols of artist mystics; and thus to present a united front to materialism. The artist, represented by Aleel, is involved, almost against his will, in the common struggle of love, patriotism, and belief against the dominant new philosophy of the age.

Nationalism provides a drastic and terrible end to the dilemma. Only by sacrificing to the destiny of a people can art be more than

9. *The Countess Kathleen* (1892), p. 38; *Variorum Plays,* pp. 58, 60.

aestheticism, love more than desire, religion more than opiate. In the sacrifice, however, art, love, and religion reach their apotheosis. Cathleen's action is beauty, charity, passion, faith.

The Countess Cathleen, like later dramas, concludes where "The Zodiac is changed into a sphere,"[10] where the antinomies are resolved, where the contradictories, through the very intensity of their opposition, call upon the unity that transcends them. The play ends at a moment of revelation, of passionate perception, when ordinary human seeing and suffering melt away.

The first version of *The Countess Cathleen* is set in the sixteenth century. Poetic drama is perhaps easier to accept for a modern audience if set in the time of its greatest flourishing. At that time, moreover, the Christian belief could still claim universality, the Irish tradition vitality. And the chivalrous tradition was still productive of Petrarchan love-songs and of unhappy courtly loves like that of the Irish bard in this play. The feudal system would allow Yeats's heroine to be a focus of religious, economic, social, and artistic life. She represents the kind of aristocracy in which Yeats believed.

There is no attempt at historicity, however. In later editions the scene is laid simply "in Ireland, and in old times." Already Yeats is moving away from presentation of actuality. He wrote in the first number of *Beltaine* that he had

tried to suggest throughout the play that period, made out of many periods, in which the events in the folk-tales have happened. The play is not historic, but symbolic, and has as little to do with any definite place and time as an *auto* by Calderon. One should look for the Countess Cathleen and the peasants and the demons not in history, but . . . in one's own heart.[11]

Regrettably, they must perhaps have more of a local habitation and a name than Yeats gives them before we can find them even in our hearts. The ruined house and bare tree of *Purgatory* are somehow more

10. "Chosen," *Variorum Poems,* p. 535; cf. *Poems,* p. 273.
11. "Plans and Methods," *Beltaine* 1 (May 1899), 8.

evocative of the ideas of nation and land than is all the tapestry of *The Countess Cathleen*. And in *Purgatory's* fusion of symbolism and realism there is a truer marriage of heaven and earth. Yet the continuing validity of the Christian myth, the credibility of the peasants' belief in it, and the traditional form of the fable all lend *The Countess Cathleen* a kind of supra-personal authenticity that later dramas lack.

Yeats's 1892 version is much closer to the narrative form of the story as it appears in *Fairy and Folk Tales* than are the later versions. The division into scenes follows the change of place and time in the story, without the attempts to unify and elaborate the action that are evident later. Yeats has even borrowed dialogue (such as "Their claws were clutched under their gloves of leather").[12]

The conception of the chief characters, both Countess and demons, is not basically altered—although the parallel between British imperialists and the demons is suggested. The characters Yeats adds—principally Shemus Rua, keeper of the hostelry; Teig, his son; Mary, his wife; Oona, Cathleen's foster-mother; Kevin, a young bard—are not motivated so as to direct the action significantly.

In later versions there is revision towards unity shown by the progressive reduction of the number of characters; the fusing of characters whose functions may be combined; the growing tendency to portray, not human inconsistency and idiosyncrasy, but passionate types; the growing prominence of Aleel, who is ultimately the second major character and the primary interpreter of the action; the addition of the love scenes between Aleel and the Countess in order to motivate Aleel's centrality and to shift the whole center of the play from the traditional and outer toward the private and inner; the alteration of the final scene from supernaturalism based on naturalism to an elaborate and vague angelic show in which the objective world dissolves.

In the first version (1892), scene I, Mary Rua and Teig, her son, await in their peasant cottage the coming of Shemus Rua, Mary's husband. When he comes, bringing a dead wolf, he is bitter because the famine

12. *Fairy and Folk Tales*, p. 213. Cf. *Variorum Plays*, pp. 146, 151.

has reduced them to such straits. In this mood he rails recklessly, and inadvertently calls on demons. They come in the form of two merchants, give Teig and Shemus magic wine, and buy their souls.

In scene II at Cathleen's castle, Cathleen is seeking peace from her people's troubles by hearing her foster-mother Oona talk and sing to her. They are interrupted by a servant who admits first a gardener and then a herdsman. Both tell of depredations by starving men. Later the servant admits Cathleen's steward. The latter brings with him a peasant who had stolen apples and a peasant who had stolen sheep. They have gained money by selling their souls to the demons and come to restore what they stole.

In scene III the demons rob Cathleen's treasure room with the aid of spirits—Sheogues, Soulths, and Tevishes and the ghosts of the two robbers, who have now killed each other. The demons deceive Cathleen into thinking that the grain and cattle she has ordered brought from a distance have been delayed. They leave as she is thanking God that she still has the treasure to help her people. Then peasants enter with the discovery that the treasure is gone. The porter reports that demons have passed his gate.

In scene IV, at the inn of Shemus Rua, the Merchants buy souls: that of a Middle-aged Man and that of a Young Woman. The bard, Kevin, enters, desperate with sympathy for Cathleen, and tries to give his soul away, but is led off by Shemus and Teig. This is the first appearance of the young minstrel who, as Aleel, is almost as important as Cathleen herself in the final version. An Old Woman sells her soul, and another peasant ludicrously tries to sell half his soul, but even the demons will have none of him. Then the Countess enters and completes her fatal bargain.

In scene V, in the castle, Oona and Peasants are disturbed by screeching noises. None of these peasants have appeared previously and yet Yeats takes time to individualize them in this final scene: First Peasant, Second Peasant, Neal (an old peasant), and a Young Peasant who questions Oona about Kevin and the nature of love. After the others leave to investigate the noises, Oona, alone, finds owl feathers on the steps of the oratory in which Cathleen has secluded herself. Thinking some hawk has killed an owl, she enters the oratory, but backs out immediately seeing a vision of angels who carry in Cathleen's body and announce that she is saved. The peasants return and join Oona in mourning.

Skipping the intermediate versions of the play, one may turn to *A Selection from the Poetry of W. B. Yeats* (1913) and observe what has happened. Many characters are eliminated. Aleel has taken on numerous minor functions as well as a major role. He appears in almost every scene. Shemus and Teigue have increased in prominence, taking all the functions of the earlier minor characters on the bad side and developing a considerable opposition to Aleel. In scene I Shemus and Teigue have become blacker characters and Mary whiter. Aleel, the Countess, and Oona are introduced momentarily before the demons come, to serve a number of unifying functions. Shemus and Teigue, instead of selling their souls immediately, now have to serve the Merchants through the rest of the action.

In scene II the Steward meets Aleel, Oona, and the Countess as they near the castle and tells them all the unfortunate news without the aid of the Servant, the Gardener, and the Herdsman. Teigue and Shemus run in and give news of the soul-selling, thus cutting out the scene in which the peasant robbers confess and make the same announcement. Five characters are dropped in these changes. Instead of the servant's pursuit of the peasants in an attempt to buy back their souls with Cathleen's money, we have Aleel's fruitless but brave pursuit of Shemus and Teigue.

In scene III Aleel comes to the castle to say that he has had a vision and to warn Cathleen that she must leave with him or die there. She recognizes that she is being tempted to find escape in love and beauty (perhaps in Tir-nan-oge) from a patriotic, religious, and human responsibility and refuses to go. She simultaneously intimates her love for Aleel and renounces it. Aleel is enlarged here into a symbol of her spiritual sacrifice. The rest of the scene is the robbery of the treasure and the suggestion to Cathleen by the demons that her soul is marketable.

Scene IV, done before the curtain to give time for the changing of

sets, is not in previous versions. Various peasants cross, talking about
gold; the demon merchants follow them, and Aleel tags behind singing "Impetuous heart be still, be still."[13] Scene V, the marketing of
souls, is elaborated but not fundamentally changed until Cathleen sells
her soul and goes out to distribute the wealth to the peasants. Then
Aleel has his elaborate vision of angels warring upon devils and learns
that Cathleen is saved. The last scene is almost entirely Aleel's.

Let us look in more detail at the most significant change, the change
in the ending. Scene V of *The Countess Cathleen* (1892) is completely
altered when it appears as the last part of act III in 1895, and (with no
change) in 1899. With few and minor alterations it becomes the last
part of act IV in 1901, but is not essentially changed in 1912.

Scene V (1892) is laid in the castle at dawn. "A number of peasants
enter hastily, half dressed, as though aroused suddenly from sleep."[14] A
screeching noise has awakened them and they search for the cause of it.
All but Oona and a young peasant go to search the northern tower.
The young peasant has seen Kevin wandering in the woods:

> They say he hears the sheogues down below
> Nailing four boards.
> *Oona.*   For love has made him crazy,
> And loneliness and famine dwell with him.[15]

The young peasant goes to ask old Neal about love. Oona, not
hearing Cathleen in the oratory, where she has been pacing all night,
goes to the steps and finds them covered with owl feathers. Thinking
some hawk has chased its prey through an open window, Oona goes
into the oratory to investigate. She returns immediately, overcome by a
vision.

13. *Variorum Plays*, pp. 129, 23. As Russell K. Alspach has pointed out, Aleel's song was
moved from Scene I, "where it had been from the 1895 printing up to and including the
three 1912 printings," to Scene IV (*Variorum Plays*, p. xiii).
14. *Ibid.*, p. 154.
15. *Ibid.*, p. 158.

My dear mistress
Must have dropped off to sleep. All night
She has been pacing in the chapel there.

[*She goes over to the oratory steps and finds them covered with feathers.*]

I know what clamour frighted them—some bird,
Some hawk or kestrel, chased its prey to this;
These are owls feathers. I will go and see
What window has swung open over-night.

[*She goes into the oratory and returns hastily, leaving the door open. A bright light streams through the open door.*]

My hour has come, oh blessed queen of heaven,
I am to die, for I have seen a vision.
O, they are coming, they are coming, coming.[16]

Spirits carry in the body of Cathleen from the oratory and lay her head on Oona's knees. They are singing the Pre-Raphaelitish lyric beginning *"All the heavy days are over,"* and ending

> She goes down the floor of heaven,
>   Shining bright as a new lance,
> And her guides are angels seven,
>   While young stars about her dance.[17]

The spirits report to Oona that God commanded them to save Cathleen.

We are angelical.
She gave away her soul for others—God,
Who sees the motive and the deed regards not,
Bade us go down and save her from the demons,
Who do not know the deed can never bind.
We came and waited; some score minutes since,
As mortals measure time, her body died,
For her heart broke. The demons, as two owls,
Came sweeping hither, murmuring against God.
We drove them hence; and half our company

---

16. *Ibid.*, pp. 158, 160.
17. *Ibid.*, pp. 162, 164.

> Bore the bright spirit to the floors of peace,
> And half now give the body to your care.
> Let it have noble burial; build a high
> And ample tomb, for she who died and lives
> Was noble in her life and in her beauty;
> And when men gaze upon the flying dawn,
> We bid them dream of her.[18]

Having honored the body with lines echoing Shakespeare's *Hamlet,* Yeats honors the soul with Dante, or at least with Dante Gabriel Rossetti:

> Farewell! the red rose by the seat of God,
> Which is among the angelic multitude
> What she, whose body lies here, was to men,
> Is brightening in my face, I bear no more
> The heavy burden of your mortal days.[19]

The vision over, Oona is silent for a moment, but then, realizing the Countess is dead, she shrieks and the peasants rush in. Each mourns Cathleen in a simple line, until Oona cries:

> Be silent. Do you dare to keen her? Dare
> To set your grief by mine? Stoop—lift her up;
> Now carry her and lay her on her bed,
> When I have keened I will go be with her,
> I will go die, for I have seen a vision.[20]

And the peasants go out, carrying the body.

In the revision of 1895 the merchants depart to capture Cathleen's soul, and Aleel, who has been thrown to the ground by Shemus and Teig, crawls to the middle of the room. It grows dark and a storm arises. Aleel, as poet and seer, now becomes narrator and raisonneur, describing the supernatural events that form the conclusion. He sees demons come, and many of them are evil figures from Celtic myth. Balor, Yeats's notes tell us, is "the Irish Chimaera, the leader of the

---

18. *Ibid.,* pp. 164, 166.   19. *Ibid.,* p. 168.
20. *Ibid.*

hosts of darkness at the great battle of good and evil. . . ." Barach deceived the great Fergus in order to betray Deirdre and Naisi. "The Druid Cailitin and his sons warred upon Cuhoollin with magical arts." Concobar or Conhor was the king who pursued Deirdre and her love, finally killing the latter by treachery.[21]

These are specifically Irish demons, who betrayed the best in Irish manhood—Cuhoollin—and in Irish womanhood—Deirdre.

> And all their heads are twisted to one side,
> For when they lived they warred on beauty and peace
> With obstinate, crafty, sidelong bitterness.[22]

Oona enters, searching solicitously for Cathleen, who had not told her that she was going to Shemus Rua's to sell her soul. Aleel warns her, "Crouch down . . . out of the blind storm" of demons.

> Cathleen has chosen other friends than us,
> And they are rising through the hollow world.[23]

One of them is the sorceress Orchil, type of the damned beauty, accompanied by carnal sinners. This is the sort of company Cathleen has chosen. Oona prays that her own soul, rather than Cathleen's, may be condemned.

As Aleel gazes down through the earth, the peasants carry in Cathleen, who awakens for long enough to struggle with the demon host.

> O hold me, and hold me tightly, for the storm
> Is dragging me away.[24]

She gives direction for the division of money after her death.

Two peasant women are given contrasting speeches—one worrying whether Cathleen will leave enough money, the other ready to sacrifice everything to save Cathleen.

After her last beautiful speech, the most remarkable in the play, Cathleen dies.

21. *Ibid.*, p. 1285.
23. *Ibid.*, p. 157.

22. *Ibid.*, p. 155.
24. *Ibid.*, pp. 159, 161.

Cathleen. Bend down your faces, Oona and Aleel;
 I gaze upon them as the swallow gazes
 Upon the nest under the eave, before
 She wander the loud waters. Do not weep
 Too great a while, for there is many a candle
 On the High Altar though one fall. Aleel,
 Who sang about the dancers of the woods
 That know not the hard burden of the world,
 Having but breath in their kind bodies, farewell!
 And farewell, Oona, you who played with me,
 And bore me in your arms about the house
 When I was but a child and therefore happy,
 Therefore happy, even like those that dance.
 The storm is in my hair and I must go.

Oona tests Cathleen's breath with a mirror, as is done in Lear, and half-screams "O, she is dead."[25] Aleel shatters the mirror, since it can no longer show her live face, and tells his heart to die, since

 . . . she whose mournful words
 Made you a living spirit has passed away
 And left you but a ball of passionate dust.[26]

He calls for the end of earth, sea, Time, Fate and Change—left empty of value by her death. He then beholds an actual battle of angels and demons. When this is over, the darkness is broken by a visionary light. The peasants seem to be kneeling on a mountain slope. Above them stand angels with drawn swords who have driven off the demons.

The others fall to the ground, but Aleel, now standing, seizes one of the angels and demands to know the fate of Cathleen. He learns that she is saved, that

   The Light of Lights
 Looks always on the motive, not the deed,
 The Shadow of Shadows on the deed alone.[27]

25. *Ibid.,* p. 163.   26. *Ibid.,* p. 165.
27. *Ibid.,* p. 167.

The play ends with a humble speech of Oona's, asking to be reunited with Cathleen.

If, after reading the 1895 ending, we go back to the 1892 version, the latter seems most unworkmanly, introducing new characters at the very end—Neal and the Young Peasant—and leaving the last view of Cathleen for the loyal but pedestrian Oona, who acts simply as witness not as interpreter. In the early version we are not even told whether or not Oona knows what happened in the previous scene. Kevin, who does know, is left wandering around behind the scenes. Cathleen, who has carried the play thus far, appears only as an eloquent corpse. The struggle, in her, of good and evil forces is not represented, nor any of her sorrow and pity at leaving her friends. It is the effect of her action on herself that an audience would be primarily interested in—not merely in the fact of her dead body—and our interest is not satisfied in this version.

It is interesting, however, that the simplicity and concreteness of the symbolism is something Yeats returned to in his later plays. The discovery of owl feathers on the steps as a proof of the defeat of the demons—however clumsily managed in this play—is the sort of thing out of which Yeats built later plays—a well, a heartbeat, an egg, some words cut on a window-pane. Later he would support the concrete symbol with symbolic dance or action so that there would be no pretense of a superficial one-level realism which the play itself would question. A symbolic superstructure carefully worked out in action on several levels would go a long way towards convincing one of the concrete reality—on one level—of those owl feathers.

The revised version of 1895 shows much more competent stagemanship, yet is almost pure show. Although reassured by a dim vision of angels that the demons are defeated, one misses the conviction of owl feathers between the finger tips. The transformation of the usual and concrete into the symbolic or supernatural was the insight Yeats later found valuable in the Japanese Noh plays, which were the models for such plays as *At the Hawk's Well, The Dreaming of the Bones, The Only*

Jealousy of Emer, and *Calvary.*[28] The owls have their analogue in the hawk of *At the Hawk's Well.*

In this 1895 version, as in all later versions, instead of using natural *and* supernatural as he did in his last plays, Yeats allows the "real world" to dissolve into the cloudy mist of the Celtic twilight.

> *Aleel.* I shatter you in fragments, for the face
>   That brimmed you up with beauty is no more:
>   And die, dull heart, for she whose mournful words
>   Made you a living spirit has passed away
>   And left you but a ball of passionate dust.
>   And you, proud earth and plumy sea, fade out!
>   For you may hear no more her faltering feet,
>   But are left lonely amid the clamorous war
>   Of angels upon devils.
> [*He stands up; almost every one is kneeling, but it has grown so dark that only confused forms can be seen.*
>   And I who weep
>   Call curses on you, Time and Fate and Change,
>   And have no excellent hope but the great hour
>   When you shall plunge headlong through bottomless space.
> [*A flash of lightning followed immediately by thunder.*
>
> *A Peasant Woman.* Pull him upon his knees before his curses
>   Have plucked thunder and lightning on our heads.
>
> *Aleel.* Angels and devils clash in the middle air,
>   And brazen swords clang upon brazen helms.
>   [*A flash of lightning followed immediately by thunder.*
>   Yonder a bright spear, cast out of a sling,
>   Has torn through Balor's eye, and the dark clans
>   Fly screaming as they fled Moytura of old.
>   [*Everything is lost in darkness.*

28. This Noh-like transformation may be found in Yeats's earliest plays. See the two contrasting appearances of Ebremar in *Mosada* (1886) (*Variorum Plays,* pp. 1263–78); the discovery that an old peddler is Time in *Vivien and Time* (above) and *Time and the Witch Vivien* (1889) (*Variorum Plays,* pp. 1279–81); the dramatization first of the external and then the internal action of the knight who unknowingly seeks infamy in *The Seeker* (1889) (*Variorum Plays,* pp. 1259–63); the metamorphosis of Naschina from mortal shepherdess to immortal queen in *The Island of Statues* (1885) (*Variorum Plays,* pp. 1223–58).

An Old Man. The Almighty wrath at our great weakness and sin
   Has blotted out the world and we must die.
[*The darkness is broken by a visionary light. The Peasants seem to be
kneeling upon the rocky slope of a mountain, and vapour full of storm and
ever-changing light is sweeping above them and behind them. Half in the
light, half in the shadow, stand armed angels. Their armour is old and worn,
and their drawn swords dim and dinted. They stand as if upon the air in
formation of battle and look downward with stern faces. The Peasants cast
themselves on the ground.*[29]

It remains to discuss the differences between the alternate endings in
the 1912 version.[30] Yeats's note in the 1912 edition stated:

Now at last I have made a complete revision to make it suitable for performance at the Abbey Theatre. The first two scenes are almost wholly new, and
throughout the play I have added or left out such passages as a stage
experience of some years showed me encumbered the action; the play in its
first form having been written before I knew anything of the theatre. I have
left the old end, however, in the version printed in the body of this book,
because the change for dramatic purposes has been made for no better reason
than that audiences—even at the Abbey Theatre—are almost ignorant of
Irish mythology—or because a shallow stage made the elaborate vision of
armed angels upon a mountain-side impossible. The new end is particularly
suited to the Abbey stage, where the stage platform can be brought out in
front of the proscenium and have a flight of steps at one side up which the
Angel comes, crossing towards the back of the stage at the opposite side. The
principal lighting is from two arc lights in the balcony which throw their
lights into the faces of the players, making footlights unnecessary. The room
at Shemus Rua's house is suggested by a great grey curtain—a colour which
becomes full of rich tints under the stream of lights from the arcs.[31]

The Abbey version may be contrasted with the ending quoted above.

Aleel. I shatter you in fragments, for the face
   That brimmed you up with beauty is no more;
   And die, dull heart, for you that were a mirror

---

29. *Variorum Plays,* pp. 165, 167.

30. An alternate end for the Abbey Theatre was added in an appendix in *The Countess
Cathleen* (1912), pp. 124–28 (*Variorum Plays,* pp. 173–76).

31. *Variorum Plays,* pp. 173–74, 176. By the "old end" Yeats means the 1895 end.

Are but a ball of passionate dust again!
And level earth and plumy sea, rise up!
And haughty sky, fall down!
A Peasant Woman.   Pull him upon his knees,
His curses will pluck lightning on our heads.
Aleel. Angels and devils clash in the middle air,
And brazen swords clang upon brazen helms.
Look, look, a spear has gone through Belial's eye!
[*A winged Angel, carrying a torch and a sword, enters from the R. with eyes
fixed upon some distant thing. The Angel is about to pass out to the L., when
Aleel speaks. The Angel stops a moment and turns.*][32]

Irish ignorance of Celtic mythology has caused Balor, Barach, the
Cailitin, and Concobar to be replaced by the biblical and Miltonic
Asmodel and Belial in Aleel's vision. Orchil and her multitude of
alluring women are omitted. The storm of evil that is dragging
Cathleen is not given a concrete physical counterpart in the Abbey
ending. The stage darkens, but directions such as *The wind roars* and
speeches such as

And while we bore her hither cloudy gusts
Blackened the world and shook us on our feet.
Draw the great bolt for no man has beheld
So black, bitter, blinding and sudden a storm.[33]

are omitted. Did the Abbey not have a wind machine? From Aleel's
speeches are pruned not only the rich symbolism of Celtic mythology
but all the operatic largeness meant to build up to the vision of the
angels on the mountain side.

The remaining lines are the same in both versions except that the
Abbey ending drops the final stage direction, the melting away of the
vision.

[*A sound of far-off horns seems to come from the heart of the light. The vision melts
away, and the forms of the kneeling Peasants appear faintly in the darkness.*][34]

There would seem to be no reason to quibble with Yeats's judgment

32. *Ibid.,* pp. 175–76.   33. *Ibid.,* p. 159.
34. *Ibid.,* p. 169.

that only deficiencies of his theatre and audience made necessary the changes in the alternate ending for the Abbey Theatre.

Yeats was not unsatisfied with the final version of *The Countess Cathleen*. He had vastly improved it in construction, characterization, and style. He had begun the play in reaction against Shelley's *The Cenci* and Tennyson's *Becket*. Shelley and Tennyson had been "deliberately oratorical; instead of creating drama in the mood of *The Lotos-Eaters* or of *Epipsychidion* they had tried to escape their characteristics, had thought of the theatre as outside the general movement of literature." Yeats, on the other hand, began *The Countess Cathleen,* "avoiding every oratorical phrase *or* cadence."[35] He was trying to keep within that area—the drama—where theatre and literature overlap, and he was not at first successful. The version produced in 1899 "was ill-constructed, the dialogue turning aside at the lure of word or metaphor. . . ."[36]

Yeats was aiming at organic work, dialogue being inseparable from structure and yet written in verse approaching that of the best romantic poetry—a difficult ideal, involving a careful discipline of each passage in terms of the development of the whole. On these grounds he objected violently to Wilde's *Salomé:* "The general construction is all right, is even powerful, but the dialogue is empty, sluggish and pretentious. It has nothing of drama of any kind, never working to any climax but always ending as it begun. . . . He thought he was writing beautifully when he had collected beautiful things and thrown them together in a heap."[37] This passage shows that from the beginning Yeats aimed, not at a dramatic frame of events upholstered in poetry, but at what Eliot has called "the perfection of verse drama, . . . a design of human action and of words, such as to present at once the two aspects of dramatic and of musical order."[38]

35. "Preface," *Letters to the New Island*, p. 4.
36. *Autobiographies*, pp. 416–17.
37. *Yeats and Sturge Moore Correspondence*, pp. 8–9.
38. Eliot, *Poetry and Drama*, p. 43.

Yeats's alterations in structure and style brought the play a long way toward this goal. The "first meagre version"[39]—Yeats hoped, after finishing the first version—was "very different . . . from the play as it is to-day after many alterations, every alteration tested by performance."[40] Yeats was satisfied, too, with the improvement in characterization. "My *Countess Cathleen* . . . was once the moral question, may a soul sacrifice itself for a good end? but gradually philosophy is eliminated until at last the only philosophy audible, if there is even that, is the mere expression of one character or another." Representing the sacrificial passion of the Countess Cathleen is a different thing from posing a philosophical query. Yet it is a different thing too from painting a realistically individuated person. The characterization goes deeper than individuality. It avoids both abstraction and surface particularity. Cathleen is neither an idea nor an accurately mirrored individual. She is a heroic motive. Yeats's play went through the same process in being written as that by which "in Christianity what was philosophy in Eastern Asia became life, biography and drama."[41] The Countess's own history becomes like the life of Christ, the miraculous incarnation of what was a religious conception.

One should not, however, without realizing its limitations, approve the "triumphant thing"[42] that Yeats has made of the final version. The play does not present the full tragic rhythm from purpose, through passion (or suffering), to perception, accepting the old myth and varying it only in expression, rather than in content or arrangement. The love scene between Aleel and the Countess is not part of the original fable. This addition represents the way a modern journalistic playwright, as opposed to the old masters Yeats admired, would handle a traditional story. "The old playwrights took old subjects, did not even arrange the subject in a new way. They were absorbed in expression, that is to say in what is most near and delicate. The new playwrights invent their subjects and dislike anything customary in

39. *Autobiographies*, p. 200.   40. *Ibid.*, p. 417.
41. *Ibid.*, p. 468.
42. Lennox Robinson, "The Man and the Dramatist," in *Scattering Branches*, ed. Stephen Gwynn (New York: Macmillan, 1940), p. 72.

the arrangement of the fable, but their expression is as common as the newspapers where they first learned to write."[43] One is reminded of Eliot's disapprobation of Tennyson for tampering "unscrupulously with the meagre records" in his *Becket*, "introducing Fair Rosamund, and . . . suggesting that Becket had been crossed in love in early youth."[44]

The first version of *The Countess Cathleen,* however meagre, had its values, which Lionel Johnson sympathetically distinguished at the time. The "very absence of all complexity strengthens the power of the poem; it has the moving appeal of nature . . . the entanglement, the estimate of motives, the casuistry, unasserted in the play, are present, as it were, in the minds of God and of His angels."[45] In his revisions Yeats regrettably left this narrow path of the traditional fable.

Nor is *The Countess Cathleen,* in any version, a tragedy of vision in a realist sense. Cathleen is not transformed, does not "horrify the peasants in the midst of their temptations,"[46] as she might have done in a dance play by the late Yeats. In his "delight in the moment of exaltation, of excitement, of dreaming," Yeats worked, through revision, toward an art that diminished "the power of that daily mood," summoning in its place "rhythm, balance, pattern, images that remind us of vast passions, the vagueness of past times, all the chimeras that haunt the edge of trance."[47] That art refined away the real world as others see it and have seen it for centuries, replacing it with his own imaginative world. This sort of drama, which he explored more fully in *The Shadowy Waters, The King's Threshold,* and *Deirdre,* neither retains the full tragic rhythm nor achieves, as do his last plays, a new drama of passionate perception, an idealist drama which nevertheless dramatizes the third stage of the tragic rhythm, the moment of revelation, or epiphany, and presents the total rhythm in an essentialized form.

43. *Autobiographies*, p. 521.

44. Eliot, *Poetry and Drama*, p. 29.

45. Lionel Johnson, "The Countess Kathleen and Various Legends and Lyrics," *The Academy* 42 (July–December, 1892), 278.

46. *Autobiographies*, p. 417.

47. *Essays and Introductions*, pp. 242–43.

🌿 *Deirdre:* The Rigor of Logic

A S WE HAVE SAID, the action of a typical Yeats play is not to demonstrate purpose or to express passion but to reveal perception. The particular form this action takes in *Deirdre* is to discover the tragedy of trust. This play, however, uses both the syllogistic progression of logical relationships and the qualitative progression of feeling.[1] These are present as the necessary conditions of moments of revelation. Reason demonstrates its narrowness and superficiality; passion expresses its undirected force. The insufficiency of either is momently revealed. Their opposition causes repeated deadlocks during which the characters pause in their acting or suffering, startled by sudden insights that correct their previous misapprehensions of life.

In this play each character shares with the others in four fatalities— each is fated to trust another; to betray and to be betrayed; to be motivated by a love; and to shape (or distort) that love to fit the requirements of a code.

Because of his love for all men, which appears in the form of optimistic good faith, Fergus must trust Conchubar and be betrayed by him. Moreover, Fergus must unconsciously betray others through lack of insight. Naoise must trust in Fergus, and through him in Conchubar, not only because of his warrior's code of honor but also because of his friendship for Fergus and his love for Deirdre. This love takes the shape of expecting ideally honorable behavior from both her and himself. Thus he cannot stoop to the dishonorable doubt that would save him. Therefore he must be betrayed and must involve Deirdre in

---

1. "Mr. Kenneth Burke, in an essay entitled 'Psychology and Form,' distinguishes two kinds of literary composition, 'syllogistic progression,' in which the reader is led from one part of the composition to another by means of logical relationships, and 'qualitative progression' . . . in which the reader is led, according to a 'logic of feeling,' by means of association and contrast" (Fergusson, pp. 80–81).

the same fate in spite of her warnings. That his honor is based on her love is shown by the change in him when she pretends to care for Conchubar.[2]

Deirdre must trust Naoise because she loved him and thus must be fellow victim with him of Conchubar's betrayal. Even though her love makes her more fearful and perceptive than the others, it also binds her to assume the honorable pose Naoise believes in. In her death, however, her love takes its honor and dignity from its own integrity. And yet Deirdre too must betray. Her love for Naoise has made her deceive Conchubar once. At the end of the play she again escapes to her lover by deceiving the king. She has even pretended to betray Naoise, at points in the play, but she can never actually do so, even to save him, because the love to which she is true assumes an ideal honor between the lovers.

Conchubar's love for Deirdre is distorted by his sovereign pride. This pride forces him to betray the lovers in order to get Deirdre back and to punish Naoise. Yet it forces him to trust them, too. His intrigue depends on the good faith of Fergus and the honorableness of Naoise. His pride forces him to trust Deirdre at the end and brings about his betrayal by her and her suicide. He is surrounded by "traitors" as Fergus brings in the aroused people.

The theme of the play seems to be something like this: The movement of the whole soul in romantic love gives truer knowledge, nobler courage, and more controlled passion than do abstract public virtues such as humanitarian good faith, kingly pride, and even heroic honor. Each of the four fatalities, while found in all four chief characters, is most fully dramatized in one. To betray is Conchubar's chief action. To trust is Fergus's. To love is Deirdre's. And to adhere to a code of honor is Naoise's. Yet in the deepest sense, Deirdre is the most successful of the four chief characters in remaining true to trust, although seemingly she is the one most moved by other motives: fear and passion. She fears lest she not be allowed to keep faith with Naoise. Her passion is a faithful love for Naoise.

2. *Variorum Plays,* pp. 365–66.

Naoise is a person of great nobility whose public code (he must behave honorably with Conchubar) comes into conflict with his private faith-keeping with Deirdre. In a sense he betrays her by leading her into the unfortunate situation in which we find them. But one cannot seriously blame him. He has the vice of his virtue: nobility.

Fergus stands surety for the lovers and for the King. He tries to keep faith with both. If he admits the validity of Deirdre's fear, he has to admit the baser motives in Conchubar. Then the pattern of decorum will break down, fear and anger will be admittedly stronger than honor, reason, and policy. Being a humanitarian, he cannot admit this possibility without cancelling his fundamental assumption—that decorous (but unsacrificial) righteousness and goodwill unfailingly bring out those qualities in others. Therefore, he deceives himself constantly. There is in him no sufficient recognition of evil, no recognition of the risk, or of the complete willingness to renounce and sacrifice that his attitude must involve in order to work. There is perhaps, too, not a sufficient awareness of the sacrifice he is requiring Conchubar to make.

Conchubar has been betrayed, he feels. But his self-centeredness has caused the betrayal. His love is self-centered. An old man choosing a young girl as his bride is not thinking of her happiness. His honor, too, is more a dedication *to* self than a dedication *of* self. He breaks faith, yet maintains that it was only honorable for him so to do. He has his kingly office from which to rationalize his self-centeredness. It was treason for Deirdre and Naoise to run away. It was to keep faith with his office that he should choose "her most fitting to be Queen," and conspire to get her back. It was a king's duty also to punish treason, to let "no boy lover take the sway."[3]

Both he and Deirdre are willing to break faith, but in different senses. In being true to himself and his office, he must betray the lovers, or so he feels. Deirdre betrays to be true to another. Deirdre's love is for

3. *Ibid.,* p. 388.

Naoise, not for herself. She does not hate even Conchubar. Her honor too is a dedication of self. She is willing to sacrifice the appearance of it, in order to have the reality.

Naoise, similarly, feels no responsibility to die in a great display of physical courage. He would rather die quietly, exercising a genuine moral courage. Yet if Conchubar would fight him chivalrously, he would be glad; more glad to share with his enemy an honorable code than to display individual honor, whether publicly on the field or privately by playing chess to the end with Deirdre.

The fact that Fergus rallies fighting men to the defense of Deirdre and Naoise perhaps shows that his values are changed. But he was never pacifist, merely long-suffering and overtrusting. His uprising, it may be noted, accomplishes no end. Conchubar's motives are indeed unchanged. He learns the consequences of his selfish pride, but he does not reject it. The discovery that each character (with the exception of Fergus) makes is that, although he was "right" in his values, he was incompletely aware of the price of living by them. In the case of Deirdre and Naoise, their struggle purifies their motives, leading them to reject all other values. It does not change their values.

Oedipus' proud purpose, in *Oedipus Rex,* is to find the murderer. His resulting *pathos* is to suffer disruption of his confident kingship. His perception is to discover his own guilt. In *Deirdre,* where the action for each of the characters is to discover the tragedy of trust, only the optimism of Fergus and the pride of Conchubar are qualities capable of bringing about a Sophoclean tragic rhythm, and these are not the chief tragic characters. Trust is not a vice but a virtue. Naoise's honor is not a mistake, nor is Deirdre's love. What does each perceive but what he already knows? The characters do not undergo any fundamental changes in moral being—they are merely perfected and pay the price of their finishing.

The function of the chorus in this play is different from that in Greek tragedy because of the difference in the sort of action imitated and the difference in the conception of tragedy. It is different also from the use in Neoclassic French drama. Fergusson says that the Neoclassic tragedians did not know what to do with the chorus because they imitated action as rational.

The pathos pictured by the Sophoclean chorus is a moment of change in the moral being: it includes the breakdown of one rationalized, moral *persona;* the suffering of feelings and images suggesting a human essence capable of both good and evil, and always underlying the individual with his desperate reasons and his fragile integrity. The Sophoclean pathos can only be conveyed by the chorus, with its less than individual mode of being; its musical and kinesthetic mimicry, and its sensuous dreamlike imagery, precisely because it has to convey a change in the highly realized and rationalized individual moral being.[4]

The "chorus" of women musicians in *Deirdre* has no great function to perform in representing the breakdown of the rationalized moral beings of the characters. Its function is to hold before characters and audience the outcome of the drama, the recognitions that they will soon experience. In the very opening lines of the play, the musicians hold before us the action as fiction, as artistically (if not actually) completed story or song.

> I have a story right, my wanderers,
> That has so mixed with fable in our songs
> That all seemed fabulous.[5]

The First Musician has "entered hurriedly" to announce to the others her discovery that they are "come, by chance, / Into King Conchubar's country" where "Queen Deirdre grew," and she tells the familiar story up to the elopement of Deirdre and Naoise. Then the musicians gather around her to hear a close secret about present developments in that affair. Conchubar's house is being elaborately prepared and in particular one "great room"[6]—but here the entrance of Fergus interrupts them, turning what was to have been a narrative into a dramatic showing forth of the remainder of the tale.

That the imminent revelation of Conchubar's evil purpose by the

4. Fergusson, p. 52.   5. *Variorum Plays,* p. 345.
6. *Ibid.,* p. 345–47.

First Musician is prevented by Fergus's interruption does not merely mark the place where exposition leaves off and drama begins. It establishes a pattern basic to the play in which again and again the revelation of Conchubar's intent is frustrated by characteristic attitudes and actions of Fergus or Naoise. When, a little later, the First Musician attempts to tell Fergus about that "great room," he will not listen. We must wait until Deirdre is left alone with the musicians to discover the untold secret: In that room is a bed into which are sewn "strange, miracle-working, wicked stones" which have power "to stir even those at enmity to love."[7] This is evidence enough of Conchubar's plot. The musicians are consciously aware of the impending danger. Their conscious awareness points up the unconscious fear from which the other characters suffer. They hold in our attention the consequences of trust, the price these characters, including Conchubar, will have to pay. They also hold up, in their lyrics, an ideal of behavior for Deirdre and Naoise. The heroic and all-sufficient marriage of love and honor is praised by them before Naoise and Deirdre dramatize it in their lives. Thus the outcome of the tragedy, both in terms of the catastrophe and of values displayed, is present from the beginning in the persons of the musicians, who never leave the stage.

The musicians, then, are there partly to put the audience into a frame of mind in which they will accept the legendary material. This is a tale that Irish minstrels have handed down. But further, the tale is one of lovers whose lives seemed shaped by characters and events into a structure like that of art. Deirdre's death seems an artistic achievement, and the form implicit in it cries out—as she herself does to the musicians—for representation in song.

Still further, the musicians combine the function of chorus with that of seer. Their knowledge is a surer one than the narrow reasoning of a Fergus, a Naoise, or a Conchubar. Only Deirdre, who thinks with her emotions as well as her head, shares it.

Acting mainly as seers, the musicians oppose their arguments to those of Fergus. Thus they demonstrate a reasoned purpose contrary to

7. *Ibid.,* p. 361.

his. Acting mainly as chorus, they express for Deirdre and Naoise their passion and devotion. But acting as spectators and transmitters, artistic apprehenders and perfecters of the story, they discover the meaning of the whole. They are always the first to know what is going to happen and what it means. They wait from the beginning in expectancy of a fitting end to the story which is already a legend even before it is over. They are the discoverers of the tragedy of trust. The other characters act that the musicians may see, remember, and praise. The musicians' revelations are the discoveries of poetry, however, not of philosophy or science; they are not, on the other hand, the revelations of religion. The musicians are not oracles, only artists. The discoveries represented by the play are terminal stages in movements alternating craft and feeling—as if the characters were periodically granted insights as they practiced the art of their lives, training their passion to the model of some form of decorum. Further aspects of the working out of this pattern may be seen as we go through the play in more detail.

The scene of *Deirdre* is a guest house in a wood near Conchubar's palace. ". . . *Through the doors and some of the windows one can see the great spaces of the wood, the sky dimming, night closing in.*"[8] The perspective through the window is symbolically important. The woods and the approaching darkness remind us of "that first night in the woods" when Deirdre and Naoise

> . . . lay all night on leaves, and looking up,
> When the first grey of the dawn awoke the birds,
> Saw leaves above . . .[9]

and of their death together when they are gone "Into the secret wilderness of their love."[10] The perspective draws our mind off toward "the things [which] come after death."[11]

The interior arrangement is also symbolic as well as functional.

8. *Ibid.*, p. 345.
9. *Ibid.*, p. 375.
10. *Ibid.*, p. 387.
11. *Ibid.*, p. 375.

There is a door to right and left, and through the side windows one can see anybody who approaches either door, a moment before he enters. In the centre, a part of the house is curtained off; the curtains are drawn. There are unlighted torches in brackets on the walls. There is, at one side, a small table with a chess-board and chessmen upon it. At the other side of the room there is a brazier with a fire; two women, with musical instruments beside them, crouch about the brazier.[12]

The guest house is a trap, a cage. The perspective without of the darkening woods represents a liberty to be achieved only in a love-death. The mysterious glimpses, through the windows, of whoever approaches either door provide moments of ominous suspense and focus the attention on the threat from the hunter, Conchubar, who will soon come to claim his quarry.

The curtain closing off the central part of the house is also mysterious. What is behind it? Why is it there? In the context the audience cannot avoid a certain alarm about this question. Both the characters and the audience examine the interior of the room for evidence of Conchubar's intention or for any hint of what is to come. Nothing waits behind the curtain, however, except the fate of Deirdre and Naoise, who will die there, and the fate of Conchubar, whose purpose will be defeated there. The curtain will deceive Deirdre while Naoise is murdered, and will deceive Conchubar while Deirdre kills herself. The curtain conceals the unexpected and shocking tragedy, which is not recognized until too late, but for which destiny and the dramatist have reserved a place from the beginning.

The betrayal of guests in a guesthouse would be one of the most treacherous sorts of fraud, yet there has been an ominous lack of preparation for these guests. The torches are unlighted, though it is getting dark. An old chess board has not been moved for their coming. The only fire has been prepared by wandering musicians whom chance has made the only persons ready to receive the lovers. The unlighted torches convey the sense of dismal loneliness. The lovers suffer from this fear and depression until they finally see Conchubar's purpose. Then they prepare to meet death in a heroic spirit. At that point Naoise cries, "Light torches there and drive the shadows out, /

12. *Ibid.*, p. 345.

For day's grey end comes up,"[13] and the musicians light the torches in the sconces. The falling darkness, then, suggests the "grey end" of their coming death, the torchlight their growing courage. Later, when Deirdre's triumphant death is taking place behind the curtains, Fergus enters with the people, Deirdre's friends, armed. Then *The house is lit with the glare of their torches.*"[14] Life burns highest in these last minutes.

The brazier around which the wandering musicians crouch is the source of the torchlight—both literally and figuratively. The fire of the brazier suggests natural instinctive emotion—the desire to live, the fear of death, and above all the passion of love. This is a woman's play and the fire is a visible symbol of a woman's sensibility. The musicians about the brazier make that space the women's side of the stage. The men's side is over by the chess board, which represents sometimes code and decorum, sometimes craft and the struggle of wills.

The women are wanderers like Deirdre. Like her they value only love. "There is nothing in the world," says the First Musician, "That has been friendly to us but the kisses / That were upon our lips."[15] The women are lowborn and need not consider honor as a motive. Thus their direct apprehension of the situation is not confused by noble scruples. Naoise finds Deirdre unqueenly in listening to them. They are musicians, and, according to Fergus, full of

> wild thought
> Fed on extravagant poetry, and lit
> By such a dazzle of old fabulous tales
> That common things are lost, . . .[16]

Yet the imaginative truth they grasp proves more trustworthy than the "truth" based on reason and code. They are simultaneously the sympathetically suffering chorus of this tragedy and the Tiresias or Cassandra whose warnings, unheeded, prove to have a deeper truth than that of reason.

In short, they and their brazier externalize Deirdre's passion, fear, and demanding vitality. It is meaningful that Deirdre and Naoise have

13. *Ibid.,* p. 374.
15. *Ibid.,* p. 360.
14. *Ibid.,* p. 387.
16. *Ibid.,* p. 351.

been "paid servants in love's house / To sweep the ashes out and keep the doors,"[17] that after their death Deirdre and Naoise will be "Imperishable things, a cloud or a fire"[18] and that the musicians, showing Deirdre's token in afterdays will find "the doors of kings / Shall be thrown wider open, the poor man's hearth / Heaped with new turf."[19] The torches of Deirdre and Naoise's spiritual triumph are lit by these women from their symbolic brazier.

On the opposite side of the stage is the chess table suggesting that the action has many qualities of a game played according to rules. Although, as has been said, the men usually stand near the chess table and the women near the brazier, Deirdre moves back and forth as she fluctuates between passion and craft, fear and honor. When Deirdre and Naoise first enter, Deirdre has gone toward the women, who put her jewels on her as she expresses her fear of Conchubar. *"Naoise has stood looking at her, but Fergus brings him to the chess-table."*[20] Naoise says: "I have his word and I must take that word, / Or prove myself unworthy of my nurture."[21] Fergus replies, "We'll play at chess," and argues that both Deirdre's fear and Conchubar's tardiness have an innocuous explanation. The chessboard thus externalizes Naoise's heroic honor and Fergus's statecraft based on optimistic good faith. Naoise, whose code does not require him to deceive himself as Fergus's does, notes that the chessboard is an ominous sign:

> It is the board
> Where Lugaidh Redstripe and that wife of his,
> Who had a seamew's body half the year,
> Played at the chess upon the night they died.[22]

The chessboard thus becomes an objective correlative for their complete tragedy. Like Lugaidh Redstripe and his wife they will play a game of honor and good faith while they are being betrayed.

Deirdre senses Naoise's apprehension of danger, and now the whole stage becomes a chessboard on which passion and honor oppose each

---

17. *Ibid.*, p. 378.
19. *Ibid.*, p. 377.
21. *Ibid.*, p. 355.

18. *Ibid.*, p. 376.
20. *Ibid.*, p. 354.
22. *Ibid.*, pp. 355–56.

other. Deirdre protests her fear; Fergus and Naoise leave rather than listen to her unqueenly distrust. Then she must evoke and sift the hints of the musicians who are afraid to tell her what they suspect. When she has won that knowledge, she calls back Naoise. He again counters her fear with his honorable scruples, but she tricks him into thinking she cares for Conchubar and thus makes him jealous. When Fergus makes her see the vanity of this action, she is ready to blacken her beauty and thus avoid Conchubar's passion. All this were like an intense game, were it not also like the struggle of a bird in a net.

Conchubar's servant enters and announces that Deirdre is invited to Conchubar's table and his bed, but that Naoise is to be held as a traitor. This event is the betrayal foreshadowed by the earlier reference to Lugaidh Redstripe. Conchubar's cold craft is now added to the suggestions emanating from the chessboard symbol. Conchubar has cheated in the game.

An extension of the impersonal and inexorable quality of the chess game is found in the foreign mercenaries hired by Conchubar to carry out his intention. They are foreigners using force, in security, for gain. They are the opposite of the musicians, who are of the Irish people yet insecure wanderers, and who act for love. Note also that the mercenaries are opposed at the end not by an Irish army, but by the aroused, undisciplined people. The confusion of the "reaping-hooks"[23] stands partly for the insufficient preparation of Fergus in the face of evil, but also for the natural and instinctive horror of evil as opposed to Conchubar's calculation.

When "the game is up," so to speak, Naoise desires to die, not "fighting and passionate" but like "Lugaidh Redstripe and that wife of his" who

> Sat at this chess-board, waiting for their end.
> They knew that there was nothing that could save them,
> And so played chess as they had any night
> For years, and waited for the stroke of sword.

23. *Ibid.,* p. 387.

I never heard a death so out of reach
Of common hearts, a high and comely end.[24]

Deirdre agrees to play, saying,

> . . . though I have not been born
> Of the cold, haughty waves, my veins being hot,
> And though I have loved better than that queen,
> I'll have as quiet fingers on the board.

The torches are lighted, and they play. The musicians sing at the bidding of the lovers:

> *Deirdre.*   Make no sad music.
> What is it but a king and queen at chess?
> They need a music that can mix itself
> Into imagination, but not break
> The steady thinking that the hard game needs.[25]

This scene is of the highest importance, for it brings together the images of fire, light, music, and womanly passion with the images of the hard masculine game. The substance of Deirdre's passion is being given the form of Naoise's honor.

She breaks off the game, not to lapse back into fear, but to prefer a higher game, the game of love. Deirdre's victory over fear is passionate, and therefore superior to that of the stoical seamew's victory.

> I cannot go on playing like that woman
> That had but the cold blood of the sea in her veins.
> *Naoise.* It is your move. Take up your man again.

She does so, but in the game of love, not chess. She says:

> Do you remember that first night in the woods
> We lay all night on leaves, and looking up,
> When the first grey of the dawn awoke the birds,
> Saw leaves above us? You thought that I still slept,
> And bending down to kiss me on the eyes,

24. *Ibid.*, p. 373.
25. *Ibid.*, p. 374.

Found they were open. Bend and kiss me now,
For it may be the last before our death.
And when that's over, we'll be different;
Imperishable things, a cloud or a fire.
And I know nothing but this body, nothing
But that old vehement, bewildering kiss.[26]

Death is here figured as a dawn rather than a sunset. A transformation has taken place. Deirdre has joined to her passion the language of honor which Naoise uses in referring to the seamew and her lover:

... those two,
Because no man and woman have loved better,
Might sit on there contentedly, and weigh
The joy comes after.[27]

In this game of love Deirdre and Naoise have been opposites, he honorable and she passionate. But now she has penetrated into his area of this psychological chessboard and he into hers. From this time on she is heroical and controlled. Love appears in her speeches now in the forms of decorum, honorable courage, and masterful craft. He, on the other hand, becomes passionate in his desire to kill Conchubar, losing his earlier determination not to "die like an old king out of a fable, / Fighting and passionate."[28]

The temptation comes in the form of honor. Conchubar appears, seemingly inviting Naoise to the noble game of single combat.

Naoise [laughing]. He has taken up my challenge;
Whether I am a ghost or living man
When day has broken, I'll forget the rest,
And say that there is kingly stuff in him.

Conchubar, however, disappears. It is not the game of war he is playing, but the ignoble one (when human beings alone are involved) of hunter and hunted.

Naoise. A prudent hunter, therefore, but no king.
He'd find if what has fallen in the pit

26. Ibid., pp. 375–76.   27. Ibid., p. 373.
28. Ibid.

Were worth the hunting, but has come too near,
And I turn hunter. You're not man, but beast.
Go scurry in the bushes, now, beast, beast,
For now it's topsy-turvy, I upon you.[29]

This angry lack of restraint leads to Naoise's capture.

Conchubar. He cried 'Beast, beast!' and in a blind-beast rage
He ran at me and fell into the nets. . . .[30]

From this moment on there is no conflict, in Naoise's speeches, between honor and love, the law of one being the law of the other, both games following the same rules. Deirdre is ready to sacrifice herself to Conchubar to rescue Naoise. This sacrifice Naoise will not accept:

Naoise. . . . If you were to do this thing,
And buy my life of Conchubar with your body,
Love's law being broken, I would stand alone
Upon the eternal summits, and call out,
And you could never come there, being banished.[31]

Deirdre bows to his decision; she obeys always the law of love.

As Deirdre begins her dignified and decorous pleading, she stands on the women's side of the stage and slowly approaches Conchubar who is on the other side. When she kneels before Conchubar, asking for him to pardon her obedience to the law of love, she has come completely across the stage—from the side of fear and passion to the side of honor. Naoise is then killed. Deirdre staggers back to the other side with the musicians.

Now she opposes to Conchubar's seven-year game of plotting her own skillful deception. She begins to move again towards the center of the stage. She pretends to a passion she does not feel—"There's something brutal in us, and we are won / By those who can shed blood," and a conventional honor with which she is not concerned—

I shall do all you bid me, but not yet,
Because I have to do what's customary.

29. *Ibid.,* p. 376.   30. *Ibid.,* p. 378.
31. *Ibid.,* p. 381.

We lay the dead out, folding up the hands,
Closing the eyes, and stretching out the feet,
And push a pillow underneath the head,
Till all's in order; and all this I'll do
For Naoise, son of Usna.[32]

Earlier she used her sophistry to get Naoise to give in to her fears. Now she uses it to deceive Conchubar and achieve an honorable love-death.

She appeals to the code of love—"It is so small a gift and you will grant it / Because it is the first that I have asked." Conchubar is not moved. She appeals then to selfish pride and wins her end.

Deirdre. . . . He shall be mocked of all.
   They'll say to one another, "Look at him
   That is so jealous that he lured a man
   From over sea, and murdered him, and yet
   He trembled at the thought of a dead face!"
                              [*She has her hand upon curtain*
Conchubar. How do I know that you have not some knife,
   And go to die upon his body?
Deirdre.   Have me searched,
   If you would make so little of your queen.
   It may be that I have a knife hid here
   Under my dress. Bid one of these dark slaves
   To search me for it.   [*Pause.*
Conchubar.   Go to your farewells, Queen.[33]

As Naoise and Deirdre had to trust Conchubar, because not to do so would be dishonorable, so now Conchubar has to trust Deirdre, or else be humiliated—kingly pride being his code of honor.

Deirdre now goes behind the curtain from the women's side, as Naoise has been dragged from the men's. The curtain is halfway between the symbols of brazier and chessboard. Deirdre stabbing herself upon the body of Naoise, has played her game of honorable love and won. Fergus enters with rescuers, playing out his game of

32. *Ibid.,* p. 384.
33. *Ibid.,* pp. 385–86.

keeping faith. He will not allow Conchubar to touch the body of Deirdre, for which he still stands surety. Conchubar's game, that of deception used to enhance his sovereign pride, is lost. However, even he feels justified by the rules.

> *Conchubar.*   I have no need of weapons,
>   There's not a traitor that dare stop my way.
>   Howl, if you will; but I, being King, did right
>   In choosing her most fitting to be Queen,
>   And letting no boy lover take the sway.[34]

The whole play has been a tragic chess game in which each player followed the rules sacred to him: Conchubar, sovereign pride, Fergus, statesmanly good-faith, Naoise, heroic honor, and Deirdre, the laws of love. In a sense, the finish was determined before the start and all the action was like that of Lugaidh Redstripe and his bride: "They moved the men and waited for the end."[35]

Just as legitimately, however, one could say that the whole play has been a rising fire of passion against the night sky of death. In terms of stage properties, the fire spreads from the brazier, to the torches in the sconces, to the torches in the hands of Deirdre's belated defenders. All four chief characters show themselves in an intensity both of passion and of control in that last flaring scene.

The stage movement, like the psychological movement of the whole play, follows that of a pendulum. The early scenes show a great distance between Deirdre's passion and Naoise's honor, and the action shifts obviously back and forth from one side to the other. These movements, both physical and psychological, become briefer and briefer as passion becomes honor and honor passion and as Deirdre and Naoise converge upon their place of death and triumph behind the central curtain.

Deirdre, like the plays of the theatre of reason, never allows the rationalized moral persona to be completely dissolved in passion. On

34. *Ibid.,* p. 388.
35. *Ibid.,* p. 356.

the other hand it is destructive of all codes but a completely individualistic ethic. Fergus and Conchubar are wrong. Naoise and especially
Deirdre—whose code is a truth to individual emotion—are right. To
be most human, according to the play, is to trust to feeling, not to
abstract conceptions of social duty. (Naoise's honor is individualistic,
not social.)

This play, then, is not for the theatre of reason; nor is it for the
theatre of passion. It borrows elements from both and attempts to fuse
them. They become each other. Naoise's loyalty to his honor is motivated by his love. His purpose gives form to an ideal wholeness.
Deirdre's passion provides the content, inseparable from the form in
that whole.

The play says that honorable purpose and passionate love are both
essential to an ideal relationship, but that the two are in practice
incompatible in life. The hero and heroine achieve this ideal relationship only in death. The way of knowing which the play underwrites is
neither that of reason nor that of passion but that harmonious movement of the whole soul indicated in the perfect love of Deirdre and
Naoise and in the symbol of music and poetry.

The play presents not a genuine tragic rhythm of purpose, passion,
and perception, but the discovery that the first two are complementary
parts of the third. Yeats has still to create the heroes whose central
reality would be, not to demonstrate reason or express emotion, but to
see, to recognize, to discover the tragedy of vision.

The Mask Maker

❦ "That struggle of a dream with the world"

T
HE TRAGEDY OF vision is the art form in whose service the Poet would enlist the Actress in the dialogue to which we now turn. "The end of art is ecstasy, and that cannot exist without pain. It is [a] sudden sense of power and of peace, that comes when we have before our mind's eye a group of images which obeys us, which leaves us free, and which satisfies the need of our soul" [SB22(1p207)]. The tragic poet "shows the pain side by side with the ecstasy.... He must be able to see reality without flinching" [SB22(1p210)].

The Poet wishes for the birth of an "unreal theatre" sired upon the world by philosophy, not by science like modern realism. The philosophical speculations that ultimately resulted in *A Vision* have fathered this new form. Yeats wishes "a new instrument where nothing will be possible but poetry or music" [SB22(1p193)]. In the place of bad scene painting, "some plain unbroken surface . . ." will "display every movement" of the actor. "I would not disguise the real properties, and the real light and shadow of the stage" [SB22(1p194)]. The form will be that of a dance play. Yeats exclaims, "You know [how] important the dance is in the Japanese theatre" [SB22(1p195)]. The mask will be central, and the supposed occasion of the dialogue is a mask that the Poet has brought from Fez for the Actress to wear in his next play.

The Actress calls this new form the "Theatre of Beauty" [SB22(1p211)], and the description of the scenery is close to that in Yeats's 1911 lecture of that title.[1] Yet it is clear that this dialogue, which Mrs. Yeats dates 1916, heralds Yeats's plays for dancers, the first of which, *At the Hawk's Well*, was produced on 2 and 4 April of that year.

The tone of the dialogue is light, but Yeats is very serious about the

---

1. *Uncollected Prose*, II, 399–401.

nature of his drama. Why are masks necessary? asks the Actress and prompts the Poet to expound the doctrine of the mask. All admirable art is the result of battle. The new drama, unlike the realistic theatre, is a battle that "takes place in the depths of the soul, and one [of] the antagonists does not wear a shape known to the world or speak a mortal tongue" [SB22(1p200)]. Clearly we are in the presence of the anti-self of "Ego Dominus Tuus"[2] and of "Anima Hominis."[3] Lady Gregory and Mrs. Patrick Campbell are cited, not by name, as friends who wear the mask in their art, and the descriptions echo "Anima Hominis," where Lady Gregory's "only fault is a habit of harsh judgment with those who have not her sympathy, and she has written comedies where the wickedest people seem but bold children."[4] Mrs. Patrick Campbell, "in private life, is like the captain of some buccaneer ship holding his crew to good behaviour at the mouth of a blunder-buss, and upon the stage she excels in the representation of women who stir to pity and to desire because they need our protection. . . ."[5] It was shortly before this date that Yeats had a breakthrough in his long struggle to write *The Player Queen,* which also illustrates the theory of the mask.[6]

Dante and Keats are important examples in the dialogue, as they are in "Ego Dominus Tuus," where we read of Dante,

> He set his chisel to the hardest stone.
> Being mocked by Guido for his lecherous life,
> Derided and deriding, driven out
> To climb that stair and eat that bitter bread,
> He found the unpersuadable justice, he found
> The most exalted lady loved by a man

2. Composed October 5, 1915, according to Ellmann, *Identity,* p. 290, and published in October 1917 (*Variorum Poems,* p. 367; cf. *Poems,* p. 160).

3. "Anima Hominis" is dated February 25, 1917 (*Mythologies,* p. 342).

4. *Ibid.,* p. 326.

5. *Ibid.,* pp. 326–27.

6. Curtis Bradford dates this breakthrough November 1915 (*W. B. Yeats: The Writing of the Player Queen,* ed. Curtis Baker Bradford [DeKalb: Northern Illinois University Press, 1977], pp. 269–70).

and of Keats,

> His art is happy, but who knows his mind?
> I see a schoolboy when I think of him,
> With face and nose pressed to a sweet-shop window,
> For certainly he sank into his grave
> His senses and his heart unsatisfied,
> And made—being poor, ailing and ignorant,
> Shut out from all the luxury of the world,
> The coarse-bred son of a livery-stable keeper—
> Luxuriant song.[7]

Indeed the new form will be the anti-self of circumstantial realism. In it the battle is the soul's "battle with reality itself" [SB22(1p198)].[8] Not only must mask, music, dance be used, not only must speech be heightened to poetry, but "there must be [a] whole phantasmagoria, through which the life long contest finds expression. There must be fables, mythology that the dream and the reality may face one another in visible array" [SB22(1p204)]. In this dialogue we see the motives that led Yeats to abandon the stage temporarily and to attempt his dance plays based on Noh drama, to do "what the Japanese did centuries ago to scene and player alike" [SB22(1p201)].

A Note on the Transcription of *The Poet and the Actress*

This transcription was made while the present National Library of Ireland MS 30,410 was still number 410* in Senator Michael Yeats's collection.

The dialogue exists in manuscript and typescript. The manuscript, untitled, is in W. B. Yeats's hand (see "A Description of the Manu-

---

7. *Variorum Poems*, pp. 369–70; cf. *Poems*, pp. 161–62; cf. also *Autobiographies*, pp. 272–75.

8. There are even intimations of the future—as far ahead as "Among School Children" (1927). There Yeats dreams "of a Ledean body" (*Variorum Poems*, p. 443; cf. *Poems*, p. 216) and "Both nuns and mothers worship images" (*Ibid.*, p. 445; cf. *Poems*, p. 217). In *The Poet and the Actress,* the "lover . . . thinks of Helen and the mother forgets her own child, so full of idiosyncracy, to dream of the child at Bethlehem" (p. 178).

script." Words difficult to read have been underlined in pencil, and
Mrs. Yeats has written glosses over them. This was probably done for
the typist, who seems to have been someone other than Mrs. Yeats. The
typescript, entitled "THE POET AND THE ACTRESS," is corrected in Mrs. Yeats's hand and some of the typing errors demonstrate
a greater struggle with Yeats's handwriting than Mrs. Yeats would
have had. Some of the illegible words are left unglossed, and un-
transcribed, however, and many glosses are questioned. Yeats himself,
then, was not available for consultation when the typescript was made.
Mrs. Yeats has made editorial decisions, changing minor words in
order to complete or to clarify sentences, and one suspects that at some
time after Yeats's death she was preparing the piece for possible
publication.

I have transcribed Yeats's manuscript from the microfilm in the
William Butler Yeats Microfilmed Manuscripts Collection (MC 294),
Department of Special Collections, Library, State University of New
York at Stony Brook, and have checked my transcription against the
original. While not accepting all of her readings, I have taken full
advantage of Mrs. Yeats's work and am greatly indebted to it. Moreover, when one of two equally possible readings has her authority, I
have chosen that one. Mrs. Yeats's own corrections are not always easy
to read, and in need I have profited from the late Liam Miller's
transcription of her own corrected typescript. (Indeed I am grateful to
Miller for urging me to transcribe and present the original.)

I have not followed Mrs. Yeats's punctuation, but that, rather erratic,
of Yeats's manuscript. (I have supplied end stops and apostrophes
where he has neglected them.) My purpose is not to give the work a
finished appearance but to present it as an unpolished draft which
Yeats never fully revised for publication. The commas that Yeats
dropped in when pausing for breath or thought would have been
replaced, as in the typescript, by others marking grammatical units.
But Yeats's original punctuation may interest the reader, and having to
construe the sense without the usual aids may serve as a reminder that
this is not a finished work. Some sentences that Mrs. Yeats completed I
have left in their mysterious inconclusiveness.

Yet I have broken part of the spell by exorcising Yeats's daemonic illegibility and orthography. This is a reading text with spelling and capitalization normalized and the fascinating stages of Yeats's cancellations and revisions omitted. Only when cancelled words are necessary to complete the sense do I include them. Some interesting cancelled passages and some alternate readings by Mrs. Yeats are added in the notes. I have normalized the styling of Yeats's speakers' names. Broken words are silently joined or hyphenated except where, in the context, the division adds emphasis: "our selves." Editorial additions other than silent are in square brackets. When, as in moving from one page to the next, Yeats has repeated a word ("of/of"), I omit the first appearance.

Each page is introduced by its number in the Yeats Archive at Stony Brook. The manuscripts are reproduced there both on microfilm and in bound volumes. "SB22(1p192)" means that the page may be found in reel 22 and on page 192 of the first of the bound volumes which reproduce that reel. Yeats's page numbers at the top right of each page are reproduced exactly as Yeats left them, for accuracy of identification, in spite of their evident inconsistency: "(1", "(1a", "2", "2a", "4.3", etc.

The Poet and the Actress†

BY W. B. YEATS

[SB22(1p192)]   (1

The Poet.

I have just returned from the city of Fez and have in this box a mask, which was made for you by the artists modelling in continual consultation with the poets of that[1] city. You will wear it in my next play.

The Actress.

Yes my friend let us talk of the theatre. There are going to be different plays and a different playhouse it seems. You will have grown tired of the theatre before it comes and I shall have grown too old for anything but Juliet's nurse. So let us discuss it. We are impartial. I may even come to understand why the poets and artists of Fez have sent me that mask.

The Poet.

I see that even this—a supreme compliment coming from such illustrious artists has not convinced you, and yet there are every [where] stages[2] of change. Putting aside, the criticism[3] and creation[4] of Fez itself you [have] the

---

†The following textual footnotes are not meant to be exhaustive in noting cancelled passages but only to call items of special interest to the reader's attention. I note most divergences (except for capitalisation and punctuation) between Mrs. Yeats's corrected typescript and my transcription. Some of these she would probably have changed if she had polished her transcription. "GY" stands for Mrs. Yeats's typescript; "MS" for Yeats's original manuscript.

Explanatory notes, marked with manuscript page numbers and indicated in the text by asterisks following key words or phrases [*], are set at the end of the text, beginning on page 183.

Yeats's MS is untitled. Mrs. Yeats's typescript is titled "THE POET AND THE ACTRESS."

1. *that:* the, GY.   2. *every[where] stages:* every signs, GY.
3. *criticism:* criticisms, GY.   4. *creation:* creations, GY.

[SB22(1p193)]   (1a

success of Claudel in Paris, so much more significant than that of Maeterlinck, for Claudel has an elaborate language and then there is[5] Hoffmansthal[,] D'Annunzio and less known men, and still more significant the[6] creation of an unreal theatre, of a new instrument where nothing will be possible but poetry or music, and in all the arts there is a revolt against mimicry, realism, the mere copying of the surface of life. The world having brought forth the realistic theatre to her lover science, is about to bear a child to her husband philosophy. He was indignant but he forgave her though he has not made up his mind what he is going to do with his[7] illegitimate son. He could not expose him on a shovel* in this humane age, and will probably leave him to the father's care.

The Actress.

I am surprised—and science so respectable since he was taken up by the religious press. I suppose they will prefer even his child to the child of philosophy. But why are you so anxious to turn out realists.[8] I have always tried to be as real as possible in my acting.

The Poet.

I wish to have the stage itself real, though it must always suggest

[SB22(1p194)]   2

a dream. I would not disguise the real properties, and the real light and shadow of the stage and I would recognise the reality of the actor so much, that I would put him against some plain unbroken surface that will display every movement. I would not allow any bad landscape painter to compete with him. I would not drive player, and stage out of sight in the delusion that I can copy some imaginary scene exactly, or that it would be worth doing if I could. It is that attempt which only began when the enthusiasm of the Italian renaissance for painting got

---

5. *then there is:* ~~then~~ there is, GY.   6. *the:* of the, GY.
7. *his:* so GY. It could just as well be "her".
8. *realists:* so GY. It could also be "reality".

into the theatre a wholly different art, and compelled the actors—
always impressionable people[9]—to create the picture stage. Once understand that you must use what is in front of you, the light and
shadow of sun or lamp, and not painted light and shadow, the architecture of the stage, and not Mr. So and So['s] garden walk, who realised
when he was twenty-five that he would never sell a picture—once
prefer the beauty and expressiveness of the actor's mind and body to
their suppression in mimicry as do clerk[10] or lawyer whose life has
been obedience to mechanical habit, and all will become powerful and
beautiful. Player, playwright, decorator would at once discover, that
they were[11] doing what they had always longed for.

[SB22(1p195)]   2a

Take anything you will. Theatre or speech or a man's body and
develop its emotional expressiveness, and you at once increase its
power of suggestion, and take away from its power of mimicry, or of
stating facts. The body begins to take poses, or even to move in a dance,
and you know [how] important the dance is in the Japanese theatre.
Speech becomes rhythmical full of suggestion, and as this change takes
place, we begin to possess instead of the real world of the mimics
solitudes and wilderness peopled by divinities, and demons, the vast
sentiments, the desires of the heart cast forth into forms, mythological
beings, a frenzied parturition. In the middle ages, certain clowns made
a great reputation by the skill, that[12] they had acquired, of imitating
animals. Can you not imagine a country, where the violin its old use
forgotten, had become an instrument for imitating the crying and
wailing of cats. Presently a violinist discovers, that the strings have also
a sweet sound

[SB22(1p196)]   2.b

which is curiously deepened by the resonance of the wood and to the

9. *actors—always impressionable people:* actors— not a very intelligent class —always
impressionable people, MS.

10. *clerk:* the clerk, GY.

11. *were:* are, GY.

12. *that:* Yeats wrote "they they", meaning "that they". GY omits first "they".

despair of his admirers, and amid the mockery of critics begins the
evolution of an art which has nothing for the lovers[13] of mimicry, and
has to create its own lovers. That is the way with the theatre, but once
we have banished that[14] crying out of cats, we shall [have] an art, which
[is] as[15] illimitable as the mind itself.

The Actress.
Well I will admit that I am annoyed when I have to play a slut or a
tousled hoyden. A good many men have told me that I am charming.

[SB22(1p197)][16]   4.3

Next time I play a queen for you you may not perhaps compel me to
make up dark, which does not in the least become my blond hair, and
all because you are such a realist in spite of your principles, that you
wanted me to appear sunburnt.

The Poet.
You have forgotten the mask.

13. *lovers:* lover, GY.
14. *that:* this, GY.
15. *art, which [is] as:* art, which ~~shall be able to suggest, every fancy that passes before the mind's eye~~ as MS; art as, GY.
16. SB22(1p199), the original of which SB22(1p197) and SB22(1p198) are the revision, is transcribed only in these notes. It is not transcribed in GY. I include some, not all, cancelled words.

(3

charming. Next time I play a queen for you, you will perhaps allow me to wear my high heeled shoes.

The Poet.
Next time I may perhaps put upon your face, a mask with certain severe Egyptian lines, that when I listen to your beautiful voice I may believe that you are the goddess, that only boys of seventeen will believe in now.

The Actress.
There you go taking away in one moment all that you promised the moment before—but I forgot we shall both be old before these dreadful things happen. ~~I shall not mind a mask the~~ [= it] ~~may be if Mr. Ricketts is [not] too old to make it.~~ I may have come to prefer Mr. Ricketts handiwork to God's. But why have you taken such a dislike to my face.

The Poet.
Alas I like it so well that I shall never perhaps, ask Mr. Ricketts for the mask. And yet great art does not express the visible world, but some dream created by a contest with reality, and ~~that above all with the real self.~~ It only becomes possible, when we have seen beyond circumstance, and conquered our selves, and the more violent the contest, the loftier the dream, the greater the art. ~~When the contest is deliberate, we have a moral genius.~~ We have to do with ourselves, with the whole world, what Mr. Craig, and Mr. Barker and the other [. . .]

The Actress.

So you take away with one hand what you give with the other—but I forgot we shall both be dead before a theatre exists such as you describe, and till that day comes I will do as I like. But I wish you would explain[17] to me why I am not to make my face as expressive as possible.

The Poet.

You ask that because you have been so admirable

[SB22(1p198)]   3a

in those plays of the new scientific kind.[18] Now those plays like all admirable art—and I admit that even mimicry can be admirable mimicry [—] are the result of battle, but I want to show you another battle, which has the insatiable[19] charm for a good fighter that it can never be won, the battle with reality[20] itself.

The Actress.

Have I been taking part in a battle?

The Poet.

[SB22(1p200)]   3a/3.b

Do we not call Strindberg a woman hater, and did not he call Ibsen a male blue-stocking, and do not you call him a feminist, and then think of Mr. Galsworthy's convictions. They are overpowering. They weigh upon us like a nightmare—I have even heard two girls during [one] of

---

17. After *explain* the MS continues:

The Poet.
I wished you to look sun burned, not out [of] a love [of] reality but because a sun burnt queen suggests a strange intense world.

18. A cancelled passage in SB22(1p200) may be of interest here:

I shall always offer you the flattery of being false to my principles but you ask me these questions because you have been so admirable in ~~The Dolls House, & Hedda Gabler, in Strindberg & Ibsen, &~~ the plays of the new scientific kind. Now those plays like all organic art are the result of a battle.

19. *insatiable:* irresistible, GY.

20. *with reality:* will realise, GY. Curtis B. Bradford, *Yeats at Work* (Carbondale and Edwardsville: Southern Illinois University Press, 1965), p. 215, confirms my reading.

his plays discussing the obvious offence of eating chocolates ~~when~~ at[21] such a serious play. But even the dramatists who have no doctrine, they too have their battle—for they have satire—is not all comedy a battle, a sham fight often—but still a battle. Now the art I long for is also a battle but it takes place in the depths of the soul, and one [of] the antagonists does not wear a shape known to the world or speak a mortal tongue. It is that[22] struggle of a dream with the world. It is only possible when we transcend circumstance and ourselves, and the greater the contest the greater the art.[23] We have to do with our selves what Mr. Barker and Mr. Craig* and the other

[SB22(1p201)]   4

craftsmen of the theatre are doing with the scene, or what the Japanese did centuries ago to scene and player alike. When the contest is deliberate we have a moral genius. Dante at the death of Beatrice, imagined an ideal mistress, and imagined excited by his banishment, and the violence of his time an ideal justice. Every artist is a starving man, who creates imaginary drink and food, which content[24] him while the want lasts.[25]

The Actress.
Then he is merely like any reformer, preacher or philanthropist.[26]

21. ~~when~~ *at:* in, GY.
22. *that:* the, GY.
23. *is not all comedy . . . the greater the art.* Bradford, *Yeats at Work,* p. 215, quotes these lines normalising punctuation, though somewhat differently from Mrs Yeats. Bradford's papers contain a transcription of the whole dialogue which I have not seen. See James L. Allen and M. M. Liberman, "Transcriptions of Yeats's Unpublished Prose in the Bradford Papers at Grinnell College," *Serif: Quarterly of the Kent State University Libraries* 10: 1 (Spring 1973) 16.
24. *content:* contents, GY.
25. After *lasts* the MS has this cancelled passage:

~~If he did not create that vision he would [die?] for he must imagine something [or?] be full of bitterness and regret.~~

26. After *philanthropist* there is an interesting cancelled passage difficult to decipher:

philanthropist ~~or preacher or journalist, who is convinced that when he is at or young lover separated from his sweetheart. If I believed that I would never be not be touring about the provinces with a~~

My friend I believe you have begun to roll down hill[27] and that you will end in the ditch with Tolstoy.

The Poet.

Dante did not create the Divine Comedy to bring[28] Beatrice back from the grave, or even in the main to reform his time. If he had wished to reform his time, he would have been a rhetorician, as Milton was in part. He was himself a violent man, full of hatred and of lust, and he created beauty and justice to give peace to his own soul. Guido,* who was no fastidious moralist remonstrated with Dante for his disordered life after the death

[SB22(1p202)]

5

of Beatrice and there is[29] a sonnet of   * complaining of his injustice. The beauty he created was his victory over himself, a sign that he so ordered his thoughts that neither the spectacle of his time, nor of his own life could break his peace. I know no writer whose life is known to us, either because of the minuteness of the record, or the greatness and plainness of the events ~~where one cannot discover this contest, thought it is conscious~~ only ~~in the great moralists.~~[30] The men of tragic genius give us not only their ideal vision, but the reality that excited it, but there are others Keats for instance who give[31] us the vision only. Keats the son[32] of a livery stable keeper, reading Greek in translation, and kept[33] out of the luxurious world by his obscurity, and his lack of training, creates the vision of luxury and of Greece and alters the history [and] the direction[34] of our poetry. Cannot you see[35]

~~manager with people with disaggreable people and living in proffered lodgings. I would join a strike committee, or go to Italy with a lover.~~

27. *hill:* the hill, GY.   28. *to bring:* to reform, bring, GY.

29. *there is:* then in, GY.

30. *events . . . moralists:* GY stops the sentence at ~~contest~~ and does not transcribe ~~though it is conscious~~ only ~~in the great moralists.~~

31. *give:* gave, GY.

32. *Keats the son:* Keats the ~~ill bred ill educated~~ son, MS.

33. *and kept:* kept, GY.

34. *history [&] the direction:* history ~~of the English imagination~~ [&] the direction, MS.

35. *cannot you see:* can you not see, GY.

him like a boy with his face glued to the glass window of a sweet shop.
We can see it in the few people of creative power we know intimately. I
know one writer of comedy* who is a stern judge of herself and others
giving an obedience, which I would call heroic but you would accuse
me [of] romanticism

[SB22(1p203)]   9.6

to a self-chosen moral law and in her comedies no one is judged, even
the wicked people are seen as indulgently as if they were naughty[36]
children. Her exquisite art is the glorification of indulgence, perpetual
pardon and charity. Then we both know an actress, who in daily life is
over masterful,[37]* and restless, as if she were in command of a perpetual pirates' cave, where power must always be apparent. On the
stage she excels in the representation of Maeterlinck's faint and selfless
heroines, and has there not been Synge, always ill and constitutionally
timid and reserved, whose imagination was busy with the spectacle of
violent, or confident persons, full of noise and braggadocio. Carlyle
said of Scott* that he was lucky to have but a club foot, that left
his mind healthy, and not some inner morbidity—perhaps Carlyle
thought of himself—and yet some morbid trait, or bodily[38] disease,
which would have troubled the mind, might have so deepened, so
roused into self consciousness the mind of Scott that he would have
been a Balzac or a Tolstoy instead of a writer for boys. All over Europe
was coming again the tragic man, the revealer of the invisible[39] life of
the soul, and Carlyle obsessed with Victorian rhetoric saw perhaps, as
the newspapers still do, the morbidity and not that victory.

The Actress.

[SB22(1p204)]   10 7

I understand that, but I do not yet fully understand, why [we] must
get away from reality to express this victory. I notice, that you spoke of
Claudel's language—and I know he writes in very eloquent verse
libre—as if for that reason he could say more than let us say Maeter-

36. *naughty:* ~~bold, charming,~~ naughty, MS.
37. *over masterful:* masterful, GY.   38. *bodily:* brooding, GY.
39. *invisible:* insoluble, GY.

linck, with his simple language. I understand that as a poet you want to bring back verse, but after all that is an ornament. One doubts if Shakespeare if he had lived now would have used it, was not everything written in verse once,—even books on agriculture. The stage is a place for acting, and you who object to its imitating the easel picture, should not ask it to do what is so much better done in a volume of lyrics.

The Poet.

Rhythmical speech, is only the most heightened form of speech but heightened speech of some kind you must have. Dante could choose from the real speech of this day, fitting words for the living Beatrice, and the injustice of his time cried out in the streets but what words had he for the world of his [or her?] victory. In every great play—in Shakespeare for instance you will find one group of characters— Hamlet Lear let us say—who express the Dream and another group who express its antagonist & to the antagonist,[40] Shakespeare gives a speech close to that of daily life. But it is not only the mere speech that must be heightened, there must be [a] whole phantasmagoria, through which the life long contest finds expression. There must be fables, mythology that the dream and the reality

[SB22(1p205)]   8

may face one another in visible array. Even when real life moves us deeply, so profound is the scorn the heart feels for all created things, so unutterably proud it is we cease to be realists. The lover forgets [the] living woman who has set fire to his haystack,* and thinks of Helen and the mother, forgets her own child, so full of idiosyncrasy, to dream of the child at Bethlehem. Only the intellect is humble despite that false fable of the fallen angels, is content with what the eye sees, and the intellect only wishes to understand. That is why we poets pass on age after age an artificial language, inherited from the first poets, and always full of reminiscent symbols, which grow, richer in association

40. *express its antagonist & to the antagonist:* so GY. It could also read "express the antagonist to the antagonist".

every time, they are used, for new emotions. In primitive communities, where men are not yet crowded together, and so are able to find time when they speak[41] to express emotion as well as describe facts is real language fit for the use of a great artist. Yet even Synge concentrated, and enriches[42] the language he found in Arran, or in the Blaskets, and in the one play where he expresses his vision, without its antagonist the grotesque, he throws the events backward in time that he might obtain a more powerful phantasmagoria.

[SB22(1p206)]   9.

In Deirdre of the Sorrows, he expressed through the symbolism of an old Irish story his own thoughts as to fate,[43] and made up his mind to die. The dream is the group of images and emotions by which he created peace. Setting the thought of his own approaching death, into a world of vast sentences [= sentiments][44] he saw it as all men's death—as though his own life gathered up the general lot like a burning glass the sunlight. He kept before his mind for those last months death—it was never out of his mind one friend told me—and in making Deirdre renounce life, because life could but mar what it had already given, and the answer Shelley gave, when the spirit came to him in a dream before his drowning and said are you satisfied.* Both answered 'I am satisfied.'

The Actress.

I understand that art is the expression of an ideal—all the old writers used to say that though we have got tired of the word but I do not understand this contest. I think art is just our pursuit of happiness—and that when we put into play or poem the thoughts that make us happy we create beautiful art. I do not think there can be much

41. *when they speak:* for their speech, GY.

42. *enriches:* enriched, GY.

43. *as to fate:* ~~as to faith,~~ GY. In the left margin of GY's typescript she writes "[William?] Becker/'to the full'." This is a possible reading.

44. *sentences [= sentiments]:* GY strikes out the typed "sentiments" and writes in "sentences". Yeats wrote "sentenes" or "sentmes".

happiness about thoughts that come out of such a battle as that[45] with the fear of death. Why not say that Synge was merely trying to make a beautiful thing.

[SB22(1p207)]   10

The Poet.

Those who try to create beautiful things without this battle in [the] soul, are mere imitators, because we can only become conscious of a thing, by comparing it with its opposite. The two real [or new?] things we have are our natures, and the circumstance that surrounds us. We need in both a violent antithesis, nor do I believe art has anything to do with happiness. When we say we are happy we mean that we are doing all kinds of pleasant things, that we have forgotten all painful things. The end of art is ecstasy, and that cannot exist without pain. It is [a] sudden sense of power and of peace, that comes when we have before our mind's eye a group of images, which obeys[46] us, which leaves[47] us free, and which satisfies[48] the need of our soul.[49]

[SB22(1p208)]   11

We all desire certainty—that is to say that the imagination shall be at rest—no longer troubling about all kinds of things and no longer bitter—and beauty is the emotion of a[50] soul in the presence of this certainty. Synge in Deirdre of the Sorrows has given us his own reverie over his approaching death and he weighs life and death, and decides that death is best and as [for] what sorrow remains, he forgets himself in those last wonderful lamentations, in which he speaks the sorrow of

---

45. *that:* this, GY.   46. *obeys:* obey, GY.
47. *leaves:* leave, GY.   48. *satisfies:* satisfy, GY.

49. *soul:* After *soul* the MS. has the following cancelled passage, of which GY transcribes and includes only the first sentence:

But we must believe in it, and if we left out a single painful fact, we would be unable to believe in those images. Synge had to think of death perpetually,—to hold before himself all the images of fear that the emotion that broke forth at last might be as I believe it was the greatest ecstasy he had known. He must be certain that he had conquered the last antagonist and he was a great writer but he never as do the sentimentalists, [hid from himself?] the reasons for despair. Beauty is deliberately chosen emotion, but we cannot choose till we have escaped from the last obsession the last antagonist. There cannot be new beauty without obsession.   /   /   /

50. *a:* the, GY.

all men. He had death perpetually in his mind. He left out nothing of
the pain for if he had he would not have believed in his ecstasy. His
imagination like that of Dante said all is well, but that would have
been an unreal peace, a mere sentimentality if he had hidden from
himself any cause of despair. The goal of the imagination is ~~that~~ when[51]
the imagination gives assent to the order of the world and is satisfied
with it and it resembles religious faith which is the assent of the moral
nature

[SB22(1p209)]   ƴ 12

just as there cannot be religious faith without doubt. Beauty is the
soul's gift to the world, faith is the soul's gift to god, but that faith may[52]
be real, the whole nature emotion and intellect alike, must give assent,
and that faith is a[53] false faith—a creation of priests—if the whole
being has not been excited into activity. It is the business of the intellect
to call forth, to create the antagonist. The greater the intellect, the
nobler is the faith, the nobler the beauty.

The Actress.
I saw Mr. Shaw's Candida last night. There was a poet there who
shudders to the depths of his soul because he sees his sweetheart
cutting onions. I had always thought a poet was like that, that everything moved him, and so[54] commonplace things can become subjects[55]
of poets. That he was just like the rest of us only more emotional.

The Poet.
Do you know any great poet, or great writer who is easily moved.

The Actress.
Well now that I think of it, I have found all poets great or small,
exceedingly blasé. It has done more for my chastity

[SB22(1p210)]   13

even than my knowledge of their unfaithfulness. When they have paid

---

51. *is ~~that~~ when:* is when, GY.   52. *may:* must, GY.
53. *a:* to, GY.   54. *so:* all, GY.
55. *become subjects:* be the subjects, GY. The MS has "bec", elliptical for "become".

me compliments I have wondered if they were laughing at me. Even you my friend wish to cover my face with a mask.

The Poet.

You will acknowledge at once that bad poets, and the bad musicians and bad novelists are full of charming illusions. They are like statesmen and founders of great businesses perpetually deceiving themselves and others. There [= They] are in fact men of action, and all men of action are kept from contemplation by an egregious belief in life. They believe in happiness, in love, in money, in progress, and if they are single taxers, in land nationalisation, in the millennium. They have an immense popularity. But everywhere the poet in his way, and the realist in his way is their enemy. The realist shows the pain, they are trying to forget, and the tragic poet shows the pain side by side with the ecstasy. In their[56] perpetual fermentation of their happiness, they turn from the realist with terror, and refuse to the tragic artist, even the pain that is the price of his ecstasy. If the poet were emotional he would not endure, the vision created by his intellect long enough, to attain to certainty. He must not feel that the intellect has shown him reality. He must be able to see reality without flinching.

[SB22(1p211)]   14

The Actress.

The realist should therefore help to bring the Theatre of Beauty*— which I confess I desire as much as you do.

The Poet.

Yes—for a hundred years we have had the rose pink sentimentalist created by the press of the linen drapers, by[57] a priesthood that the linen drapers pay for. All painful things have been hidden and now the reaction has come. There is a passion for reality all through Europe. The religious men created a false faith and they have lost the world, and the popular writers have created a false beauty, and they are losing the world.

56. *their:* this, GY.
57. *by:* and by, GY. MS has "or a by".

The Actress.

The first piece is over, and I shall have to go on the stage. I really believe you have convinced me but convinced or not I shall never wear that mask and you can pack it straight back to Fez.

The Poet.

There is no mask. I have never been in Fez.

Explanatory Notes to *The Poet and the Actress*

The Poet and the Actress is a densely allusive work, which overlaps at many points with Yeats's published texts. No attempt has been made to annotate it exhaustively in the notes that follow. The references are to page numbers and key words in the manuscript.

SB22(1p193)

expose him on a shovel: Yeats would have been familiar with the Irish belief that to "take a clean shovel and seat . . . the changeling on its broad iron blade, and [to] convey . . . the creature to the manure heap" was a mode of enforcing the fairies to give back a stolen child—E. S. Hartland, *The Science of Fairy Tales* (London: Walter Scott, 1890), pp. 118–22. On Yeats's interest in the contemporary expression of such beliefs, see Genevieve Brennan, "Yeats, Clodd, *Scatalogic Rites* and the Clonmel Witch Burning," *YA* 4 (1986) 207–15. See also Seán Ó Súilleabhain, *A Handbook of Irish Folklore* (Detroit: Singing Tree Press, 1970), pp. 392, 475, 476. I am grateful to Deirdre Toomey and Dr. Maria Tymoczko for these allusions.

SB22(1p200)

Mr. Barker and Mr. Craig: I have not annotated most of the names. They are either self-evident or easily looked up. Harley Granville-Barker (1877–1946) and especially Edward Gordon Craig (1872–1966), however, figured in Yeats's development as a dramatist, the former as a leading experimental producer of modern plays and Shakespeare, the latter as a revolutionary stage designer who much influenced Yeats, starting in 1901.

SB22(1p201)

Guido: Guido Cavalcanti (*c.* 1255–1300) was a friend of Dante and author of the sonnet "Io vengo il giorno a te infinite volte," which Yeats knew in the Rossetti translation as "I come to thee by daytime constantly"—Dante Gabriel Rossetti, *Dante and his Circle*, ed. William M. Rossetti (London: Ellis and Elvey, 1892), p. 144. See "Ego Dominus Tuus," l.33. See also *Mythologies*, p. 330.

SB22(1p202)

*and there is a sonnet of——:*Cino da Pistoia (*c.* 1270–*c.* 1336) was a friend of Dante and possibly author of the sonnet "In verità questo libel di Dante," although its authenticity has been questioned. Yeats would have known it in the Rossetti translation, where it is ascribed to Cino, as "This book of Dante's, very sooth to say" (*Dante and his Circle*, p. 176).

See *Mythologies*, p. 330. Yeats derives from Cino/Rossetti the line "Are flung into some corner like old nut-shells" of *The Only Jealousy of Emer* (1919; *Variorum Plays* 539).

one writer of comedy: Lady Gregory. See *Mythologies*, p. 326 ("one close friend," etc.).

SB22(1p203)

an actress who in daily life is over masterful: Mrs. Patrick Campbell (1865–1940). In 1908 she had given the performance of his *Deirdre* which most satisfied Yeats: "Deirdre was only once played and that was by Mrs. Pat Campbell" (*Letters*, p. 674). At the time of Yeats's composition of *The Poet and the Actress*, he still hoped that she would do his *The Player Queen* (*Letters*, p. 625), and it is clear that he thought her the only right actress for it (*Letters*, p. 654). Yeats describes Mrs. Campbell's temperament in *Letters*, pp. 539–40, and in *Mythologies*, pp. 326– 27.

Carlyle said of Scott: "A vigorous health seems to have been given by Nature; yet, as if Nature had said withal, 'Let it be a health to express itself by mind, not by body', a lameness is added in childhood; the brave little boy, instead of romping and bickering, must learn to think; or at lowest, what is a great matter, to sit still. No rackets and trundling-hoops for this young Walter; but ballads, history-books and a world of legendary stuff, which his mother and those near him are copiously able to furnish. Disease, which is but superficial, and issues in outward lameness, does not cloud the young existence; rather forwards it towards the expansion it is fitted for. The miserable disease had been one of the internal nobler parts, marring the general organisation; under which no Walter Scott could have been forwarded, or with all his other endowments could have been producible or possible. 'Nature gives healthy children much; how much! Wise education is a wise unfolding of this; often it unfolds itself better of its own accord' "— Thomas Carlyle, "Sir Walter Scott" (1838), in *Critical and Miscellaneous Essays: Collected and Republished* (1839, 1869), 2 vols. (Boston, Mass.: Dana Estes, n. d.) II, 418–19.

SB22(1p205)

woman who has set fire to his haystack: the woman who has bowled him over, I suppose, but I defer to the folklorists.

SB22(1p206)

are you satisfied: "One night, loud cries were heard issuing from the saloon. The Williamses rushed out of their room in alarm; Mrs. Shelley also endeavored to reach the spot, but fainted at the door. Entering the saloon, the Williamses found Shelley staring horribly into the air, and evidently in a trance. They waked him, and he related that a figure wrapped in a mantle came to his bedside, and beckoned him. He must then have risen in his sleep, for he followed the imaginary figure into the saloon, when it lifted the hood of its mantle, ejaculated, '*Siete sodis fatto?*'* [*Are you satisfied?*] and vanished"— Lady Shelley (ed.), *Shelley Memorials: From Authentic Sources* (Boston, Mass.: Ticknor and Fields, 1859), p. 207. I cannot find that Shelley (or Synge, or Deirdre) literally answered "I am satisfied." Yeats is interpreting their attitudes toward death.

SB22(1p211)

the Theatre of Beauty: In a letter of March 17, 1903, to Gilbert Murray, Yeats suggested "a Theatre of Beauty" which should produce "Marlowe's Faustus, your translation of the

Hippolytus, a translation of Edipus Tyrannus, a play of Congreve's & contemporary work of Robert Bridges (his 'Return of Ulysses') & myself—." The letter, in Lady Gregory's hand, is in the Bodleian Library, Oxford. At an organization meeting on March 28, Walter Crane presiding, the name was changed to "The Masquers." The Committee consisted of Yeats, Gilbert Murray, Sturge Moore, Edith Craig, Pamela Colman Smith, and Arthur Symons. The brief career of the Masquers is described in Ronald Schuchard, "W. B. Yeats and the London Theatre Societies, 1901–1904," *Review of English Studies*, n. s., 29: 116 (Nov 1978) 415–46, esp. pp. 430–46. Although the Masquers disbanded about November 12, 1903, Yeats clung to his concept under its original name. He spoke on "The Theatre of Beauty" at Harvard on October 5, 1911, and his address appeared in *Harper's Weekly* for November 11 (*Uncollected Prose* I, 397–401). That address is mainly about scene as this is mainly about the player. Already in 1911, as here, Yeats is looking toward the Japanese.

❦ The Whirlwind of Lovers

CERTAIN OF Yeats's plays (and I do not speak of the Cuchulain cycle) seem to me interrelated in the most fundamental way by a basic situation, perhaps even by a common visual image, which, as it had once been for years before the playwright's eyes, may have been in his mind when he wrote these plays. John Masefield tells[1] that on one wall of Yeats's chief room at Woburn Buildings there hung for many years William Blake's first Dante illustration, *The Whirlwind of Lovers.* The subject of this illustration is indeed an action of perception, and to contemplate it can be to know "that tragic ecstasy which is the best that art—perhaps that life—can give," in which one is "carried beyond time and persons to where passion, living through its thousand purgatorial years, as in the wink of an eye, becomes wisdom." It is as if one "had touched and felt and seen a disembodied thing."[2] Based on Canto V of the *Inferno,* the illustration represents Dante swooning in pity at the tale of Francesca and Paolo. It is a striking engraving, "the most finished" of the group, according to Yeats. "It is not, I think, inferior to any but the finest in *Job,* if indeed to them, and shows in its perfection Blake's mastery over elemental things, the swirl in which the lost spirits are hurried, 'a watery flame' he would have called it, the haunted waters and the huddling shapes."[3]

At the left, as one regards the picture, is a long serpent-like swirl of wind or flame within which numbers of carnal sinners—male and female nudes in postures of desperate abandonment—are being pulled about by a current. In the center foreground is the body of the unconscious Dante. A cone-shaped flame seems to emerge from his

---

1. John Masefield, *Some Memories of W. B. Yeats* (New York: Macmillan, 1940), p. 7.
2. *Essays and Introductions,* p. 239.
3. "William Blake and His Illustrations to *The Divine Comedy,*" *ibid.,* pp. 126–27.

FIGURE 6. William Blake, *The Whirlwind of Lovers.* Engraving. (*The Tate Gallery, London*)

body and in this are the draped figures of Paolo and Francesca, in attitudes of tension. They lean back energetically away from each other at the same time as their hands are joined in a fixed grip, as if to prevent their being separated by the storm. At the right, by Dante's head, stands Virgil, his figure massive and serene, expressing the quality that Yeats describes elsewhere as "a placid, marmoreal, tender, starry rapture."[4] Virgil's head appears within the light from a large luminous circle, suggesting a halo. In the center of this light the eye can just make out two nude human figures, seated facing each other in absolute poise and serenity, the man gently embracing the woman. One is reminded of Dante's description of the Empyrean, where ardour is peace and peace ardour.[5] One remembers also Blake's words as quoted by Yeats, "The treasures of Heaven are not negations of passion, but realities of intellect, from which the passions emanate uncurbed in their eternal glory."[6]

Virgil, Dante's representative of Human Reason, stands enlightened by the true nature of love. Dante is overcome by pity of the souls deprived of that love. There is no narrow legalistic condemnation in Blake's illustration, only a piercing vision of the truth. As Yeats wrote, "It was a profound understanding of all creatures and things, a profound sympathy with passionate and lost souls, made possible in their extreme intensity by his revolt against corporeal law, and corporeal reason, which made Blake the one perfectly fit illustrator for the *Inferno* and the *Purgatorio*. . . ."[7] In other words, Blake's insight penetrated beyond abstract law and logic on the one hand and beyond the melting, changing flow of emotion on the other. Neither will nor feeling was his absolute. His view included them, but was a higher, more complex, more intense contemplation, a vision of the whole.

In another form, Blake's art had achieved what Yeats felt was

4. *Ibid.,* p. 127.
5. "Quando scendean nel fior, di banco in banco / porgevan della pace e dell' ardore, / 'ch' egli acquistavan ventilando il fianco." Canto XXXI, 16–18. *The Paradiso of Dante Alighieri* (London: J. M. Dent & Sons, 1941), p. 376.
6. *Essays and Introductions,* p. 138.
7. *Ibid.,* p. 144.

lacking in realistic drama. Blake, of course, did not rob his persons of the energy of their souls. To use Fergusson's terms, he represented the action of his protagonist "with all its moral and intellectual depth." "The acceptance of the catastrophe, leading to the final vision or epiphany"[8] was present. As we have seen, it is toward the representation of such vision that Yeats's own dramatic art evolved.

It is noteworthy that three of these "dramas of perception," three middle and late plays that are quite different from each other in form and that cover the most significant periods of Yeats's dramatic development, have as their common subject the essential Francesca-Paolo-Dante situation. *The Dreaming of the Bones*[9] is one of the plays for dancers with which Yeats experimented after studying the Noh drama of Japan—the very anti-self of circumstantial realism. *The Words upon the Window-pane,*[10] in which the spirit of Swift interrupts a séance, uses realistic set, characters, and method. However, Yeats has picked the one occasion on which realism must testify against its own completeness or sufficiency as truth. *Purgatory*[11] is a third sort of drama, showing a realism simplified, stylized, reduced to barest essentials, so that the play becomes symbolical without being cut off from the recognizable world. It successfully fuses elements of the two previous forms.

In each of these plays ghostly lovers recall their passion and their suffering before one or more moved observers. Each, although all are brief, has the form of a play within a play, as does the Dante episode. In *The Dreaming of the Bones* two ghosts from the twelfth century,

8. Fergusson, pp. 156–57.

9. First published in *The Little Review,* January 1919. Wilson, *Yeats's Iconography,* notes the Dante parallel to this play, pp. 207–8.

10. First performed at the Abbey Theatre, November 17, 1930. First published in *The Words upon the Window Pane* (Dublin: Cuala Press, 1934).

11. Dated April 1938. First performed at the Abbey Theatre, August 10, 1938. First published in *Last Poems and Two Plays* (Dublin: Cuala Press, 1939). Ure, in *Yeats the Playwright,* p. 84, comments, "These plays . . . are at first sight very different from one another, and perhaps they are not commonly thought of together." He devotes chapter 5, "From Grave to Cradle," to this group. The three plays are again related in Vendler's *Yeats's* Vision and the Later Plays, pp. 185–202, as "the three purgatorial plays" (p. 185).

Diarmuid and Dervorgilla, who betrayed Ireland for love at the time of the English invasion, plead with a young Irish patriot to forgive them. Their ghosts are together, but "Though eyes can meet, their lips can never meet."[12] Only "If some one of their race forgave at last/Lip would be pressed on lip."[13] But the hero of 1916, however deeply moved, will not forgive those who brought about the Norman invasion of Ireland. In *The Words upon the Window-pane* the ghost of Swift, before an audience of spiritualists, again rejects love of the flesh with Vanessa for love of the mind with Stella, only to face, in his repeated dream, tragic loss of health, friends, and mind. *Purgatory,* Yeats's last play but one, presents the unending remorse of an Irish lady who desired her own groom and married him, with disastrous consequences—her own early death, the destruction of her stately house, her husband's murder at the hand of their son. That son, now an old peddler, returns with a rascal son of his own to the haunted house. He is spectator while the lady relives the transgression of her wedding night in ceaseless sorrow. In each of the three plays the action is that, through the presence of an observer, passion becomes knowledge— whether for the ghostly sufferer, the observer, or the audience. The meaning of the relived episode, *sub specie aeternitatis,* becomes plain. Similarly, Dante swoons when Francesca tells her story, not simply because he is moved, but because he has seen a vision, because he understands now the full loss, the terrible irony in "If the King of the Universe were our friend" and "He who shall never be divided from me."[14] This perception is not of the mind alone, but of the whole soul.

That these plays, with some of the Noh plays he studied, show a marked similarity in subject is only an instance of the general similarity among Yeats's plays. His favorite action of recognition often

12. *Variorum Plays,* p. 771.

13. *Ibid.,* p. 773.

14. "Se fosse amico il re dell' universo," Canto V, 91, and "questi, che mai da me non fia diviso," Canto V, 135, *The Inferno of Dante Alighieri* (London: J. M. Dent & Sons, 1941), pp. 54, 56. Cf. T. S. Eliot, "Dante," *Selected Essays* (New York: Harcourt Brace, 1932), pp. 206–8.

appears as the recognition of some sort of supernatural manifestation. This action is often given a twist, the recognition being not only of the manifestation but of the witness's own nature or circumstance. To see the ghost is often to live over, but symbolically, simultaneously, in full knowledge of its fateful meaning, one's moment of greatest passion or suffering. The external manifestation parallels and dramatizes an internal recognition.

🌿 *The Dreaming of the Bones* and the Anti-Self of Circumstantial Realism

The Noh of Spirits[1]

Of the five sorts of Noh plays, Yeats and Pound were especially interested in only one—the Noh of spirits. The direct cause of their interest in this form is that in it everything known to Western drama is lacking except the final vision or epiphany. The latter is the whole play.

The Noh plays were performed in cycles and are of a meaningful variety, the Noh of spirits being fourth. A cycle of six plays would consist of: (1) A congratulatory piece ("Shugen"), connected with religious rite, about God's immemorial protection of Japan; (2) A "Shura," or battlepiece, which puts out devils by sympathetic magic; (3) A "female Kazura" in contrast to the male battle-piece. ". . . After battle comes peace, or Yu-gen, mysterious calm, and in time of peace the cases of love come to pass"; (4) The Noh of spirits; (5) A piece "bearing upon the moral duties of man. . . . This fifth piece teaches the duties of man here in this world as the fourth piece represents the results of carelessness to such duties"; (6) Another Shugen, praising the lords and the reign, and asking a blessing—"To show that though the spring may pass, still there is a time of its return, this Shugen is put in again just as at the beginning."[2]

Pound points out that, unlike Western drama, each cycle of six plays "presents a complete service of life . . . a complete diagram of life and recurrence."[3] This aspect alone would appeal to both Pound and Yeats,

---

1. F. A. C. Wilson's *Yeats's Iconography* interprets the dance plays in terms of traditional symbolism and thus supplements this present study of the evolution of a dramatic-poetic language appropriate to the drama of perception.

2. From the *Ka-den-sho,* or secret book of Noh, *'Noh' or Accomplishment,* pp. 14–16.

3. *Ibid.,* p. 17.

with their antiprogressive historical view. However, the individual mysteries, battle pieces, and moralities will "be interesting only to students of folk-lore, or of comparative religion."[4]

The lover of the stage and the lover of drama and of poetry will find his chief interest in the psychological pieces, or the Plays of Spirits. . . . These plays are full of ghosts, and the ghost psychology is amazing. The parallels with Western spiritist doctrines are very curious. This is, however, an irrelevant or extraneous interest and one might set it aside if it were not bound up with a dramatic and poetic interest of the very highest order.[5]

The description of this type of Noh given in the *Ka-den-sho* is as follows:

The fourth piece is Oni-No, or the Noh of spirits. After battle comes peace and glory, but they soon depart in their turn. The glory and pleasures of man are not reliable at all. Life is like a dream and goes with the speed of lightning. It is like a dew-drop in the morning; it soon falls and is broken. To suggest these things and to lift up the heart for Buddha . . . we have these plays of spirits ('Oni'). Here are shown the struggles and the sins of mortals, and the audience, even while they sit for pleasure, will begin to think about Buddha and the coming world. It is for this reason that Noh is called Mu-jin-Kyo, the immeasurable scripture.[6]

In these plays the tragic rhythm of life is seen in its final moment— where will and passion become insight.

A reading of Yeats's "Anima Mundi," which contains many references to Japanese drama, will show that the particular fascination of Noh plays for Yeats was partly a result of his belief in spiritism.[7] Whether or not we share this belief, we must realize its value to Yeats as an assurance of ultimate insight into the meaning of the soul's history.

We may see at certain roads and in certain houses old murders acted over again [cf. *Purgatory*], and in certain fields dead huntsmen riding with horse

---

4. *Ibid.,* p. 18.   5. *Ibid.,* pp. 18–19.
6. *Ibid.,* p. 15. Pound adds in a note: "These pieces are the most interesting because of their profound and subtle psychology and because of situations entirely foreign to our Western drama, if not to our folklore and legend."
7. Cf. "Anima Mundi," *Mythologies,* esp. pp. 352–61.

and hound, or ancient armies fighting above bones or ashes. We carry to *Anima Mundi* our memory, and that memory is for a time our external world; and all passionate moments recur again and again, for passion desires its own recurrence more than any event, and whatever there is of corresponding complacency or remorse is our beginning of judgment. . . .[8]

The dead, as the passionate necessity wears out, come into a measure of freedom and may turn the impulse of events, started while living, in some new direction, but they cannot originate except through the living. . . .[9]

When all sequence comes to an end, time comes to an end, and the soul puts on the rhythmic or spiritual body or luminous body and contemplates all the events of its memory and every possible impulse in an eternal possession of itself in one single moment. That condition is alone animate, all the rest is fantasy. . . .[10]

To illustrate his conception, Yeats alludes directly to *Nishikigi*, one of several Noh plays that repeat the outlines of the Francesca episode in Dante and that may have been models for *The Dreaming of the Bones*, *The Words upon the Window-pane*, and *Purgatory*.

There are two realities, the terrestrial and the condition of fire. All power is from the terrestrial condition, for there all opposites meet and there only is the extreme of choice possible. . . . In the condition of fire is all music and all rest. Between is the condition of air where images have but a borrowed life, that of memory or that reflected upon them when they symbolise colours and intensities of fire: the place of shades who are "in the whirl of those who are fading," and who cry like those amorous shades in the Japanese play:—

> That we may acquire power
> Even in our faint substance,
> We will show forth even now,
> And though it be but in a dream,
> Our form of repentance.[11]

8. *Ibid.*, p. 354.
9. *Ibid.*, pp. 355–56.
10. *Ibid.*, p. 357.
11. *Ibid.* Cf. also note, p. 356, and "Swedenborg, Mediums, and the Desolate Places," section xi, *ibid.*, pp. 60–69. Ure, *Yeats the Playwright*, p. 93n., argues that these ghosts are in the state later called *Phantasmagoria* in the second edition of *A Vision*. This state is " 'self-created' by the spirit, which undergoes during it emotional suffering due to remorse for sin committed in life (*A Vision*, 1937, pp. 225–31). The punishments which it must live through are its 'own conscience made visible' (*A Vision*, 1925, p. 225)." Wilson, *Yeats's*

In *Nishikigi* the ghosts of two lovers are kept apart because the girl had for three years refused the man's offer of charm sticks. She had gone on weaving as he waited fruitlessly at the gate. The ghosts are united at last through the coming of a wandering priest.[12] This play reminded Yeats "of the Aran boy and girl who in Lady Gregory's story come to the priest after death to be married."[13]

In *Sotoba Komachi* and *Kayoi Komachi* is told the story of how the beautiful Ono told Shosho, her lover, that if he would court her for one hundred nights she would grant him her love. Whether or not she would have kept her bargain:

... Shosho ... came to me in the moonlight and in the dark night and in the nights flooded with rain, and in the black face of the wind and in the wild swish of the snow. He came as often as the melting drops fall from the eaves, ninety-nine times, and he died. And his ghost is about me, driving me on with the madness.[14]

In *Kayoi Komachi* it seems that what finally kept, or at least keeps, the lovers apart is that Shosho would not accept Buddhism. Now his spirit struggles to prevent a priest from bringing Ono no Komachi's spirit to Buddha.[15] The priest interrupts the quarrel of the spirits to

---

Iconography, also speaks of this phantasmagoria, but does not relate it specifically to the 1937 edition of *A Vision,* which of course greatly post-dates the play. However, Wilson does not, as Ure does, seem to foresee other stages of discarnate existence and an ultimate cleansing for these souls: "Hell was for him a condition of eternal fixation in the purgatorial state, which is precisely the situation of his Dermot and Dervorgilla" (Wilson, p. 224).

12 *'Noh' or Accomplishment,* pp. 131–49.

13. *Essays and Introductions,* p. 232. Wilson, *Yeats Iconography,* pp. 213–23, has studied the parallels between *Nishikigi* and *The Dreaming of the Bones* in his full account of the sources of the latter play and the influences upon it. He finds, p. 221, that Yeats's play "has nothing of the lyricism of its Japanese counterpart" and is marked by "a certain heaviness of statement." The passages he compares do not bear him out, but I think that is because the fragile beauty of *Nishikigi* in the Pound-Fenollosa version is not really in the isolated passage but in the whole.

14. *'Noh' or Accomplishment,* p. 24.

15. The Irish influence on Pound's "finishing" of these translations is evident. Some of the lines bear the mark of the tongue perfected by Lady Gregory and especially Synge and imitated by Yeats. The following has some of the *Playboy* verve: "It is a sad heart I have to

suggest that they show forth the story of the one hundred nights' courtship, which they do in a dance. Apparently this purgatorial reliving of her cruelty and his arrogant unbelief has some effect, for the chorus concludes: "Both their sins vanished. They both became pupils of Buddha, both Komachi and Shosho."[16] But as Pound points out, "Without the last two lines of the chorus one could very well imagine her keeping up her tenzone with Shosho until the end of time."[17] Except for this tag, the two Komachi plays are Dantesque in conception, more so than *Nishikigi*.

There are two events in the drama *Nishikigi:* the priest's decision to go to the love-cave and the appearance of the supernatural lovers in their ancient guise, playing their story. In scene 1 the priest establishes the circumstantiality of the place by his interest in it, and in scene 2 he establishes its sanctity by perceiving the vision of the lovers' dance. He is the most important character. His questing, non-possessive attitude makes the action possible. He has his "heart set upon no particular place . . . no more than a cloud. . . ." He wonders "would the sea be that way or the little place Kefu that . . . is stuck down against it."[18] The lovers tell him, "You tread the border and nothing/Awaits you."[19] It is to such a man that vision will come. Lack of the qualities which he has—humility and sympathy—has kept the lovers apart.

---

see you looking up to Buddha, you who left me alone, as I was diving in the black rivers of hell. Will soft prayers be a comfort to you, you in your fine quiet heaven, you who know that I'm alone in that wild, desolate place? To put you away from me! That's all he has come for, him and his prayers. Will they do any good to my sort?" *The Drama* V, 18 (May 1915), pp. 215–16. Pound revised much of the Irishness out of the version in *'Noh' or Accomplishment,* cf. p. 30.

16. *'Noh' or Accomplishment,* p. 36.

17. *Ibid.* Another Noh play relevant is *Motomezuka,* which Wilson says, p. 311, Yeats read in M. C. Stopes's version. "A ghost in a Japanese play is set afire by a fantastic scruple, and though a Buddhist priest explains that the fire would go out of itself if the ghost but ceased to believe in it, it cannot cease to believe" (*Mythologies,* p. 354). Ure, *Yeats the Playwright,* p. 93, points out that to end *The Dreaming of the Bones* "with the dance of the unappeased shades was to imitate *Motomezuka.* . . ."

18. *'Noh' or Accomplishment,* p. 132.

19. *Ibid.,* p. 149.

The priest is a sight-seer, and the play dramatizes the sight he sees. His sight-seeing moves from the objective to the subjective, or rather from the natural to the supernatural world. He is spectator of the visionary dance of the lovers, as we are spectators of the whole play. As a result, the Noh play seems to us both firmly rooted in place and yet a symbolic manifestation of supernatural reality.

The Circumstance and Sanctity of Place

The paradox of *The Dreaming of the Bones* and Yeats's other plays for dancers is that they are a return to a deeper realism through cleansing away all devices of circumstantial realism. *At the Hawk's Well, The Only Jealousy of Emer,* and *Calvary* are more "convincing" than *Deirdre, On Baile's Strand* and *The King's Threshold,* although the latter plays are much closer to modern realism in their representation of character and action. In the earlier plays the pretense that Deirdre, Cuchulain, and Seanchan are real people involved in real events can only be disturbing. External action and character are cut down to such an extent that what is left is obviously a mere token. Character and event are so restricted by the central conception that it would be better to drop the pretense and show that conception itself in frankly symbolic terms. Yeats's art moved in the dance plays from inadequate representation of the struggle of purpose and of the suffering of passion directly to imitating the moment when passion becomes perception.

The actions of the dance plays are appropriate to the method. In *The Dreaming of the Bones,* a young patriot faces eternal spectres of Ireland's own guilt, spiritual enemies more potent than the English, and, though deeply moved, he refuses to forgive treason or to commit it in subtle form. In *At the Hawk's Well,* Cuchulain is once for all driven from content by the attraction of an impossible high life. Emer, in *The Only Jealousy of Emer,* renounces her essential illusion in order to preserve the object of her futile hope. In *Calvary,* Jesus Christ discovers that his life-sacrifice was based on a narrow understanding of the nature of things and was futile. These conceptions are realities from "the deeps of the mind."[20] It remained only to give them their recognizable (because strange) costumes from myth and dream. The Noh of spirits showed Yeats how.

I have talked as if there were an absolute conception to be clothed in symbolic characters and action. The conception is, of course, an abstraction that one makes from the final play. A better statement of the case might be that the symbolic characters and actions of the dance plays are more effective and convincing than similar elements in earlier plays exactly because they are like images that might appear in "the deeps of the mind." They do not claim reality on any but the deepest level. In the earlier plays Yeats had not delimited his scope and perfected his art within it. The elements used in *Deirdre, On Baile's Strand,* and *The King's Threshold,* because still within the realm of possibility, are weak representations. The reality of the dance plays can only be here, now, in the soul's own experience. This is what Yeats must have meant in speaking of the Japanese dancer in his *At the Hawk's Well.* In the studio or drawing room

... where no studied lighting, no stage-picture made an artificial world, he was able ... to recede from us into some more powerful life. . . . One realised anew, at every separating strangeness, that the measure of all arts' greatness can be but in their intimacy.[21]

One means of attaining a deeper realism was Yeats's use of place as circumstance, metaphor, and symbol. This technique he learned from the Noh plays. "These Japanese poets, too, feel for tomb and wood the emotion, the sense of awe that our Gaelic-speaking countrypeople will sometimes show when you speak to them of Castle Hackett or of some holy well; and that is why perhaps it pleases them to begin so many plays by a traveller asking his way with many questions, a convention agreeable to me."[22]

In the early plays, such as *On Baile's Strand* and *The King's Threshold,* Yeats had not dramatic time to call up objective place and give it value.

20. *Essays and Introductions,* p. 224.
21. *Ibid.*
22. *Ibid.,* pp. 232–33. Wilson, *Yeats's Iconography,* p. 222, finds in this play "passages where Yeats makes use of the poetry of place-names as never before or after. . . ."

When I first began to write poetical plays for an Irish theatre I had to put away an ambition of helping to bring again to certain places their old sanctity or their romance. I could lay the scene of a play on Baile's Strand, but I found no pause in the hurried action for descriptions of strand or sea or the great yew-tree that once stood there; and I could not in *The King's Threshold* find room, before I began the ancient story, to call up the shallow river and the few trees and rocky fields of modern Gort. But in the *Nishikigi* the tale of the lovers would lose its pathos if we did not see that forgotten tomb where "the hiding fox" lives among "the orchids and the chrysanthemum flowers."[23]

The descriptions of place in Noh drama are often echoed throughout the texture of the plays in the metaphorical language. The scene becomes symbolic. Yeats found in *Nishikigi*

a playing upon a single metaphor, as deliberate as the echoing rhythm of line in Chinese and Japanese painting. In the *Nishikigi* the ghost of the girl-lover carries the cloth she went on weaving out of grass when she should have opened the chamber door to her lover, and woven grass returns again and again in metaphor and incident. The lovers, now that in an aëry body they must sorrow for unconsummated love, are "tangled up as the grass patterns are tangled." Again they are like an unfinished cloth: "these bodies, having no weft, even now are not come together; truly a shameful story, a tale to bring shame on the gods." Before they can bring the priest to the tomb they spend the day "pushing aside the grass from the overgrown ways in Kefu," and the countryman who directs them is "cutting grass on the hill"; and when at last the prayer of the priest unites them in marriage the bride says that he has made "a dream-bridge over wild grass, over the grass I dwell in"; and in the end bride and bridegroom show themselves for a moment "from under the shadow of the love-grass."[24]

Although the use of metaphor of which Yeats speaks is very much the sort of thing he had already done himself in *Deirdre,* where the symbols of brazier and chessboard, trap and forest, are worked into the texture of the poetry in countless suggestive parallels, nevertheless the objective reality of place is less convincing in *Deirdre.* The setting exists only for its subjective value. The rigorous unity into which the play is pressed is an exclusive, univocal and idealist unity. Yeats had

23. *Essays and Introductions,* p. 233.
24. *Ibid.,* p. 234.

already learned that "obvious all-pervading rhythm"[25] made his first plays seem merely subjective and lyrical, rather than dramatic. Moreover, even though he still (as always) demanded not just an abstract unity of construction but the correct tone in every word, he was learning that "occasional prosaic words gave the impression of an active man speaking."[26] Later, however, the Noh plays taught him how to achieve that more realistic, analogical unity in which the poet, fixing on an objective scene in the present, makes a symbol of it by which to leap into the past and into the subjective or supernatural.

The objective reality of place is quite convincing in *Nishikigi,* while from the grass over the actual path is made a symbol of the weaving done by a long-dead woman and of the eternal entanglement of the lovers. Conversely, the long-silent loom, when it was anciently used by Hasonuno, made a sound like the song of crickets—a song still heard in the present. The metaphorical language, because based on objective fact, has a validity as dramatic speech while avoiding the complete and superficial objectivity of modern realistic prose.

Like the settings of the Noh plays, the scene of *The Dreaming of the Bones,* a mountainside near the village of Abbey in County Clare, gives a validity of existence to both the subjective dream world of the dead and the objective world of the living and active. Past and present are joined through a location. Subjective reality and objective reality, supernatural and natural, share a spot and therefore a convincing validity. The language of the play, however, is not firm, sure, and consistent in the simultaneous communication of two levels of reality. Yeats exploits the weakness as if it were a virtue and makes it a successful part of the form. Carefully designed contrasts work within the limited aims of the play. But the play as a whole avoids the ultimate problem of creating a speech that fuses the dramatic and the poetic. The problem is all the more clearly revealed, however, as the play attempts to solve it by avoiding it. The First Musician sings an opening lyric which fills the valley with ghostly suggestion. Immediately after-

25. *Autobiographies,* p. 435.
26. *Ibid.,* p. 434.

wards, however, he speaks lines of comparatively objective place description.

> *First Musician [or all three Musicians, singing].*
>> Why does my heart beat so?
>> Did not a shadow pass?
>> It passed but a moment ago.
>> Who can have trod in the grass?
>> What rogue is night-wandering?
>> Have not old writers said
>> That dizzy dreams can spring
>> From the dry bones of the dead?
>> And many a night it seems
>> That all the valley fills
>> With those fantastic dreams.
>> They overflow the hills,
>> So passionate is a shade,
>> Like wine that fills to the top
>> A grey-green cup of jade,
>> Or maybe an agate cup.

> [*The three Musicians are now seated by the drum, flute, and zither at the back of the stage. The First Musician speaks.*

>> The hour before dawn and the moon covered up;
>> The little village of Abbey is covered up;
>> The little narrow trodden way that runs
>> From the white road to the Abbey of Corcomroe
>> Is covered up; and all about the hills
>> Are like a circle of agate or of jade.
>> Somewhere among great rocks on the scarce grass
>> Birds cry, they cry their loneliness.
>> Even the sunlight can be lonely here,
>> Even hot noon is lonely.[27]

The simile of wine filling a jade cup is used forthrightly in the lyric, but is hidden or merely echoed in the spoken passage of blank verse. There is nothing wrong in this division except that Yeats has not yet achieved a verse that can convey at once both the objective and the subjective drama in complete fusion.

27. *Variorum Plays*, pp. 762–63.

The figure of the wine cup is not without its objective counterpart in the gradual darkening of a valley from stream to summit. Primarily, however, wine is a rather arbitrary sign for the coming of the spirits that "fill waste mountains with the invisible tumult/Of the fantastic conscience."[28] That the connection was firmly established in Yeats's mind is shown in "All Souls' Night," where ghosts come "to drink from the wine-breath"[29] and in "A Drunken Man's Praise of Sobriety" in which "all dead men are drunk."[30] The arbitrariness is nevertheless a flaw in the symbol. Taken literally, wine has nothing to do with the events of the play, and the jade cup is probably introduced merely in honor of the Japanese source of Yeats's form.

After the musicians have set the scene and the mood, a Young Man enters wearily. He has fought at the Post Office in the Easter Rising of 1916 and fears being taken and shot. When he meets a Stranger and a Young Girl, he places himself in their hands. They agree to lead him to a shelter on the summit from where he can see an Aran coracle put in to shore for him in the morning. He is warned, however, of a danger he had not expected.

> *Stranger.*   I will put you safe,
>   No living man shall set his eyes upon you;
>   I will not answer for the dead.
> *Young Man.*   The dead?
> *Stranger.* For certain days the stones where you must lie
>   Have in the hour before the break of day
>   Been haunted.
> *Young Man.*   But I was not born at midnight.
> *Stranger.* Many a man that was born in the full daylight
>   Can see them plain, will pass them on the high-road
>   Or in the crowded market-place of the town,
>   And never know that they have passed.
> *Young Man.*   My Grandam
>   Would have it they did penance everywhere;
>   Some lived through their old lives again.

28. *Ibid.*, p. 766.
29. *Variorum Poems*, p. 471; cf. *Poems*, p. 227.
30. *Ibid.*, p. 592; cf. *Poems*, p. 313.

Stranger.   In a dream;
    And some for an old scruple must hang spitted
    Upon the swaying tops of lofty trees;
    Some are consumed in fire, some withered up
    By hail and sleet out of the wintry North,
    And some but live through their old lives again.
Young Man. Well, let them dream into what shape they please
    And fill waste mountains with the invisible tumult
    Of the fantastic conscience. I have no dread;
    They cannot put me into gaol or shoot me. . . .[31]

The ghosts' speeches are often in what Richards called an "exclusive" verse. They use the associationism of "pale passion" and remind us of Yeats's own early narrative and dramatic poems. The Young Man's speeches are usually, although not always, objective and full of circumstance. Thus the verse tends to fall into two categories. However appropriate dramatically, this contrast shows the difficulty of fusing objective and subjective. The play makes a virtue of avoiding the problem and thus more clearly reveals it. Yet, although the Young Man's speeches are often too direct, too single-mindedly accurate in thinking and observation to carry a depth of suggestion, at their strongest they achieve a fusion of realism and symbolism. There is a promise in some of the Young Man's speeches of the fusion later achieved in Yeats's *Purgatory,* a beauty not "in the line or the isolable passage, but woven into the dramatic texture itself."[32]

The difference between the speeches of the ghosts and the speeches of the Young Man is not, of course, merely that the first make use of landscape while the second do not. The speeches of the ghosts continually dim the immediacy of the landscape, even while describing it. They put a veil before its objective reality. The Young Man's speeches are true to the clear outlines of the landscape, but not always to its tide of passionate associations.

Stranger. We're almost at the summit and can rest.
    The road is a faint shadow there; and there

31. *Variorum Plays,* pp. 765–66.
32. Eliot, "The Poetry of W. B. Yeats," p. 451.

The Abbey lies amid its broken tombs.
In the old days we should have heard a bell
Calling the monks before day broke to pray;
And when the day had broken on the ridge,
The crowing of its cocks.

Young Man.   Is there no house
Famous for sanctity or architectural beauty
In Clare or Kerry, or in all wide Connacht,
The enemy has not unroofed?

Stranger.   Close to the altar
Broken by wind and frost and worn by time
Donough O'Brien has a tomb, a name in Latin.
He wore fine clothes and knew the secrets of women,
But he rebelled against the King of Thomond
And died in his youth.

Young Man.   And why should he rebel?
The King of Thomond was his rightful master.
It was men like Donough who made Ireland weak—
My curse on all that troop, and when I die
I'll leave my body, if I have any choice,
Far from his ivy-tod and his owl.[33]

The ghosts, more conscious of the past than of the present, remove
the mind to an ancient scene, leaving the landscape of the present a
"faint shadow." This characteristic they share with the Yeats of the
early poetry and of many of the early and middle plays. It is the
tendency to dissolve away "this pragmatical, preposterous pig of a
world."[34]

Nevertheless, the style of the ghosts' speeches is dramatically appropriate. The play falls into three movements, an exposition, a temptation, and a revelation, and the above speech appears in the middle
section. The Young Man is being tempted to fail to see Ireland before
him at all times, to overlook the crimes against her. The Stranger
arouses the Young Man's curiosity about the ghosts upon the summit,
presenting their pitiable plight before revealing that they are the

33. *Variorum Plays,* pp. 768–69.
34. "Blood and the Moon," *Variorum Poems,* p. 481; cf. *Poems,* p. 238.

traitors Diarmuid and Dervorgilla who invited the Norman invasion
of Ireland.

> *Young Girl.* Although they have no blood, or living nerves,
>   Who once lay warm and live the live-long night
>   In one another's arms, and know their part
>   In life, being now but of the people of dreams,
>   Is a dream's part; although they are but shadows,
>   Hovering between a thorn-tree and a stone,
>   Who have heaped up night on wingéd night; although
>   No shade however harried and consumed
>   Would change his own calamity for theirs,
>   Their manner of life were blessed could their lips
>   A moment meet; but when he has bent his head
>   Close to her head, or hand would slip in hand,
>   The memory of their crime flows up between
>   And drives them apart.[35]

The Young Man resists the temptation. His sturdy speeches repeatedly rend the veil that the story of the suffering ghosts casts over the
scene.

> *Young Man.* What crime can stay so in the memory?
>   What crime can keep apart the lips of lovers
>   Wandering and alone?
> *Young Girl.*   Her king and lover
>   Was overthrown in battle by her husband,
>   And for her sake and for his own, being blind
>   And bitter and bitterly in love, he brought
>   A foreign army from across the sea.
> *Young Man.* You speak of Diarmuid and Dervorgilla
>   Who brought the Norman in?
> *Young Girl.*   Yes, yes, I spoke
>   Of that most miserable, most accursed pair
>   Who sold their country into slavery; and yet
>   They were not wholly miserable and accursed
>   If somebody of their race at last would say,
>   'I have forgiven them'.

35. *Variorum Plays,* pp. 771–72.

Young Man.   O, never, never
  Shall Diarmuid and Dervorgilla be forgiven.[36]

But he is not yet aware who the lovers are.

The moment of revelation occurs when the party reaches the summit just at dawn. The Young Man looks out over the landscape, which was ruined by a continuous invasion starting 700 years ago when Dermot asked Norman help to war against Dervorgilla's husband. He speaks of this, but the lovers are lost in a dance representing their attraction and the guilt that keeps them apart. They do not see what he sees. He at last realizes that they are Dervorgilla and Dermot, ghosts of Ireland's own guilt, which has been more formidable in ruining the country than English armies have. The subjective and interior peril is seen as greater than the objective peril. Then, as dawn breaks and the birds of March begin to crow, the ghosts disappear.

The setting has provided the means by which the opposition of the characters is shown. Dawn defeats the ghosts and releases the Young Man. The subjectivity of the ghosts has been presented through the darkness, the calls of night birds, the blinding of clouds, the wind (so the Young Man thinks) blowing out the lantern, the dim path to the ruined abbey and on up to the ridge where the grave of the lovers is. All these are symbols of the dizzy dreams that spring from the dry bones of the dead, the consciousness of tragic guilt in the past.

On the other hand, the Young Man's objectivity is presented through the dawn and sunlight, the crowing of the cocks and the panorama of the landscape ruined by a civil war. Devoted to serving his nation, the Young Man looks out upon the objective world of action.

The characters are not mere individuals, but symbolic embodiments of directions in Irish history and in the history of modern civilization. In terms of the "system" that was later to emerge in *A Vision,* the time ("The hour before dawn and the moon covered up") is the end of an antithetical or subjective era and just before the birth of a new primary or objective civilization. "The strong March birds a-crow"[37] suggest

36. *Ibid.,* pp. 772–73.

37. *Ibid.,* p. 776. Wilson, *Yeats's Iconography,* pp. 234–40, finds in the "red March cock" a "clinching symbol: a device which will weld together aesthetically . . . Yeats's two themes of

both the martyrs of 1916 and the announcers of the end of the ancient year, of a death and a birth. No longer caught in its subjective consciousness of guilt, Ireland starts objectively, and, one must admit, somewhat unimaginatively, into its new day. Having reached the summit of one kind of consciousness, the nation begins to move in the other direction, as the Young Man starts climbing down the mountain toward his freedom.

To get back now to the image dwelt upon in the first lyric—that of wine filling an agate cup—we find that the closest thing to wine in the action is the heroic Irish blood, which "has returned to fields" of the valley that "have grown red from drinking blood."[38] However, the filling of the cup is analogous to the direction the action takes: the characters gradually mount the path to the summit; the night darkens gradually toward dawn; the ghostly lovers' preoccupation with their dream "Draws to its height,"[39] that is, to a summit or brim of intensity. "The memory of their crime flows up."[40] The cup (which the mountains form) is filled when the travelers have reached the summit and when the lovers become lost in their dance, unconscious of the contemporary ruin revealed to the Young Man in the dawn light.

> They have drifted in the dance from rock to rock.
> They have raised their hands as though to snatch the sleep
> That lingers always in the abyss of the sky
> Though they can never reach it. A cloud floats up
> And covers all the mountain-head in a moment;
> And now it lifts and they are swept away.[41]

Through the arbitrary figure of filling a wine cup, the setting of the

---

politics and ghosts" (p. 234). The " 'cock of the springtime' . . . is a more powerful defence against the supernatural than any other" and "the cock serves as a reincarnation emblem" (p. 235); "the bird is the red symbolic bird of Mars, regent of war and in Yeats's system . . . of the first bloody phases of a new historical cycle. We know . . . that Yeats expected 'the cycle of freedom' to begin with world-wide wars—involving among other things the liberation of Ireland—at a full moon in March, the month of Mars . . . the Easter Rising of 1916 came almost exactly at this time . . ." (pp. 236–37).

38. *Variorum Plays,* p. 766.   39. *Ibid.,* p. 771.
40. *Ibid.,* p. 772.   41. *Ibid.,* p. 775.

play is, not statically, but actively, dynamically, involved in both the physical and the spiritual movement of the action. Yet the uncertainty with which the figure enters passages other than the most subjective lyrical interludes is symptomatic of a failure to fuse the communication of subjective truth and that of objective truth. There is in this play a pattern of movement and countermovement in action and symbol, which, while it clarifies the significances of the characters, provides the excuse for a lack of integration in the language.

This generalization, however, is not true of the speech that comes closest to the fusion of symbol and circumstance later achieved in *Purgatory*. Although the dream of the ghostly lovers has cast a veil over the landscape, the Young Man's words, as he finally thrusts off the temptation, tear the veil away completely:

> So here we're on the summit. I can see
> The Aran Islands, Connemara Hills,
> And Galway in the breaking light; there too
> The enemy has toppled roof and gable,
> And torn the panelling from ancient rooms;
> What generations of old men had known
> Like their own hands, and children wondered at,
> Has boiled a trooper's porridge. That town had lain,
> But for the pair that you would have me pardon,
> Amid its gables and its battlements
> Like any old admired Italian town;
> For though we have neither coal, nor iron ore,
> To make us wealthy and corrupt the air,
> Our country, if that crime were uncommitted,
> Had been most beautiful.[42]

No longer do the suggestions "Mix in a brief dream-battle above" their circumstantial counterparts, or "in the hurry of the heavenly round / Forget their earthly names"[43] as that wine-cup image hovered above the actuality of the mountains. This is the language of an active man speaking, not elaborating his symbolism but compressing it un-

42. *Ibid.*, pp. 773–74.
43. *Ibid.*, p. 770.

consciously into place-names, into natural symbols ("the breaking light"), into what Yeats called "dull and numb"[44] words, and idiomatic expressions ("toppled roof and gable," "known / Like their own hands").[45] The movement is no longer that of revery. The young patriot is moved by the situation and the scene to a passionate impromptu defense. In his mouth, the new realism is dramatically appropriate. The passage promises well for the developing speech of passionate perception.

Just as Ibsen was forced to move from circumstantial realism toward metaphorical vine-leaves[46] and symbolic pistols, so Yeats, in the other direction, moved from the Celtic twilight toward an objective (but richly suggestive) scene. The imitative quality of Yeats's dance plays is enhanced by the scene painting in words that the lack of scenery makes necessary. The action takes place, not in a cardboard world, but in the real world, recognized and colored by the imagination. The objective solidity of place gives a reality to event and a concreteness to speech that simultaneously make the ghostly action more intangible (by contrast) and more convincing (by having a local habitation). The play is no longer "made-up," happening in a void. The strange action expresses the spirit of an actual place and borrows objectivity from it; the place, on the other hand, receives value from the expression in action of its history or meaning.

Yeats seemed at first to think of this interest in place as a romantic "delight in remembering celebrated lovers in the scenery pale passion loves."[47] But the objective reality of the setting, its importance not as a romantic companion to emotion but as an immediately and historically real frame of reference, is a new note in *The Dreaming of the Bones*. This note was to be heard more plainly in *The Words upon the Window-pane* and *Purgatory*.

44. *Autobiographies*, p. 435.
46. *Essays and Introductions*, p. 274.
45. *Variorum Plays*, pp. 773–74.
47. *Ibid.*, p. 233.

The Later Yeats

❧ "Into the desolation of reality"

Yeats's imitations of the Japanese Noh of spirits were not a passing interest but a discovery of his proper dramatic form. His early dramas contain that form by expectancy. In his last dramas he has consciously retained but submerged it. His first experiments in the Noh form show the germination of the dramatic-poetic speech he later matured. These "dramas of perception" imitate the third stage of "the tragic rhythm," that climactic stage which modern realism must of necessity slight. By fusing the spirit drama with an action and language full of objectivity, Yeats restored the epiphany to a drama that had lost it.

In the plays from 1892 to 1903, in contrast to later plays, Yeats's drama was still "realistic" in its imitation of the total tragic rhythm. He used traditional stories without tampering with their structure. The revisions of *The Countess Cathleen* (1892–1912) show Yeats losing this grasp of reality as he individualized his craft and gained in constructive power.

From 1903 to 1912 Yeats wrote "idealist" dramas, in which passion is praised as our chief means to perception. In *Deirdre* Yeats dissolved the traditional story, remolding it about his individual thought. All is eliminated from structure and style but what will express exclusive preoccupation with a great passion. The verse is rich in metaphor and association.

In the Japanese Noh of spirits Yeats found the model for a true drama of perception. His plays for dancers (1916–1921) concentrate on the moment of vision by eliminating stage and scene and by substituting chorus, dance, and mask for circumstantially realistic action and character. *The Dreaming of the Bones* (1919) shows objective place and action, eliminated from spectacle, entering the dialogue to objectify subjective reality. Having discovered the structure of the drama of perception, Yeats had to perfect its language: in a series of prose plays culminating in *The Words upon the Window-pane* (performed 1930), he learned to eliminate poetical ornament, letting the structure of the fable provide symbolic richness.

Between 1934 and 1938 Yeats applied these structure-baring principles to his dramatic poetry. He found it necessary to abandon blank verse for an experimental verse, in short lines, with a close approximation to the rhythms of speech. These experiments reached fruition in *Purgatory* (1938), where speech and poetry, objective reality and subjective reality are fused.

The Death of Cuchulain (1939) reveals Yeats's doctrines that character is passion and that tragedy is the struggle of will with mask. While abandoning the use of actual masks, Yeats retains the essential Noh of spirits form, in a submerged state, by using characters who are themselves masks, symbolic representations of fundamental, opposed passions.

Yeats's career began with a struggle to create a realistic and analogical drama expressing the common consciousness. In trying to achieve this drama he escaped from circumstantial realism to a deeper realism. He created the structure and the language of the drama of passionate perception. His perception was a highly individual one, however, and his drama an imitation of individual perception. Its actions take place, not in a traditional scene of human life, but in the theatre of desolate reality.

🌿 The Words upon the Window-pane:
A Realist Focus of Views and Voices

IN *The Words upon the Window-pane,* as in *The Dreaming of the Bones* and *Purgatory,* place is more completely objectified than in Yeats's other dramas both by reason of the paramount importance of setting to action and by the fact that the setting is modern yet rich with historical associations. The fine old house in which the Dublin Spiritualists' Association is holding a séance becomes a symbol of the historical process and of the eighteenth-century ideal fallen on evil days. The tone in which the setting is described in these completely different plays does not vary greatly from play to play.

The Dreaming of the Bones:

Young Man.   Is there no house
Famous for sanctity or architectural beauty
In Clare or Kerry, or in all wide Connaught,
The enemy has not unroofed?[1]

The Words upon the Window-pane:

John Corbet. . . . This is a wonderful room for a lodging-house.
Dr. Trench. It was a private house until about fifty years ago. It was not so near the town in those days, and there are large stables at the back. Quite a number of notable people lived here. Grattan was born upstairs; no, not Grattan, Curran perhaps—I forget—but I do know that this house in the early part of the eighteenth century belonged to friends of Jonathan Swift, or rather of Stella. . . .
John Corbet. . . . Everything great in Ireland and in our character, in what remains of our architecture, comes from that day. . . .[2]

Purgatory:

Great people lived and died in this house;
Magistrates, colonels, members of Parliament,

---

1. *Variorum Plays,* p. 769.   2. *Ibid.,* pp. 939–40, 942.

215

> Captains and Governors, and long ago
> Men that had fought at Aughrim and the Boyne.[3]

This entrance of an objective scene—otherwise absent—into the dramatic verse does for the scene what the dances (but with the ever-
increasing aid of the dialogue) do for the action in the dance plays—
bring its significance directly to the deeps of the mind with the aid of a
formal convention, making less necessary the intervention of realistic
illusion aimed directly at everyday sense perception.

A beautiful eighteenth-century mansion, now decayed, the house
has a poem on one of its windows, cut there by Stella for Swift's fiftieth
birthday. From the point of view of author and audience, if not from
the point of view of the occupants, this makes the house a shrine sacred
to the spirit of Swift. It is also a symbol of Swift's life, having decayed
like him, having the same memory cut into it. The association with
great men makes the spot a national as well as an artistic shrine. It is a
symbol of Ireland. Since the lodging house is now being used as a
séance room, the place spirits may arise, within the conventions of
circumstantial realism—i.e., through the words of the medium—as
the ghosts of Ireland's past arose on the mountainside in *The Dreaming
of the Bones.*

The latter play has as its most convincing setting the subjective
world of the imagining spirit. This veil is rent, however, in the last part
of the play, and the objective world floods in with the dawn light. The
changes of language in the play, as we have seen, follow an accompany-
ing pattern. In *The Words upon the Window-pane,* the opposite situation
is found. As the spirit of Swift interrupts a modern séance, reliving the
Stella-Vanessa story, it is the too-solid world of actuality whose limits
must be rent to let knowledge flow in from the world of spiritual
existences. Similarly, the superficially accurate reporting of the prose is
broken by lines from a poem, a hymn, an epitaph, and the Bible, lines
that communicate on a deeper level.

In the plays of the late twenties and the thirties, Yeats moved away
from all-pervading rhythm toward the terseness of the speech of active

3. *Ibid.,* p. 1043.

men. He cleansed his dramatic poetry by experimenting with techniques that avoid the mechanics of verse and the arbitrariness of
decorative metaphor. The necessary discipline was the use of modern
realistic prose. In such prose only items related to realistic action could
be used as symbols. And only the shock of contrasting style levels could
give the complex effect of interchange between material and spiritual
reality that had formerly been achieved by incantation.

It was fitting that, in writing a play about Swift, Yeats should use a
prose that abjured almost all metaphor except that of the fable itself. If
The Words upon the Window-pane shows Yeats attempting to achieve
power without poeticism, he is doing so through certain common
devices of Augustan literature.[4] That literature aimed at a surface
appropriate to public speech, and some of its principles are applicable
to drama. Yeats achieves intensity by multiplying the contexts within
which his prose must be heard. Interest is shifted from richness of
language to richness of significance, from the expression to the dramatized image or idea.

The metaphors and similes in *The Words upon the Window-pane* are
the sort of thing one finds in ordinary conversation, but they fit into
patterns of allusion, symbol, and myth that pervade the play. The most
striking metaphor compares Vanessa's body to white ivory dice, tying
in with the theme of Chance and a network of gambling, racing, and
luck references. More ordinarily the unquiet spirits are said to "go
through the same drama at both séances . . . just as if they were
characters in some kind of horrible play."[5] Here the metaphor alerts us
to the theme of dramatic poetry and to the symbolic nature of the
séance. Again, when Vanessa is likened by Swift to "some common slut
with her ear against the keyhole" the parallel is drawn between the
Swift-Stella relationship and the mystery of the séance, held behind
locked doors, and "an undesirable theme for gossip."[6]

These examples of figurative language are among the few worth

4. Cf. Maynard Mack, "Wit and Poetry and Pope: Some Observations on His Imagery,"
James L. Clifford and Louis A. Landa, eds., *Pope and His Contemporaries, Essays Presented
to George Sherburn* (New York: Oxford University Press, 1949), pp. 20–40.
5. *Variorum Plays,* p. 943.   6. *Ibid.,* pp. 949, 938.

mentioning, and only one of them attracts attention to itself. By what means, then, does Yeats's language communicate richly, as we feel it does? For one thing, it borrows strength from myth. Yeats was among the first moderns to realize the importance of myth to structure as a way of ordering experience. The number and variety of mythologies that are congruously worked into this play are amazing. There is first of all Yeats's self-created myth, the system of *A Vision*. There is the similar cyclic theory of history that Yeats finds set forth by Swift in his *Discourse of the Contests and Dissensions between the Nobles and the Commons in Athens and Rome* (1701) and that is held as his world view by the character in the play. Swift believed in the transmission of knowledge from classical civilization, and his work was an attempt to accomplish a certain amount of such transmission. Like Pope, however, he was conscious of threats to order and reason amounting to a progress of dullness, a universal darkness covering all. Yeats connects the Scriblerian critique of whiggery with cyclic philosophies of history which are very much part of a modern climate of opinion.[7]

Another self-created myth is that of the Irish eighteenth century and particularly the life of Swift as an expression of Irish nationality. The fourth of the *Drapier Letters* "created the political nationality of Ireland."[8] Yeats sought in Swift, Burke, and Berkeley for an identification of his beliefs with the nation itself. What he found admirable in the eighteenth century were "certain great minds that were medieval in their scope but modern in their freedom." With them began "the modern world, and something that appeared and perished in its dawn, an instinct for Roman rhetoric, Roman elegance."[9]

The play makes use also of the Augustan myth implicit in the myth of the Irish eighteenth century. Swift rebuilt Rome in Vanessa's mind, taught her to think "in every situation of life not as Hester Vanhomrigh would think in that situation, but as Cato or Brutus would."[10] ". . . His ideal order was the Roman Senate. . . . Such an order and such

7. *Ibid.*, pp. 962–63.   8. *Ibid.*, p. 959.
9. *Ibid.*, pp. 958, 959.   10. *Ibid.*, p. 949.

men had seemed possible once more, but the movement passed."[11] As Yeats regards Swift and the eighteenth century, so Swift regarded Brutus and ancient Rome.

The Christian myth is as important in the play as the classical myth. Yeats's Dean was learned in the Church fathers as well as in classical history and literature. He uses the words of Chrysostom as the model of his life with Stella. He prays to the Christian God that he may leave to posterity only his intellect which came from Heaven, involving the Christian concept of man's being made in the image of God. The fallen modern condition of the Christian myth is represented by the abstract fanaticism of Abraham Johnson, an evangelist from Belfast. The continuing power of the religion, however, is shown by the simplicity, sincerity, and efficacy of the hymn singing which is part of the séance.

A myth older and perhaps more widespread than either the Augustan myth or the Christian myth is that of spiritualism. Its provenience surrounds the others in both time and space.

Sometimes a spirit re-lives not the pain of death but some passionate or tragic moment of life. . . . There is an incident of the kind in the *Odyssey,* and many in Eastern literature; the murderer repeats his murder, the robber his robbery, the lover his serenade, the soldier hears the trumpet once again.[12]

Connected with this myth, which challenges the rationality of the Augustan myth and the unworldliness of the Christian myth, is the story of Job. "I feel like Job . . . the hair of my head stands up. A spirit passes before my face."[13]

The calculated abundance of proper names is another means by which the style of this play is heightened. Names of people and places are used by Yeats to establish his various structural myths, to set up oppositions between values, to characterize people by their own names and the names they mention, to intensify his prose and to give it an air of circumstantiality. Certain names may perform several of these functions. Some names are reiterated, others used only once.

11. *Ibid.,* p. 942.   12. *Ibid.,* p. 944.
13. *Ibid.,* p. 945.

Circumstantiality is lent to the prose by the mention of a little tea shop in Folkestone, of the library of Belfast University, of tips for Harold's Cross, of the Dublin Spiritualists' Association; by the frequent mention of England, London, Cambridge, Ireland, Belfast, Dublin; by reference to the Corbets of Ballymoney, and to Mrs. Piper, an actual American trance medium. The names of some of the characters are relevant to characterization; Mrs. Mallet's name suggests that practical creature whose conversation with her dead husband is upon business matters. Other names, however, constitute allusions to Irish history. John Corbet, of the Corbets of Ballymoney, comes of a distinguished Irish family, as does Dr. Trench.

The tone is heightened, the language intensified, by the heroic listing of the "famous David Home," "notable people . . . Grattan, Curran," "Bolingbroke, Harley, Ormonde, all those great Ministers," "his ideal men Brutus and Cato," "a great doctor there, Dr. Arbuthnot," "the great Chrysostom," "Swift . . . the chief representative of the intellect of his epoch."

Thus by juxtaposition of names, contrasts in values are shown. A pattern of classical ideals, of traditional religion, of traditional literature, and of Irish patriotism is allied against a pattern of commonness, of commercialism, and of abstract fanaticism: Cato, Chrysostom, Crashaw, and Curran are allied against Democracy, Folkestone, Moody, and Sankey; Ireland and ancient Rome against England and Belfast.

Like the great Augustan writers, Yeats used brief portraits whose metaphorical action is inconspicuous: "My father often told me that he saw David Home floating in the air in broad daylight."[14] David Home, Mrs. Piper, Chrysostom, Moody, Mrs. Mallet's husband and Job, none of whom are actual characters, are more than mere names. Stella, as we shall see, is presented almost completely through the portrait technique. In addition to the names and portraits, evaluative allusions of an historical, literary, religious, or patriotic sort expand and elaborate the contexts within which the play's significance spreads.

14. *Ibid.,* p. 938. Daniel D. Home (1833–1886); Myers, II, 578–79, gives a bibliography

Various levels and intensities of meaning are brought about in *The Words upon the Window-pane* through superimposing the points of view of a variety of characters, both in this and the other world, and a variety of voices—those of the characters (including Swift, Vanessa, and so forth) and also those from a variety of quotations, including the confident simplicity and clarity of some verses from Stella, the ironic proud defiance of Swift's epitaph, the childlike quality of a hymn, and awesome lines from Job. At one point we narrowly avoid hearing a medieval ritual of exorcism. The technique is in the juxtaposition of a variety of levels of speech and meaning.

The action itself is on several levels. We have here a play within a play. On the first level there is the action surrounding the séance. The first character to speak is Dr. Trench, an old, learned gentleman, who is President of the Dublin Spiritualists' Association. He has brought John Corbet, a young Cambridge student, to the latter's first séance. They are welcomed in the hall by the Secretary, Miss Mackenna, an energetic and intelligent young woman, who ushers them onstage. Dr. Trench shows Corbet the words of the poem by Stella cut on the window-pane and tells him that the house has formerly belonged to friends of Stella and Swift.

Corbet is writing a dissertation on Swift and Stella, and he and Trench discuss the tragedy of Swift's life.

> *John Corbet.* . . . I hope to prove that in Swift's day men of intellect reached the height of their power—the greatest position they ever attained in society and the State, that everything great in Ireland and in our character, in what remains of our architecture, comes from that day; that we have kept its seal longer than England.
>
> *Dr. Trench.* A tragic life: Bolingbroke, Harley, Ormonde, all those great Ministers that were his friends, banished and broken.
>
> *John Corbet.* I do not think you can explain him in that way—his tragedy had deeper foundations. His ideal order was the Roman Senate, his ideal men Brutus and Cato. Such an order and such men had seemed possible once more, but the movement passed and he foresaw the ruin

---

on this spiritualist, including *Experiences in Spiritualism with Mr. D. D. Home,* by Viscount Adare, later Lord Dunraven, also mentioned in the play.

to come, Democracy, Rousseau, the French Revolution; that is why he hated the common run of men,—"I hate lawyers, I hate doctors", he said, "though I love Dr. So-and-so and Judge So-and-so"—that is why he wrote *Gulliver,* that is why he wore out his brain, that is why he felt *saeva indignatio,* that is why he sleeps under the greatest epitaph in history. You remember how it goes? It is almost finer in English than in Latin: "He has gone where fierce indignation can lacerate his heart no more."[15]

At this point, when we have just heard about Swift's classical ideal, his fear of democratic ruin to come, his hatred of abstraction, his marvellous epitaph, the Reverend Abraham Johnson enters, epitomizing many of the things Swift hated. With a self-righteous displeasure which is perhaps a travesty of Swift's *saeva indignatio,* Johnson protests against a hostile influence that has been disturbing the séances.

I am from Belfast. I am by profession a minister of the Gospel, I do a great deal of work among the poor and ignorant. I produce considerable effect by singing and preaching, but I know that my effect should be much greater than it is. My hope is that I shall be able to communicate with the great Evangelist Moody. I want to ask him to stand invisible beside me when I speak or sing, and lay his hands upon my head and give me such a portion of his power that my work may be blessed as the work of Moody and Sankey was blessed. . . .[16] I ask you, Dr. Trench, as President of the Dublin Spiritualists' Association, to permit me to read the ritual of exorcism appointed for such occasions. After the last séance I copied it out of an old book in the library of Belfast University. I have it here.[17]

There is a touch of the mock-heroic in Johnson's use of names which is important in delineating his character. "I am from Belfast" is said importantly, yet Belfast is that portion of Ireland most narrowly Protestant, most commercial, most middle class, most English. "The great Evangelist Moody" sounds pretentious after "Brutus and Cato," before "the great Chrysostom."

In the meantime the other members have arrived—old Cornelius Patterson, who wants to find out if they race horses in the next world;

15. *Variorum Plays,* pp. 941–42.   16. *Ibid.,* pp. 942–43.
17. *Ibid.,* p. 944.

Mrs. Mallet, who wants her dead husband's advice about starting a teashop in Folkestone. They are all disturbed lest the hostile influence be felt again. Dr. Trench refuses to let Johnson read his exorcism, however. He explains that the earth-bound ghost is re-living some tragic moment of life and that only by patience and prayer can they help it to pass out of its passion and remorse.

Mrs. Henderson, the medium, enters, and prefaces her séance with a little talk, much like the opening of an informal religious meeting.

> *Mrs. Henderson.* I am glad to meet all my dear friends again and to welcome Mr. Corbet amongst us. . . . The guides try to send somebody for everybody but do not always succeed. If you want to speak to some dear friend who has passed over, do not be discouraged. If your friend cannot come this time, maybe he can next time. My control is a dear little girl called Lulu. . . . Miss Mackenna, a verse of a hymn, please, the same we had last time, and will everyone join in the singing.
> [*They sing the following lines from Hymn 564, Irish Church Hymnal.*]
> 'Sun of my soul, Thou Saviour dear,
> It is not night if Thou be near:
> O may no earth-born cloud arise
> To hide Thee from Thy servant's eyes.'
> [*Mrs. Henderson is leaning back in her chair asleep.*]
> *Miss Mackenna* [*to John Corbet*]. She always snores like that when she is going off.
> *Mrs. Henderson* [*in a child's voice*]. Lulu so glad to see all her friends.
> *Mrs. Mallet.* And we are glad you have come, Lulu.[18]

Here we enter on the second level, where the play within a play, the drama within the spirit world is reported through the medium by Lulu, the control. In what is supposed to be the speech of a child she describes the spirit of Mrs. Mallet's husband, who has approached.

> . . . A tall man . . . lots of hair on face . . . not much on the top of his head . . . red necktie, and such a funny sort of pin. . . . He has a message . . . he says, "Drive that man away!" He is pointing to somebody in the corner, that corner over there. He says it is the bad man who spoilt everything last time. If they won't drive him away, Lulu will scream.[19]

18. *Ibid.,* pp. 946–47.
19. *Ibid.,* pp. 947–48.

The sitters respond in character, Miss Mackenna, showing an attractive detestation of a spoil-sport, exclaims, "That horrible spirit again." Abraham Johnson, righteously indignant, protests, "Last time he monopolised the séance." Mrs. Mallet, with a genteel objection to rudeness and improper greediness, vouches that "He would not let anybody speak but himself."[20]

Then follows the drama on the third level. The spirits of Swift and Vanessa relive their conflict over Stella. These spirits, unlike the others, do not realize that they are dead. Our interest is captured by the opportunity to hear, in the twentieth century, an actual lifetime scene between Swift and Vanessa. That this scene, relived, is part of the purgatorial suffering of these spirits is an essential interest. Vanessa has written to ask Stella if she and Swift are married, and Swift is furious. Vanessa pleads with him to marry her and beget children. She presses his hands to her breasts, and the temptation mounts to a climax as the medium, filled with the struggle of Swift, rises and pounds on the locked door for escape.

The speeches of Swift and Vanessa are in sharp contrast, the former distinguished in diction and furious cadence, the latter undistinguished, although without vulgarity. Their dialogue is to a large extent in the form of questions and imperatives, Swift asking great unanswerable rhetorical questions which are part of a pattern of exhortation, Vanessa asking normal obvious questions, which, in their naïveté, are also unanswerable. Their dialogue thus has a basic structure of question matching question, command command.

> [*Swift*] How dare you write to her? How dare you ask if we were married? How dare you question her? . . . Did you not hear what I said? How dared you question her? . . . How many times did I not stay away from great men's houses, how many times forsake the Lord Treasurer, how many times neglect the business of the State that we might read Plutarch together!. . . .
> [*Vanessa*] Why have you let me spend hours in your company if you did not want me to love you?

20. *Ibid.*

......

[*Vanessa*] Was that all, Jonathan? Was I nothing but a painter's canvas? ...
[*Swift*] My God, do you think it was easy?

......

[*Vanessa*] If you and she are not married, why should we not marry like other men and women? ...
[*Swift*] What do I care if it be healthy? ... Am I to add another to the healthy rascaldom and knavery of the world?

......

[*Vanessa*] Look at me, Jonathan ... Give me both your hands.... Think of the uncertainty. ...
[*Swift*] O God, hear the prayer of Jonathan Swift, that afflicted man, and grant that he may leave to posterity nothing but his intellect that came to him from Heaven. ...
[*Vanessa*] Can you face solitude with that mind, Jonathan? ...
[*Swift*] Who locked the door, who locked me in with my enemy? ...[21]

Lulu the control breaks in, angry and disappointed at Swift's taking over the séance. Mrs. Mallet leads the medium back to her chair, and Lulu asks for another verse of the hymn. The singing brings Stella's influence into Swift's mind or into the room. When the medium speaks again, Swift is asking Stella if he has wronged her by keeping their friendship Platonic. "Have I wronged you, beloved Stella? Are you unhappy?"[22] Then he gratefully says that she has answered him in the poem for his fifty-fourth birthday. He quotes this poem, a testimony to the wisdom and virtue he has taught Stella, and it proves to be the poem upon the window-pane. Swift fears that he will outlive his friends—and himself—but Stella promises in the poem to outlive him and close his eyes.

"Late dying may you cast a shred
Of that rich mantle o'er my head;
To bear with dignity my sorrow,
One day alone, then die tomorrow."[23]

21. *Ibid.,* pp. 948–51. All these speeches are, of course, Mrs. Henderson's. I have ascribed them appropriately to Swift and Vanessa.
22. *Ibid.,* p. 952.
23. *Ibid.,* p. 953.

Thus Swift's monologue to Stella raises questions, as did the dialogue with Vanessa. But Swift answers the questions himself, partly in the words of Stella's own poem. Here the violent conflict generated in the prose dialogue of Vanessa and Swift is allayed, first by the serene simplicity of the hymn, then by the satisfaction of having questions fully answered instead of opposed to other questions, and finally by the controlled and dignified beauty of Stella's verse.

The séance ends with the child voice saying, "Power all used up. Lulu can do no more. Good-bye, friends."[24] The child is an important symbol. Lulu is the genius of the present—that future which Swift scorned. Her baby-talk—though it may have a subtle connection with the "little language" of the *Journal to Stella*—represents modern decay of language. She stands, moreover, for the "ignorant little girl without intellect, without moral ambition"[25] which Vanessa was before Swift's teaching and which she perhaps remained. That a child should be the "control" struggling with the spirit of Swift in the afterworld is perhaps fitting, since Swift has refused to "add another to the healthy rascaldom . . . of the world"[26] either by Stella or by Vanessa. Swift even wishes away his own childhood: "Perish the day on which I was born!"[27]

Again, Lulu may stand for the spirit of Swift, or for any spirit when confronted with the ultimate questions and the ultimate moral responsibilities. The verse sung just before the influence of Stella claims the soul of Swift, almost like a mother soothing a troubled child, is:

> "If some poor wandering child of Thine
> Have spurned to-day the voice divine,
> Now, Lord, the gracious work begin;
> Let him no more lie down in sin."[28]

Finally we remember that except as ye become as a little child ye shall not enter the Kingdom of Heaven. Without a childlike faith the manifestation would not be possible. Moreover Swift, as Shade, must,

24. *Ibid.*   25. *Ibid.*, p. 948.
26. *Ibid.*, p. 950.   27. *Ibid.*, p. 956.
28. *Ibid.*, p. 951.

according to Yeats's theory of the afterlife, dream "back through events in the order of their intensity" and again, as Spiritual Being, live "back through events in the order of their occurrence,"

> Till, clambering at the cradle side,
> He dreams himself his mother's pride,
> All knowledge lost in trance
> Of sweeter ignorance.

The Shade is said to fade out at last, but the Spiritual Being does not fade, passing on to other states of existence after it has attained a spiritual state, of which the surroundings and aptitudes of early life are a correspondence.[29]

The séance over, we return to the first level. The members take their leave, each giving the medium a sum as he goes out. The séance has been a failure, but they sympathize with Mrs. Henderson's exhaustion. Paying the medium is made into a little ceremony. She protests that she cannot take the money, but looks carefully to see what each person gives her. We hear individual character in each speech: Dr. Trench (always finding and appealing to the best in people), "You did your best and nobody can do more than that.... Of course you must take it, Mrs. Henderson"; Mrs. Mallet (always just and proper), "A bad séance is just as exhausting as a good séance, and you must be paid"; Cornelius Patterson (always a sport), "A jockey is paid whether he wins or not"; Miss Mackenna (always the lively young woman), "That spirit rather thrilled me"; Abraham Johnson (always the favorite of the Lord), "I shall ask God to bless and protect your séances."[30]

Corbet, convinced that Mrs. Henderson is an accomplished actress and scholar, rather than that the spirit of Swift has been present, gives her a pound note and asks for her opinion on a matter related to his studies.

---

29. *Ibid.*, p. 778. Ure, *Yeats the Playwright*, p. 99, points out that "the author of *A Vision* would have distinguished quite sharply between the shades in the earlier play [*The Dreaming of the Bones*] 'caught in a winding labyrinth of conscience' and those in the later [*The Words upon the Window-pane*], who are reliving, as Dr. Trench explains, 'some passionate or tragic moment of life....'"

30. *Variorum Plays*, p. 954.

Swift was the chief representative of the intellect of his epoch, that arrogant intellect free at last from superstition. He foresaw its collapse. He foresaw Democracy, he must have dreaded the future. Did he refuse to beget children because of that dread? Was Swift mad? Or was it the intellect itself that was mad?[31]

He imagines, though but for a moment [Yeats comments in his introduction], that the intellect of Swift's age, persuaded that the mechanicians mocked by Gulliver would prevail, that its moment of freedom could not last, so dreaded the historic process that it became in the half-mad mind of Swift a dread of parentage. . . .[32]

Mrs. Henderson, however, cannot answer. She knows nobody called Swift. And on being told it was Swift whose Spirit seemed present, she exclaims, "What? That dirty old man? . . . His clothes were dirty, his face covered with boils. Some disease had made one of his eyes swell up, it stood out from his face like a hen's egg."

After this description of the old, abandoned Swift, who, in Yeats's view, had sunk into imbecility or madness, Corbet departs, leaving Mrs. Henderson, half asleep, murmuring that line of marvellous simplicity and understatement, "It is sometimes a terrible thing to be out of the body, God help us all."[33] The medium begins to prepare herself a cup of tea. But suddenly we jump from the first level to the third. Mrs. Henderson, all alone, begins to speak again in Swift's voice.

Five great Ministers that were my friends are gone, ten great Ministers that were my friends are gone. I have not fingers enough to count the great Ministers that were my friends and that are gone. [*She wakes with a start and speaks in her own voice.*] Where did I put that tea-caddy? Ah! there it is. And there should be a cup and saucer. [*She finds the saucer.*] But where's the cup? [*She moves aimlessly about the stage and then, letting the saucer fall and break, speaks in Swift's voice.*] Perish the day on which I was born![34]

This last speech of the play is the final realist focus of views and voices, showing external reality shattered by the reality of the soul. The effect of the last line is not just that the spirit of Swift, without the spirit

31. *Ibid.*, p. 955.   32. *Ibid.*, p. 967.
33. *Ibid.*, pp. 955–56.   34. *Ibid.*, p. 956.

of Corbet to suggest it, is heard through Mrs. Henderson, but that an even older voice is heard through Swift's.

The implicit themes of the play, elaborated in many forms, help to strengthen the expression through the multiplying of relationships. The Job reference, for instance, is only one occurrence of the theme of enforced loss. The house is decayed; some of the sitters have lost loved ones; the medium is impoverished; the séance is a failure; the spirits lose the chance to speak, the sitters the chance to hear; Vanessa loses Swift; Stella loses money at cards as well as health and life; Swift loses Stella, his reason, his friends, his appearance; the world loses a great moment of its history; Mrs. Henderson is tired out; a china saucer is shattered.

Patterns of significant words—*intellect, spirit, friends, great, famous*—coupled occasionally with rhetorical repetition sometimes provide these themes a visible and continuous thread of outward manifestation. Culminating in the magnificent last speech, the theme of enforced loss is reiterated by the word *gone* in a funereal drumbeat. "He has gone where fierce indignation can lacerate his heart no more." "Man with funny pin gone away." "Power almost gone." "Vanessa has gone, Stella has taken her place." "Bad old man gone." "Go away, go away!" "His brain had gone."[35] The séance has come to an end and the sitters themselves have gone, one by one. Finally nothing is left, not even Mrs. Henderson's consciousness—only the suffering spirit of Swift.

All sorts of richnesses are added to the clarity of the style by the symbolic structure of the dramatic fable itself. Love, patriotism, religion, and art are among the subjects of *The Words upon the Window-pane,* along with bodily decay, mob tyranny, fanatical abstraction, and Philistinism. Yeats says in his introduction that no character upon the stage spoke his thoughts. All were people who might have been met at such a séance. Ignorant or learned, most such people have substituted the séance room for the church and taken what happens there quite

35. *Ibid.,* pp. 942, 948, 951, 952, 953, 955.

literally. "At most séances," however, "there is somebody who finds symbol where his neighbour finds fact." And such we may assume was Yeats. Not completely, however. If he had allowed his thoughts to be spoken they would be: "I consider it certain that every voice that speaks . . . is first of all a secondary personality or dramatisation created by, in, or through the medium."[36] These voices, however, "when they speak from, or imply, supernormal knowledge, when they are more than transformations of the medium, are, as it were, new beings begotten by spirit upon medium to live short but veritable lives."[37]

In short, Yeats felt that the action of his play would be possible in real life and that the spirits would have a genuine relation to the actual Swift and Vanessa.

The play, however, is not séance but symbol. In it the representative intellect of Ireland's great century, to whom "Unity of being was still possible though somewhat over-rationalised and abstract,"[38] is brought into the modern world he dreaded. There the cry of both living and dead becomes, "Drive that man away!"[39] The medium on this side and the control on the other side welcome all "dear friends."[40] But the hostile influence of Swift is outcast, condemned to the solitude it feared. This is all a symbolic "portrait of the artist." "We poets and artists [Yeats says in his introduction] may be called, so small our share in life, 'separated spirits,' words applied by the old philosophers to the dead."[41]

Except to the scholar, John Corbet, and perhaps to Dr. Trench, the struggle of Swift to reject Vanessa's desire and to keep faith with Stella has no meaning. The fanatical religionist, the genteel business lady, the old sport, representing as they do three quite broad and distinct aspects of modern life, understand not a word. For them the séance is unsuccessful. In fact, we can draw an analogy between the séance and the poet's art. The poet is like a medium before whom many possibilities clamor for speech. He is like Odysseus holding his sword above the

36. *Ibid.*, p. 967.   37. *Ibid.*, p. 969.
38. *Ibid.*, p. 964.   39. *Ibid.*, p. 947.
40. *Ibid.*, p. 946.   41. *Ibid.*, p. 964.

blood pool. This infinite fluidity of thought is the Way of the Chameleon which Stauffer too much emphasizes as the main track of Yeats's creative process.[42] It is, more exactly, the passion stage of the psychic rhythm that Burke and Fergusson find every poet repeating, the romantic poet lingering there longest. In this light, the séance is like a poem or play of Yeats's which is "unsuccessful" from the point of view of the Johnsons, Pattersons, and Mallets of this world. They do not hear what they came for. They cannot understand the voice of an influence hostile to their abstractions, the argument of genius with itself.

What should the scene mean to us? It is important to note that Stella is not present except as an influence. She does not speak, and she appears to no character, living or dead, except to Swift himself. Vanessa, on the other hand, is described by Lulu, and her voice argues strenuously against Swift's asceticism. Stella's spirit is perhaps not earthbound. In fact it would be inconsistent with what she stands for in the play for her to be a suffering, passionate spirit. Her influence is felt, but she speaks only through the words of her poem, cut in the glass of the window and repeated by Swift.

Stella is an ideal, the ideal of a spiritual and mental health of which bodily beauty is a mere corollary or indirect result. She is the symbol of Swift's "intellect that came to him from Heaven,"[43] the only thing he wishes to leave to posterity. Both Vanessa and John Corbet call this intellect "arrogant." But it is the pride of having "done one braver thing / Than all the Worthies did" and then an even braver thing "Which is, to keep that hid."[44] Yeats finds in Swift a "fakir-like contempt for all human desire; 'take from her,' Swift prayed for Stella in sickness, 'all violent desire whether of life or death' . . . .".[45]

In the poem upon the window-pane, Stella thanks Swift for teach-

42. Donald A. Stauffer, *The Golden Nightingale* (New York: The Macmillan Company, 1949), p. 22.

43. *Variorum Plays*, p. 951.

44. "The Undertaking: Platonic Love," *The Complete Poems of John Donne*, ed. Roger E. Bennett (Chicago: Packard and Company, 1942), p. 3.

45. *Variorum Plays*, p. 965.

ing her how the mind may, by freeing itself from the body, rule the body to the greater health of both. "It is the thought of the great Chrysostom who wrote in a famous passage that women loved according to the soul, loved as saints can love, keep their beauty longer, have greater happiness than women loved according to the flesh."[46]

> "You taught how I might youth prolong
> By knowing what is right and wrong;
> How from my heart to bring supplies
> Of lustre to my fading eyes;
> How soon a beauteous mind repairs
> The loss of chang'd or falling hairs;
> How wit and virtue from within
> Can spread a smoothness o'er the skin."[47]

The ideal relationship with Stella, involving the courage that is control, the freedom of intellectual adventure that is discipline, and the rich emotional rewards of temperance, stands for the Augustan ideal—applied in whatever field you will. It was this ideal that Swift feared would be engulfed in the age to come.

Did not Rousseau within five years of the death of Swift publish his *Discourse upon Arts and Sciences* and discover instinctive harmony not in heroic effort, not in Cato and Brutus, not among impossible animals—I think of that noble horse Blake drew for Hayley—but among savages, and thereby beget the sans-culottes of Marat?[48]

The classical control, the harmony of body and mind, which Stella represents suggests arrogance because of the difficulty, the impossibility, of the thing attempted. But it is not the pride of intellect scorning the body, separating itself from the body. It is not a narrow rationalism isolated from appetite, going its own way. Nor is it narrowly efficient in the service of appetite. It is Reason in the old sense, directing Will and Appetite so that the whole soul may move toward the Good. It is, by more than analogy, the same principle in the state and in the universe. It is "wisdom wound into the roots of the grass."[49]

46. *Ibid.,* p. 952.
48. *Ibid.,* p. 967.

47. *Ibid.,* p. 953.
49. *Ibid.,* p. 965.

The cry of the play, however, is different from Swift's cry. It is the cry of the Syrian in *The Resurrection:*

The Syrian. What is human knowledge?

The Greek. The knowledge that keeps the road from here to Persia free from robbers, that has built the beautiful humane cities, that has made the modern world, that stands between us and the barbarian.

The Syrian. But what if there is something it cannot explain, something more important than anything else?

The Greek. You talk as if you wanted the barbarian back.

The Syrian. What if there is always something that lies outside knowledge, outside order? What if at the moment when knowledge and order seem complete that something appears? [*He has begun to laugh.*]

The Hebrew. Stop laughing.

The Syrian. What if the irrational return? What if the circle begin again?[50]

"Everything that man esteems / Endures a moment or a day."[51] The whole Stella episode proves, in the play, to be an illusion. It has a poetic order and truth like the words cut upon the window-pane. But it does not affect the future, or at least does not correctly interpret it. Knowing that Swift fears a lonely and insane old age, Stella has promised in the poem to outlive him. It is as if the heavenly intellect should promise not to leave him. "Yes, you will close my eyes, Stella. O, you will live long after me, dear Stella, for you are still a young woman, but you will close my eyes."[52]

Yet at the end Swift is old, diseased, and ugly. Stella is long since dead, his friends are gone, and his sanity too. Like the house in which he relives his passionate struggle for the intellect, Swift's old age is a symbol of an ideal proved illusory by time. His illusion is cut into his ghostly memory as into the window of the haunted house. It is Vanessa who is in accord with the stream of time.

> Look at me, Jonathan. Your arrogant intellect separates us. Give me both your hands. I will put them upon my breast. [*Mrs. Henderson raises her right hand to the level of her left and then raises both to her breast.*] O, it is white—white as the gambler's dice—white ivory dice. Think of

---

50. *Ibid.,* p. 925.   51. *Ibid.,* p. 931.
52. *Ibid.,* p. 953.

the uncertainty. Perhaps a mad child—perhaps a rascal—perhaps a knave—perhaps not, Jonathan. The dice of the intellect are loaded, but I am the common ivory dice. [*Her hands are stretched out as though drawing somebody towards her.*] It is not my hands that draw you back. My hands are weak, they could not draw you back if you did not love as I love. You said that you have strong passions; that is true, Jonathan— no man in Ireland is so passionate. That is why you need me, that is why you need children, nobody has greater need. You are growing old. An old man without children is very solitary. Even his friends, men as old as he, turn away, they turn towards the young, their children or their children's children. They cannot endure an old man like themselves. [*Mrs. Henderson moves away from the chair, her movements gradually growing convulsive.*] You are not too old for the dice, Jonathan, but a few years if you turn away will make you an old miserable childless man.[53]

Although, when Swift rebuilt Rome in Vanessa's mind, it was as if he walked its streets,[54] she refused to be static like architecture or a painter's canvas. She is the gambler's dice. We have come upon this symbol before, in *Calvary,* where the soldiers gamble for Christ's cloak. "Whatever happens is the best, we say, / So that it's unexpected."[55] In Yeats's note on *Calvary,* we learn from his fictional old Arab that all things may be divided into Chance and Choice. Both exist in God, perfect and without limitation. God would not have freedom if he were bound by His own Choice.

If I should throw from the dice-box there would be but six possible sides on each of the dice, but when God throws He uses dice that have all numbers and sides. Some worship His Choice; that is easy; to know that He has willed for some unknown purpose all that happens is pleasant; but I have spent my life in worshipping His Chance, and that moment when I understand the immensity of His Chance is the moment when I am nearest Him.[56]

To marry Vanessa would be a throw of the dice. The possibilities—a mad child, a rascal, a knave, a saint—are not infinite, but are suggestive of God's infinite Chance. To marry her would be to tell the universe to go ahead with its next cycle, whatever it might be. But

53. *Ibid.,* pp. 950–51.   54. *Ibid.,* p. 949.
55. *Ibid.,* p. 786.   56. *Ibid.,* pp. 790–91.

Swift, who in his *Discourse of the Contests and Dissensions between the Nobles and the Commons in Athens and Rome* predicted a coming tyranny of the Many as part of a cyclic theory of history, will not throw the dice. The great ministers, the few who could make life rich for the whole state, are gone, and Swift, instead of wishing the next generation into being, cries in the words of Job, "Perish the day on which I was born!" But Yeats, as Richard Ellmann has pointed out, "is not Swift";[57] his despair, in poems such as "Crazy Jane on the Mountain," of finding a contemporary equal to the heroes of old time, is nowhere near absolute. "Whatever flames upon the night / Man's own resinous heart has fed."[58] Yeats experiences tragic zest in watching the burning of his own civilization.

Other elements in the play support the theme of Chance. Some of the living characters at the séance show a fascination with it. Cornelius Patterson wishes to know whether they race horses and whippets in the next world. He himself is a sort of lay seer, giving Miss Mackenna, who is interested in the horse races of this world, tips for Harold's Cross. Among the dead, Mrs. Mallet's husband, to whom she would turn for advice before risking her savings on a teashop in Folkestone, wears a horseshoe pin, symbol of luck.

The séance itself is a symbol of chance; the spirits present numberless possibilities and both this play and the literature of psychical research show that the sitters are gambling against odds for a desired and coherent manifestation. "The thronging multitude of the departed press to the glimpse of light. Eager, but untrained, they interject their uncomprehended cries; vainly they call the names which no man answers; like birds that have beaten against a lighthouse, they pass in disappointment away."[59] So writes F. W. H. Myers in his *Human Personality* (one of the books John Corbet has read on spiritualism) concerning the trances of Mrs. Piper (the American medium who convinced Dr. Trench of the truth of such psychic phenomena). "At first this confusion gravely interfered with coherent messages [Myers

57. Ellmann, *Identity,* p. 231.   58. *Variorum Plays,* p. 931.
59. Myers, II, 256.

adds], but through the second and third stages of Mrs. Piper's trances, under the watchful care apparently of supervising spirits, it has tended more and more to disappear."[60] The sitters at the séance in the play consider that they have gambled and lost. Yet they must pay the medium anyway. Cornelius Patterson draws the comparison when, laying down his money, he says that he would do the same for an unsuccessful jockey at a horse race.

The author of *The Mechanical Operations of the Spirit,* however, deals not with such hocus pocus nor even with the most innocent games of chance. Always the teacher, he indulgently chaffed Stella in the *Journal* "because of certain small sums of money she lost at cards probably in this very room."[61] By such a slight touch Yeats allies his hero with God's Choice and against his Chance.

I tremble to read in *A Vision* that "All these symbols can be thought of as the symbols of the relations of men and women and of the birth of children,"[62] because of the interconnections I may have missed between Yeats's play and his system. Certain passages suggest analogies with the Swift-Stella-Vanessa situation: "When my instructors see woman as man's goal and limit, rather than as mother, they symbolise her as *Mask* and *Body of Fate,* object of desire and object of thought, the one a perpetual rediscovery of what the other destroys; . . . and they set this double opposite in perpetual opposition to *Will* and *Creative Mind.*"[63]

Stella, in the play, is Swift's Mask, the ideal toward which his Will moves, a serene intelligence, rational choice, the opposite that he seeks in his passion and his insanity. Vanessa, however, presents to him his Body of Fate, the irrational flux bringing on a future he dreads. Vanessa, turning from his teaching, once again "without intellect, without moral ambition," behaving "like some common slut with her ear against the keyhole," is like the external reality that his Creative Mind and his satire scorn. Stella is the value, implicit in his work, by which that external reality is judged.

Another passage suggests that Yeats perhaps rejects neither Vanessa

60. *Ibid.*
62. *A Vision,* 1937, p. 211.
61. *Variorum Plays,* p. 940.
63. *Ibid.,* p. 213.

nor Stella, neither earth nor sky, neither Chance nor Choice, but finds them antinomies of the one reality.

When *Will* is passing through Phases 16, 17 and 18 the *Creative Mind* is passing through the Phases 14, 13 and 12, or from the sign Aries to the sign Taurus, that is to say, it is under the conjunction of Mars and Venus. When *Will* upon the other hand is passing through Phases 12, 13 and 14 the *Creative Mind* is passing through the Phases 18, 17 and 16, or from the sign Pisces to the sign Aquarius, it is, as it were, under the conjunction of Jupiter and Saturn. These two conjunctions which express so many things are certainly, upon occasion, the outward-looking mind, love and its lure, contrasted with introspective knowledge of the mind's self-begotten unity, an intellectual excitement. They stand, so to speak, like heraldic supporters guarding the mystery of the fifteenth phase.[64]

The fifteenth phase resolves these two principles. "Chance and Choice have become interchangeable without losing their identity."

Now contemplation and desire, united into one, inhabit a world where every beloved image has bodily form, and every bodily form is loved. This love knows nothing of desire, for desire implies effort, and though there is still separation from the loved object, love accepts the separation as necessary to its own existence. *Fate* is known for the boundary that gives our *Destiny* its form, and—as we can desire nothing outside that form—as an expression of our freedom.[65]

Yeats does not, like Swift, reject the white ivory dice. He refers approvingly to the statement of the "present Pope . . . that the natural union of man and woman has a kind of sacredness." Yeats sees in it "a symbol of that eternal instant where the antinomy is resolved. It is not the resolution itself."[66] The duel of the sexes, on the other hand, symbolizes the unresolved antinomy.

The whole situation of *The Words upon the Window-pane* seems tremendously ironic when we remember Swift's epitaph: "He has gone where fierce indignation can lacerate his heart no more." Immediately after John Corbet quotes this, Abraham Johnson breaks in with "Something must be done, Dr. Trench, to drive away the influence

64. *Ibid.,* p. 207. 65. *Ibid.,* p. 136.
66. *Ibid.,* p. 214.

that has destroyed our séances."[67] We soon learn that the heart of Swift is still being very much lacerated by fierce indignation. The irony is all the stronger when we reflect that Swift would never believe in such spiritualistic nonsense as the séance, although he calls up the spirits of his classical heroes in a similar scene in the third book of *Gulliver's Travels*.

What crime has Swift committed that he must suffer in this Purgatory until God gives peace? Is it simply that he must wear away in dream both the passion he felt for Vanessa and the passion of his rejection of her? Must he do the same with his fear that he was wronging Stella? Are these passions impurities that come between him and his God? "O may no earth-born cloud arise / To hide Thee from Thy servant's eyes."[68] Or is there a deeper guilt? Has he not perhaps really wronged both women by not marrying one of them? Is he not doing penance for the mad crime of defying God's Chance? Did he not through his hatred and fear of the irrational, commit a sin against the "precise inexplicable teeming life"[69] of the sacred earth? I do not mean to put a moralistic interpretation upon Swift's tragedy, but it may be that in rejecting sex and the future, Swift was rejecting the thirteenth sphere in which man's freedom from the deterministic cycles inheres.

In *The Words upon the Window-pane* Yeats experimented with the techniques of circumstantial realism and used them to communicate a reality of supernatural manifestation that is quite uncanny. The play takes Ibsen's set—the parlor with a window on the void—and uses it for Yeats's own purposes. In Ibsen there is nothing, a vast cultural and spiritual blank, beyond the window.[70] In Yeats it is beyond the "window-pane" that the real world of spiritual existences has its being. The words upon the window-pane carry us to the moment of passionate perception.

The form of the whole play is an implicit allusion. Like Lorca's *La Casa de Bernarda Alba* and perhaps like Eliot's *The Cocktail Party*, *The Words upon the Window-pane* alludes to the convention of circumstan-

67. *Variorum Plays*, p. 942.   68. *Ibid.*, p. 946.
69. *Ibid.*, p. 970.   70. Cf. Fergusson, pp. 157–61.

tial realism even while using it. All three plays seem to say that things may be seen from this limited point of view and that the persons whose lives are presented to us have difficulty in getting beyond that point of view. The convention communicates the idea of a lack of vision—quite ironic in this situation.[71]

Yeats attacks the great realist with his own weapons, using Ibsen's set, his characters, and his method. The characters include Ibsen's doctor concerned with spiritual healing, his religionist concerned with worldly power or reputation, his scholar who does not get the point, his naturally loyal and whole-minded young woman who, however, fails to see the tragedy. The method is that of discussion—Ibsen's "Let's sit down and have a little chat!"—except that part of the discussion is carried on in the spirit world. Yeats picks the occasion—a séance—where all this circumstantial realism will testify against its own completeness or sufficiency as truth. Swift, the most "real" presence in the play, never appears on the stage.

71. Ure, *Yeats the Playwright,* p. 112, notes that here "Yeats has turned the tables upon the naturalistic drama by exploding it from inside; from its shattered ruins there arises the terrible image of an utterly different kind of life."

❧ *Purgatory:* The Achieved Language of Passionate Perception

T HE REALISM of *Purgatory* is simplified, stylized, reduced to barest essentials, so that the play becomes symbolical, yet is not, as in the dance plays, cut off from the recognizable world. *Purgatory,* which has the same subject—the reliving of transgressions—as *The Dreaming of the Bones* and *The Words upon the Window-pane,* successfully fuses elements of these two kinds of drama. The dramatic speech attained in this play is representative of such a fusion. It is not the "poetic" language of romantic passion nor the prose language of reason and circumstantial realism but the achieved language of passionate perception. Closer to the language of his later poetry than to that of most of his other plays, it is nevertheless specifically dramatic speech.

The play imitates the complete tragic rhythm and has an analogical rather than a univocal form. The action, the recognition of recurrence, takes place in both this world and the other. The Old Man, protagonist of the play, goes through the complete rhythm of purpose, passion, and perception. This is perhaps as close to a realist idea of the theatre as Yeats felt that he could come in a time such as ours. He places his scene in the only one left central to our time, a "ruined house and a bare tree,"[1] "the desolation of reality."[2]

Before this background enter the Old Man and a Boy, his son. "Stand there and look," commands the Old Man, "Because there is somebody in that house." "There's nobody here," the Boy cries.

> The floor is gone, the windows gone,
> And where there should be roof there's sky,

1. *Variorum Plays,* p. 1041. Ure, *Yeats the Playwright,* p. 112, calls *Purgatory* "a Shakespearian tragedy in miniature," which seems to me a good way of putting what I am trying to get at in these two opening paragraphs.
2. "Meru," *Variorum Poems,* p. 563; cf. *Poems,* p. 289.

And here's a bit of an egg-shell thrown
Out of a jackdaw's nest.
Old Man.   But there are some
That do not care what's gone, what's left:
The souls in Purgatory that come back
To habitations and familiar spots.

"Your wits are out again,"[3] the Boy protests irritably, but the Old Man reveals that the house is his childhood home.

My mother that was your grand-dam owned it,
This scenery and this countryside,
Kennel and stable, horse and hound—
She had a horse at the Curragh, and there met
My father, a groom in a training stable,
Looked at him and married him.
Her mother never spoke to her again,
And she did right.

"What's right and wrong?" inquires the cynical son, "My grand-dad got the girl and the money." But the Old Man continues,

Looked at him and married him,
And he squandered everything she had,
She never knew the worst, because
She died in giving birth to me,
But now she knows it all, being dead.[4]

The Old Man tells the Boy that his father neglected his education and exploited the estate to pay for "what he had lost at cards / Or spent on horses, drink and women."[5] When the Old Man was sixteen years old (the present age of the Boy), his father burned down the house while drunk, and the Old Man stabbed him to death, leaving his body to burn. The Old Man escaped and took to the road as a pedlar, "No good trade, but good enough / Because I am my father's son, / Because of what I did or may do."[6] Suddenly the Old Man hears hoof-beats. These are inaudible to the Boy, but the Old Man insists that, this being the anniversary of his mother's wedding night, or of the night in which

3. *Variorum Plays*, p. 1042.   4. *Ibid.*, p. 1043.
5. *Ibid.*, p. 1044.   6. *Ibid.*, p. 1045.

he was begotten, his mother's spirit in Purgatory relives in ceaseless remorse her crime of marrying beneath her. The hoofbeats announce the coming of the drunken bridegroom. The Old Man stares at the window where the ghostly figure of his mother waits for her worthless husband. Then the window is dark and she goes down to meet him.

> Do not let him touch you! It is not true
> That drunken men cannot beget,
> And if he touch he must beget
> And you must bear his murderer.
> Deaf! Both deaf! If I should throw
> A stick or a stone they would not hear;
> And that's a proof my wits are out.
> But there's a problem: she must live
> Through everything in exact detail,
> Driven to it by remorse, and yet
> Can she renew the sexual act
> And find no pleasure in it, and if not,
> If pleasure and remorse must both be there,
> Which is the greater?
>   I lack schooling.
> Go fetch Tertullian; he and I
> Will ravel all that problem out
> Whilst those two lie upon the mattress
> Begetting me.[7]

7. *Ibid.,* p. 1046. Wilson, *W. B. Yeats and Tradition,* p. 147, comments that the Old Man can rescue his mother "from her horror at what might otherwise be an endless chain of circumstances following from the single tragic event of her marriage; but he cannot rescue her from her personal emotion, the mingled 'pleasure and remorse' that she feels as she relives the 'sexual act' from which he was conceived."

Ure, *Yeats the Playwright,* pp. 109–10, adds that at this crucial point the Old Man's learning "becomes a crazy parody of itself." If he knew "his mother's condition to its depths . . . he would not suppose that the killing of the boy could do more than momentarily assuage her torment. This state of half-knowledge is his hereditary condition entailed upon him by his polluted blood. It is his tragic fate. It is that which engineers the catastrophe." He concludes wryly, "The case is one, as the old man at length perceives, which only the 'mercy of God' can solve. . . . Yeats—can it be said?—has at last found a use for God" (p. 107).

Vendler, *Yeats's* Vision *and the Later Plays,* p. 199, finds that the point of both *The Dreaming of the Bones* and *Purgatory* is "the Yeatsian doctrine that only self-forgiveness can halt obsessive rehearsing of guilt." In the passage about pleasure and remorse, "the Old

Meanwhile the Boy has been rummaging in the pack. His father catches him at it and they struggle over a bag of money. The Boy threatens to kill the Old Man, just as the latter killed his father. They are distracted by the manifestation of the bridegroom's ghost in the window. The Boy, as well as the Old Man, sees this ghost, and while he stands in fascinated horror, the Old Man stabs him with the same jack-knife that killed the Boy's grandfather. This murder was his at least half-conscious intention in coming to the house. He feels that the sacrifice of his worthless son, "A bastard that a pedlar got / Upon a tinker's daughter in a ditch,"[8] will end the evil consequences of his mother's crime and thus give her spirit rest. But the sacrifice is futile. As the Old Man cleans his knife, picks up the money the struggle had scattered, and prepares to leave, his mother's purgatorial dream recurs.

> Hoof-beats! Dear God,
> How quickly it returns—beat—beat—!
>
> Her mind cannot hold up that dream.
> Twice a murderer and all for nothing,
> And she must animate that dead night
> Not once but many times!
> O God,
> Release my mother's soul from its dream!

Man has brought to our attention one of the difficulties of detachment, whether moral or artistic: how does the artist purify of 'complexities of mire and blood' an emotion which is integrally complex, mixed, and ambiguous? . . . Yeats's own bewilderment is reflected in the ending of the play" (p. 200). "The play ends on a tone of frustration and incomprehension, as the Old Man discovers that lashing out at the world cannot cure an inner evil" (p. 201). These are perceptive comments, but I feel that it is a mistake to confuse Yeats's bewilderment with the Old Man's, even though there are more personal elements here than anyone has yet noted. Certainly Yeats has demonstrated again and again the capacity of making great art out of the "foul rag-and-bone shop of the heart." I also believe it is a mistake to speak of the Old Man's "incomprehension" and "discovery" in the same breath. Surely he comprehends what he discovers, and states it clearly in the last four lines of the play. I do not feel that "the parable is split too many ways for coherence" or that the play is "thin and unsatisfying" (p. 201). A more powerful dose than *Purgatory* would be hard to take. Helen Vendler's preoccupation with the relation of purgation to the artistic imagination would seem to have led her to ask of the play irrelevant values.

8. *Variorum Plays,* p. 1044.

Mankind can do no more. Appease
The misery of the living and the remorse of the dead.[9]

T. S. Eliot remarks upon "the extraordinary theatrical skill with which [Yeats] has put so much action within the compass of a very short scene of but little movement...."[10] With its extreme compression and its parallel actions in the spirit world and in the "real" world, the play achieves an effect of simultaneity. It is almost as if, at the moment of the knife thrust, one might view all these actions happening together in a timeless instant: the conception of the child who would grow to be the old pedlar, the death of his mother in childbirth, the "killing" of the house, the murder of the father, the conception of the pedlar's son, and the murder of that son by his father.

Perhaps one of the most valuable things to be done in studying Yeats's *Purgatory* is to examine the grounds for Eliot's judgment that in this play Yeats "solved his problem of speech in verse, and laid all his successors under obligation to him."[11] By saying "*his* problem" rather than "*the* problem" Eliot tells us that each writer faces an individual difficulty in fusing dramatic speech and poetry, but the rest of the sentence implies that Yeats's solution follows certain general principles which other poetic dramatists may advantageously consider.

This play is the climax of a development that, as Eliot has pointed out, is marked by a "gradual purging out of poetical ornament."

The course of improvement is towards a greater and greater starkness. The beautiful line for its own sake is a luxury dangerous even for the poet who has

---

9. *Ibid.*, p. 1049. Whereas Wilson, *W. B. Yeats and Tradition*, p. 154, feels that the "murder of the Boy ... is presented as a morally desirable but ultimately unavailing act," Ure, *Yeats the Playwright*, p. 111, finds that the murder "is done by all that is good" in the Old Man and yet is "also a horrible crime.... The dramatist did not mean us to regard it in a coldly theoretical way simply as something done by the living for the sake of the dead and therefore justifiable even if largely ineffectual."

Vendler, *Yeats's Vision and the Later Plays*, p. 200, seems to agree: "The Old Man's proper function is to forgive his mother and father, since the real consequence in him of their action is his mad hatred of them both, not the coarse son he has begotten. In killing his son, he is intensifying the consequences of his mother's action, rather than abrogating them."

10. Eliot, "The Poetry of W. B. Yeats," p. 449.

11. Eliot, *Poetry and Drama*, p. 23.

made himself a virtuoso of the technique of the theater. What is necessary is a beauty which shall not be in the line or the isolable passage, but woven into the dramatic texture itself; so that you can hardly say whether the lines give grandeur to the drama, or whether it is the drama which turns the words into poetry.[12]

Perhaps Yeats knew that he had achieved this close dramatic texture when he wrote, "I have put nothing into the play because it seemed picturesque; I have put there my own conviction about this world and the next."[13]

With a design full of suggestion, the play need not use self-conscious figurative language. Such comparisons as there are either escape observation through their homeliness or call attention to the basic symbols involved in the play's structure: the spirit of the groom-bridegroom, whose coming has been announced by the sound of hoofbeats, leans in the window "like some tired beast"; "That beast there,"[14] the pedlar calls the grandfather as he kills the grandson under his window. And then the hoofbeats recur.

Although the style does not abound in figurative language, it is rich in images, and there is scarcely an image that does not reflect the multiple meanings of the whole structure by virtue of its involvement in subtly related patterns.

The "ruined house" and "bare tree" are epitomes of the decayed state of man and nature. No particular season is explicitly indicated. The tree is bare because lightning has struck it. Yet fall is inevitably suggested, and an inconclusive reference to October makes one think that it may be near Samhain, certainly an appropriate time for a spirit drama with the title of this one. Like his father, the Boy reaches his sixteenth birthday at the time of the Puck Fair, early August.[15] The conception of each child, therefore, would have taken place sometime near late October, which is possibly the time also of the two murders.

"The moonlight falls upon the path, / The shadow of a cloud upon

---

12. Eliot, "The Poetry of W. B. Yeats," p. 451.
13. *Letters on Poetry*, p. 184.   14. *Variorum Plays*, p. 1048.
15. *Ibid.*, p. 1044.

the house, / And that's symbolical. . . ."[16] The moonlight on the path stands for a period of subjective knowledge. It is perhaps a full moon, as in *The Herne's Egg* and *A Full Moon in March,* the moment of the death of one era and the beginning of another. The house is one of the great houses that meant to Yeats a tradition of distinction in Irish leadership and culture. The cloud upon it is like the smoke from its immolation, or like the curse of a crime hanging over the house. The cloud also symbolizes, as in *The Dreaming of the Bones,* the presence of spirits and the blinding remorse that can come between a guilty spirit and knowledge of God.

The symbolism of the house is made clear when, in a moving passage, the Old Man identifies it with the great few who produce all that is most valuable in beauty of architecture and landscape, in family tradition and in leadership of the state.

> Great people lived and died in this house;
> Magistrates, colonels, members of Parliament,
> Captains and Governors, and long ago
> Men that had fought at Aughrim and the Boyne.
> Some that had gone on Government work
> To London or to India came home to die,
> Or came from London every spring
> To look at the may-blossom in the park.
> They had loved the trees that he cut down
> To pay what he had lost at cards
> Or spent on horses, drink and women;
> Had loved the house, had loved all
> The intricate passages of the house,
> But he killed the house; to kill a house
> Where great men grew up, married, died,
> I here declare a capital offence.[17]

To kill the house becomes the equivalent of killing a family, a nation, or even a person—a woman such as the Old Man's mother who died bearing him to the groom. It is like killing her and the future generations with her.

16. *Ibid.,* p. 1041.
17. *Ibid.,* pp. 1043–44.

The bare tree is another good example of Yeats's symbolic use of setting and images. Since the tree is the background for the symbolic house, perhaps it is more than a natural symbol; perhaps we are to remember the conception of Burke—one of the great men in the house of Irish history—"that proved the State a tree,"[18] but who did not, like Swift, know that the tree must die.[19] At any rate it is a symbol for three conditions of the human soul: immersed in life, facing death, purified in the afterlife. The riven tree suggests age, the decay of the body, death. "What is it like?" the Old Man asks and the Boy answers, "A silly old man."[20] But the tree did not grow old naturally. It was blasted by the thunderbolt, just as the house was burned, not allowed to decay. It is the sight of this stripped tree that makes the Old Man

18. "Blood and the Moon," *Variorum Plays*, p. 481; cf. *Poems*, p. 238.

19. *Explorations*, p. 318. Wilson, *W. B. Yeats and Tradition*, relates the tree to the " 'single pine tree' that is invariably painted on the back-wall in the performance of the Noh plays" (p. 157), and, in its green-leaved state to "the tree of life of the 'Raya Mehemna' and Yeats's other Kabbalistic books" (p. 158).

20. *Variorum Plays*, p. 1041. Wilson, *W. B. Yeats and Tradition*, pp. 137–61, treats at length the theology and the philosophy of history behind the play and provides fascinating parallels from Yeats's reading. Wilson's analysis emphasizes "the next" world, and wrongly disparages John Heath-Stubbs's interpretation of the play in terms of Yeats's "conviction about this world." In Heath-Stubbs's interpretation the marriage of lady to groom "symbolizes the corruption of the old Anglo-Irish aristocracy"; the Old Man "represents the revolutionary generation or Yeats himself"; the Boy "typifies the younger generation of the new Ireland." (Quoted by Wilson, pp. 153–154, from Heath-Stubbs's *The Darkling Plain*, [London: Eyre & Spottiswoode, 1950], p. 205.) I think the historical allegory is there—Wilson in fact encompasses this interpretation—and I think it is as much a mistake to overemphasize the otherworldly as the this-worldly aspect of the play. Heath-Stubbs, on the other hand, courts the opposite misunderstanding when he says that what Yeats "derived from theosophy, and indirectly from Indian religion, forms an intrusive element, and a somewhat tiresome one, in his poetry" (*The Darkling Plain*, p. 206). This is the element, along with the neo-platonic tradition, which Wilson has so fully documented in his books, deserving the gratitude of all readers of Yeats. Yeats's phrase "this world and the next" clearly asks for a balanced reading. Helen Vendler, *Yeats's Vision and the Later Plays*, seems to me to put the political element in the right perspective, and comments grimly, "Ireland's purgation, too, seems destined to go on forever, in a sterile repetition without any new rebirth" (p. 202).

Cf. also Donald Pearce, "Yeats's Last Plays: An Interpretation," ELH, XVIII (March, 1951), pp. 67–76, for a political reading of *Purgatory*.

turn from peddling wares in the here and now to attending to the suffering of his mother's soul in the hereafter. "I saw it a year ago stripped bare as now, / So I chose a better trade."

Fifty years ago the tree was full of "Green leaves, ripe leaves, leaves thick as butter, / Fat, greasy life."[21] Then it was a "great-rooted blossomer."[22] One could not distinguish "leaf," "blossom" or "bole" as essential tree. But already a soul (the mother's) had been bruised to pleasure body, and now, the tree leafless and riven, the Old Man is planning a second time to bruise body—the body of his son—to pleasure soul—the unappeased ghost of his mother.

After having sacrificed his son, he thinks he has released his mother, and the moonlit tree becomes the symbol of achieved self-knowledge and self-forgiveness in the after-life.

> Study that tree.
> It stands there like a purified soul,
> All cold, sweet, glistening light.
> Dear mother, the window is dark again,
> But you are in the light because
> I finished all that consequence.
> I killed that lad because had he grown up,
> He would have struck a woman's fancy,
> Begot, and passed pollution on.
> I am a wretched foul old man
> And therefore harmless. When I have stuck
> This old jack-knife into a sod
> And pulled it out all bright again,
> And picked up all the money that he dropped,
> I'll to a distant place, and there
> Tell my old jokes among new men.[23]

This dramatic use of symbols makes unnecessary the importing of extraneous figurative language in order to intensify the expression.

Note that here we have a reverse of the de-animating metaphor familiar in "Sailing to Byzantium," where the dead poet's soul be-

21. *Variorum Plays*, p. 1042.
22. "Among School Children," *Variorum Poems*, p. 446; cf. *Poems*, p. 217.
23. *Variorum Plays*, p. 1049.

comes a golden nightingale on a golden bough. House and tree are animated. But Yeats is not a romantic seeking a human face in nature. The mother's soul haunts these physical objects. What Yeats finds in the tree and house is not nature's "mighty heart" but an actual human soul in its essential activity of vision, reducing itself to thought. Tree and house are external, visible tokens for the mother's tragedy and present suffering. The sounds of hoofbeats over the gravelled road toward the barns in back—although we neither hear the sound nor see the buildings—are secondary symbols of the father's beastliness, now real only in the mother's mind. The play, like house or tree, is stripped bare of any irrelevant furniture or foliage, and nothing is left but the tragedy of vision. The "purging out of poetical ornament," which Eliot calls "the most painful part of the labor, so far as the versification goes, of the modern poet who tries to write a play in verse,"[24] is here complete.

Another striking aspect of Yeats's success, Eliot found, is his escape from Shakespearean blank verse.

When [Yeats] first began to write plays, poetic drama meant plays written in blank verse. Now, blank verse has been a dead meter for a long time. . . . If you are writing a play of the same type as Shakespeare's, the reminiscence is oppressive; if you are writing a play of a different type, it is distracting. . . . Blank verse can hardly be dissociated from the life of the sixteenth and seventeenth centuries: it can hardly catch the rhythms with which English is spoken nowadays. I think that if anything like regular blank verse is ever to be re-established, it can only be after a long departure from it. . . . Yeats did not quite invent a new meter, but the blank verse of his later plays shows a great advance towards one; and what is most astonishing is the virtual abandonment of blank verse meter in *Purgatory*.[25]

The abandonment is not so astonishing when one reflects that Yeats had been moving toward a new verse and had in fact actually used a different verse for an entire play. Sixty-seven lines of dialogue (not lyric interlude) in *The Only Jealousy of Emer* are in tetrameter couplets—a

24. Eliot, "The Poetry of W. B. Yeats," p. 451.
25. *Ibid.*, pp. 450–51.

tense verse appropriate to the scene in which a supernatural woman dances temptation before the ghost of Cuchulain.[26] The verse of the attendants in *A Full Moon in March* is experimental and almost none of *The Herne's Egg* is in blank verse, whole scenes being written either in trimeter or in tetrameter, rhymed occasionally at the beginnings and ends of scenes and at moments when Attracta is possessed by her God.

Because *The Herne's Egg* is an Aristophanic comedy (or tragicomedy) which plays the intense and fantastic priestess Attracta against the clownish, but harshly actual mock-hero Congal, the alternate tightness and looseness in the verse is appropriate. This contrast is achieved by increasing or decreasing the amount of rhyme and the amount of organization of the syntax. Music and the dance, not to mention the fantastic subject matter, make this play a likely occasion for rhymed verse, and the unrhymed passages, which have the ring of real speech, do not have to carry the whole play as they do in *Purgatory*. They are like Congal's rape of Attracta, a clownish violation of the purity and integrity of her verse.

In *Purgatory* there is no rhyme. Yeats is careful, however, to indicate in the opening lines the tetrameter beat which shall be the "strong driving force"[27] throughout the play.

> *Boy.* Half-door, hall door,
>   Hither and thither day and night,
>   Hill or hollow, shouldering this pack,
>   Hearing you talk.[28]

In spite of the success with which Yeats has achieved a "subtle hesitating rhythm"[29] whenever he wants it, and occasionally, as we shall see, frustrated exact metrical investigation by presenting us lines that may be four stresses in sprung rhythm or ordinary pentameter, there is little doubt about how to read the lines of this play on the stage. "Hálf-door,

26. *Variorum Plays*, pp. 551, 553, 555, 557.
27. *Letters on Poetry*, p. 43. F. A. C. Wilson's allusion to the "free verse of *Purgatory*," *W. B. Yeats and Tradition*, p. 138, is merely confusing.
28. *Variorum Plays*, p. 1041.
29. *Letters on Poetry*, p. 43.

háll door," would have the same speech time as "Híther and thíther." But because of the Boy's exhaustion and annoyance it has the dramatic time of a full tetrameter line:

Hálf/-doòr,/háll/doòr,
Híther/and thí/ther dáy/and níght.

Of course, the actor would not say it that way. An actual isochronism between these lines would make the first line sound ridiculous. But the actor would slow down the first line beyond ordinary speech rhythm, and our minds would imagine the isochronism. These first four lines are almost Anglo-Saxon in their combination of alliteration and stress. Yeats has calculatedly arranged individually unexceptional phrases so that there will be four strong beats in each line with a pause in the syntax immediately before the first and third beats. The emphatic rhythm is dramatically appropriate. The Boy is bored and impatient with following his half-mad old father up and down the country. In "day and night" the slight difficulty of enunciating *d* and *n* together slows the phrase, dramatizing the Boy's irritated weariness.

What the Boy might actually say in this situation would differ, of course, from the lines Yeats has given him. The ellipsis in "Half-door, hall door" and in "Hill or hollow" is a mark of idiomatic speech, yet these particular expressions may be used here for the first time. "Hither and thither," on the other hand, begins to be archaic. We associate it with the folk speech we know through ballad literature. "Day and night" is usually "night and day." In other words, Yeats is giving us not common speech but the qualities of actual speech in phrases that are new-created, archaic, or distorted and, therefore, have some of the purposeful difficulty of poetry. The most evident difference from ordinary speech, however, is in the careful arrangement of individual items to create a strong regularity of stress.

The rhythm of these lines is the rhythm of the action—travelling back and forth across Ireland. More particularly it is the rhythm of common expressions that imitate the action—"back and forth," "up and down," "in and out," "over and over," "time after time." Yeats has selected from these common expressions those that fit his deeper meanings and that alliterate. "Hall door" signifies the entrance to one of the great houses whose destruction Yeats felt as a great personal and national loss. The line calls up a picture of a still half-feudal society with great houses, responsible landowners, peasant cottages, and loyal peasantry. Simultaneously the tone of irritation in which the line must be spoken obliterates the significance of such distinctions. To a pedlar with his pack, to a society increasingly mercantile and mobile, the ideals of fixed residence and local tradition are meaningless. The theme of the play, the guilt of leveling the great houses with the little ones, of destroying a high way of life to make way for a mob without traditions, thus appears implicitly in the first line.

The Boy's impulsively spoken four lines have all the shuttling movement of Yeats's cones and gyres in *A Vision*. "Hither and thither" and "day and night" are speech-like expressions, not profound or striking, yet the path and the journey on it are dramatic representations of cyclic recurrence. For, in *Purgatory* even as in "Byzantium," "Hades' bobbin bound in mummy-cloth / May unwind the winding path."[30] The winding path of life is presented to us, before conscience, in the ghost scenes that follow, must "unwind" it, reliving transgressions.

Against this impatient unsubtle beat, the Old Man introduces his complex meditative rhythms.

> Study that house.
> I think about its jokes and stories;
> I try to remember what the butler
> Said to a drunken gamekeeper
> In mid-October, but I cannot.
> If I cannot, none living can.
> Where are the jokes and stories of a house,
> Its threshold gone to patch a pig-sty?[31]

Except for one line, this speech is in tetrameter, but whereas in the Boy's opening speech the metrical pattern gave a rhythmical impulse that imposed a phrasing scarcely different from actual speech rhythm

---

30. *Variorum Poems*, p. 497; cf. *Poems*, p. 248.
31. *Variorum Plays*, p. 1041.

(though very different from the iambic pattern normal to the play), here there is a great deal of counterpoint between actual speech rhythm and rhythmical impulse, while the iambic pattern becomes more and more evident. The typical metre of the play is found in "I think about its jokes and stories," "If I cannot, none living can," "Its threshold gone to patch a pig-sty." The variation ´ ˘ / ˘ ´ / ´ ˘ / ˘ ´ however, is repeated so often in the play that it almost becomes a norm opposed to the completely iambic lines. The Old Man's first line, "Study that house," repeats the rhythm of "Hither and thither . . . Shouldering this pack / Hearing you talk." But the dramatic action it expresses—giving a mysterious command—slows the line down and puts more stress upon "that" than has been given to any previous unaccented syllable, even to "you" in the more quickly spoken line "Hearing you talk." The next line, "I think about its jokes and stories," breaks completely the trochee-plus-iamb rhythm these phrases have led us to expect. The iambic pattern becomes evident, although, the rhythmical impulse checked by actual speech rhythm, "about" almost drops out of the sentence. After four lines with an emphatic break before the strong third stress there is no caesura in this line at all. The Old Man is just talking, rambling on to justify the Boy's "Hearing you talk." Here actual speech rhythms are not distorted by dramatic passion.

In the next line, "I try to remember what the butler / Said to a drunken gamekeeper," speech rhythm and dramatic propriety further obliterate the strong beat and the medial pause which the Boy's opening lines have dramatically and idiomatically used. The syllables "what" and "keep" are minimized as to stress. Putting a subject at the end of a line, the verb at the beginning of the following line, and a modifying adverbial phrase at the start of the third line is another device that creates the swiftness and irregular rhythm of speech: "what the butler / Said to a drunken gamekeeper / In mid-October."

At the same time that Yeats is destroying the tetrameter swing, however, he subtly reasserts it by a pattern of rhythm and sound that quietly calls attention to the second and fourth feet with a repetition wholly like that of common speech:

> . . . remember . . . the butler
> . . . a drunken . . . gamekeeper
> . . . October.

My discussion of the metrics assumes that in reading any line in this play one may be aware of three possible directions from which to approach the rhythm: (1) the metrical pattern (expectation of regular iambic feet, usually but not always in tetrameter); (2) the rhythmical impulse (expectation of four beats, irrespective of number of syllables and kind of foot); and (3) the actual speech rhythms, determined by phrase divisions and meaning. (Beyond these, of course—beyond metrical pattern and rhythmical impulse, even beyond actual speech rhythm—is the rhythm of dramatic expression. The complex of rhythms in each line is there to express the dramatic tension, and the proper dramatic reading—that is the proper choice of the norm with which each syllable shall audibly accord—will best bring out the counterpoint.) In reading the line "Said to a drunken gamekeeper" one may be simultaneously aware of duties to three norms. (1) One may remember that the typical line of the play has eight syllables and that the even syllables are accented (iambic tetrameter). One is conscious of this basic metrical pattern to the extent of being somewhat disappointed that one cannot read the above line as follows: "Said tó/a drún/ken gáme/keepér." (2) One compromises, therefore, and approximates to that pattern as nearly as one can without mispronouncing words and obscuring meaning: "Sáid to/a drún/ken gáme/keéper." This rhythmical impulse has obviously done some violence to the word "gamekeeper." (3) In actual speech rhythm, "gamekeeper" will have a hovering accent, rather than a full accent, on "keep." The three ways of reading the line provide a triple tension.

The three rhythms need not be divided against each other on an equal basis. 1 (metrical pattern) and 2 (rhythmical impulse) may unite against 3 (actual speech rhythm) or 2 and 3 may join against 1. Rarely 2 may stand by itself against 1 and 3, which proves that it is an independent entity. "Said to a drunken gamekeeper," analyzed above, is an example of this third effect. An example of the second effect may be "Modern and ancient, books by the ton," where rhythmical impulse unites with actual speech rhythm in counterpoint to basic metrical pattern. An example of the first may be "I ran away, worked here and there" where metrical pattern and rhythmical impulse seem to stress "here," while speech rhythm would perhaps stress "worked." Another might be "Where great men grew up, married, died," with metrical pattern and rhythmical impulse stressing "grew," speech rhythm stressing "up." Frequently the alliance of metrical pattern and rhythmical impulse against speech rhythm preserves the four beats, as in "The moonlight falls upon the path," where speech would find but three stresses.

The variety of lines in this play is much greater than these examples reveal, because I have tried to choose examples that have close to eight syllables. One of the interesting metrical phenomena of the play is the frequent ten-syllable line, which the iambic pattern would have us read as pentameter, the rhythmical impulse as tetrameter, and about which either ordinary speech rhythm or the rhythm of dramatic expression has to make the decision. Some of these lines, in another play, would clearly be pentameter: "The shadow of a cloud upon the house"; "Because there is somebody in that house"; "Captains and Governors, and long ago"; "Bragging and drinking in the public-house." Others would be quite rough for iambic pentameter even in a blank verse play, and therefore, in a tetrameter context, are clearly four-beat lines: "Whether upon others or upon themselves," "My mother that was your grand-dam owned it." One cannot conclude, however, to read all the lines as tetrameter, because there are some that must be given five beats: "I saw it a year ago stripped bare as now"; "Men that had fought at Aughrim and the Boyne"; "Being dead she is alone in her remorse"; "I killed that lad because had he grown up . . ."

We are faced with two quite different sorts of lines here: a four-beat, often ten-syllable line in sprung rhythm and a line of straight iambic pentameter. The first violates the iambic norm, the other violates the tetrameter rhythmical impulse. Neither is the typical line of the play, but both occur frequently enough to be played against each other, the excited line of four polysyllabic feet against the longer line with fewer syllables per foot, the drawn-out, deliberate, controlled pentameter.

Greàt péo/ple líved/and díed/in this hóuse;
Mágistrates,/cólonels,/mémbers of/Párliament,
Cáptains and/Góvernors,/and lóng/agó
Mén that/had fóught/at Aú/ghrim ánd/the Bóyne.

Sometimes the metrical ambiguity of a single long line may under-
line richness in meaning. Take the line "And she must animate that
dead night," from the end of the play.

Hoof-beats! Dear God,
How quickly it returns—beat—beat—!
Her mind cannot hold up that dream.
Twice a murderer and all for nothing.
And she must animate that dead night
Not once but many times!

If the line is pentameter, the iambic pattern rules that "dead" shall fall
in an accented position. If the line is tetrameter, rhythmical impulse
rules that "that" has a right to be stressed. These alternate possibilities
suggest the reading "And shé must ánimate thàt déad níght." The
swift rhythm of "animate" is meaningfully balanced against the re-
tarded movement of the three accented monosyllables—life against
death. The accent falling on "dead," "that déad níght," brings out
several meanings: (1) that night of the dead; (2) that static, uneventful,
unpleasurable, non-existence; (3) that dead of the night—the very
darkest moment. Emphasis on "that" "thát deàd níght," adds to these
meanings the memory of a particular night: the wedding night in
which the Old Man was begotten. She must relive *that* night, resurrect-
ing it from a mercifully dead past. Emphasis on both, "thát déad
níght," brings together the two sets of meaning, making that particular
night deathly at the start and eternal in the reanimation of its deathli-
ness. For the mother to sleep with the groom was to cause her own
death, the death of her house, her husband's death, and her grandson's
death. It was to turn generations away from creation towards destruction. Her wedding night is a death that lives.

When we contrast the first line of the play, "Half-door, hall door,"
with the last line, we see what a virtuoso of metrical technique Yeats
had become.

> O God,
> Release my mother's soul from its dream!
> Mankind can do no more. Appease
> The misery of the living and the remorse
> of the dead.

"Half-door, hall door," as we have seen, has four beats in four syllables.
The last line has four beats in fifteen syllables. Here speech rhythm
and rhythmical impulse exert their greatest force against the iambic
pattern. Following several lines of fairly regular iambics, this line
pours the utmost metrical irregularity into the strong mold of the
tetrameter to produce a powerful effect. After the confusion of "Hoof-
beats! Dear God, / How quickly it returns—beat—beat—!" comes
the agonizing attempt at control in the prayer, communicated in strict
iambic tetrameter—the basic line of the play—broken before the last
foot the more to slow it down, to give the effect of momentous
supplication: "Mankind can do no more. Appease. . . ." This last foot,
an isolated hortatory verb, builds up a tremendous expectation for
what is to come. Then the Old Man bursts passionately, with a tragic
human inability to control (a central idea of the play), into the last line:
"The misery of the living and the remorse of the dead," filling the
simple rhythms of the prayer with the binding and galling complexities of human suffering.

"A poem [how much more a poetic play] is an elaboration of the
rhythms of common speech and their association with profound feeling."[32] The verse of *Purgatory* never gives one the feeling that the
language of passionate speech has been decorated or that its syntax has
been twisted to fit artificially "powerful" rhythms which are not its
own. On the contrary one has the feeling that the vocabulary, rhythm
and syntax of actual speech in a particular dramatic situation have
determined metrical questions such as number of feet and kind of feet
in a certain line. This appearance may be misleading. Yeats may have
sought far for the idiomatic expression which would have the beat he
wanted at a particular point. But " 'the natural words in the natural

32. *Essays and Introductions,* p. 508.

order' is the formula"[33] and Yeats has disciplined both vocabulary and syntax so as to avoid at least the appearance of unnaturalness and created a metric loose enough so that he can let a passage "arise out of its own rhythm"[34] and yet not so loose but that every syllable is under complete control.

In the dance plays Yeats had discovered the essential form of the drama of perception and had found the key to the future development of his dramatic style. Chorus, mask, and dance had allowed him to escape from superficial realism and had given convincing form to the revelation of a deeper reality. One reason for the greater genuineness of the dance plays was that objective scene and action could enter the poetry naturally, since realistic set and gesture had disappeared.

The poetry of the dance plays had not completely accommodated itself to this situation. Figurative language—the grey-green cup of jade of *The Dreaming of the Bones*—was often still a poetic coloring applied to the bare structure of the play. Dramatic poetry of any age, to be effective as drama, cannot be prevailingly of this kind, although such coloring may certainly enrich a verse play so long as the poetry is for the most part truly dramatic. To be essentially dramatic, the verse must take its symbols from the structure itself. That is, the structure must be so meaningful that any rich detail will have infinite relationships with the other details and the whole.

To perfect an essentially dramatic poetry, Yeats had first to submit to the discipline of prose realism. In *The Words upon the Window-pane* there are few local metaphors. The language has its metaphorical power through reverberations of the whole structure. Every intensifying name or allusion—and every plain statement—starts old echoes through the fine eighteenth-century house.

It is to be observed that the essential Noh play form lingers skeletally in *The Words upon the Window-pane* and *Purgatory*[35] after more superficial characteristics of the dance plays have proved perishable. There

33. *Letters on Poetry,* p. 56.
34. *Oxford Book of Modern Verse* (New York: Oxford University Press, 1936), p. viii.
35. In *Purgatory* "the analogy with the Noh technique is closer than in any play since *The Dreaming of the Bones*" (Wilson, *W. B. Yeats and Tradition,* p. 139).

are no dancers or chorus of musicians, yet the plays have the movement of a Noh play, from an eternal situation in this world, to a
moment of vision. The characters are witnesses and commentators like
the choruses of the dance plays, and their symbolic actions—the
preparation of a cup of tea in one play, a sacrificial murder in the
other—are as ritualistic as the motions of dancers.

In *Purgatory* a more complicated action is packed into a shorter play
through a mercilessly tight structure and a concentrated verse speech.
The heightened language of poetry seems to make this difference—
that the richness of implication becomes local, rather than general.
Through a trick of rhythm or phrase a line may not only carry us to the
macrocosm of the whole structure, but may also seem to be a rich
particular little world in which that macrocosm is reflected. In *Purgatory* Yeats applies to poetic drama the structure-baring principles
discovered in his experiment with prose realism, and develops a verse
speech appropriate to this new essentialized drama.

❧ Conclusion

Y
EATS WAS attempting to dramatize the moment of perception, of epiphany, at a time when the individual consciousness can have little faith in its own version of objective
reality. Yeats's drama does not hold the mirror up to nature
in the same sense as Shakespeare's does. It does not mirror
anything but the consciousness itself in the act of making "a super-
human / Mirror-resembling dream."[1] It is as if both dramatist and
protagonist were engaged in brightening an instrument of vision for
the moment when the dark days pass and a valid version of objective
reality appears. In *The Death of Cuchulain* that hero declares, "I make
the truth!"[2] and at the moment of death decrees his own soul's immortality: "I say it is about to sing."[3] In the lack of a valid system of belief,
the hero-artist creates his own myth. On the other hand, those who
have sinned against greatness must also create their purgatorial dream.
The ghosts of Diarmuid and Dervorgilla, in *The Dreaming of the
Bones*, the spirit of the lady who desecrated a noble house by marrying
her groom, in *Purgatory*, must "animate that dead night / Not once but
many times!"[4] They must "Re-live / Their transgressions" in imagination until they are either damned or saved in terms of their own
achieved vision or of an objective reality. For what they have done to
themselves "There is no help but in themselves / And in the mercy of
God."[5]

Action and passion are presented by Yeats primarily as the occasion of imaginative vision. Are action and suffering consummated in
knowledge? The question posed by the great sonnet "Leda and the
Swan" is central in Yeats's attitude toward his dramatic subjects.

1. "The Tower," *Variorum Poems*, p. 415; cf. *Poems*, p. 199.
2. *Variorum Plays*, p. 1056.   3. *Ibid.*, p. 1061.
4. *Ibid.*, p. 1049.   5. *Ibid.*, pp. 1042–43.

Yeats's drama may be regarded as idealist in that it takes one moment of the tragic rhythm as the clue to life and action. In so far as the moment of perception synthesizes the moments of purpose and passion, however, his drama is realist. Yet he dramatizes the soul's perception of itself—as acting, suffering, perceiving—not its perception of its place in an objective social order or cosmic whole. Yeats the playwright dramatizes the imagination's struggle for freedom and avoids binding himself to any "true" version of objective reality that might distort the soul's image. His protagonist, significantly, has no stage. In the dance dramas he plays before a wall. In the early dramas the wall is simply disguised by tapestry. The ruined house and bare tree in *Purgatory* are all that is left of the stage which in Sophocles' and Shakespeare's times was a "centrally placed mirror of man and society."[6] Yeats's protagonist is either a figure "raging in the dark"[7] or a "cry / Among the deepening shades."[8] Not only has he no stage, he has no character; he is seeing or hearing himself, not appearing to others, and therefore the actor often covers his external individuality with a mask of the soul's essence. His words, in the dance plays, are often even spoken by someone else—a musician. These marks and the consistent choice of the moment of insight or manifestation as dramatic subject are signs of an idealist theatre.

Yet he has been more successful than any other modern dramatic poet in meeting the crisis of his age. Yeats as a dramatist is not satisfied with a priori intellectual, moral, and esthetic principles. His drama, like his poetry, affirms a reality as the implied resolution of the contradictions of existence, and it appeals directly to the primitive histrionic sensibility. Yeats's great subject is one for a realist theatre. The soul recognizes that in the struggle with its opposite it transcends its incompleteness. A resolution—that completeness which is reality—is implied by the very violence of the contradictions. This subject is intensely dramatic. It is the climax of the tragic rhythm at the

6. Fergusson, p. 96.
7. *Variorum Poems*, pp. 495; cf. *Poems*, pp. 246, 200.
8. *Ibid.*, p. 416; cf. *Poems*, p. 200.

moment of passionate perception. It provides the nearest thing to a realist idea of a theatre, in Fergusson's sense of the term, that our age has achieved.

The dramatic speech that Yeats finally developed is realist. A manifold instrument of perception, it has not the exclusiveness of argument, as in the heroic couplets of the theatre of reason, or the exclusiveness of sentiment, as in the directed associationalism of the theatre of passion. It is a synthetic speech, the marriage of reason and emotion in contemplation. It is inclusive, presenting at any moment the full tragic rhythm. It is a tool of vision, ready-brightened for the moment when there is a valid image of objective reality to be accepted and perceived.

There is an evident historical appropriateness to Yeats's dramatizing the third movement of the tragic rhythm. Shakespeare's realistic and analogical[9] dramatic form represented the ideal Renaissance man's achieved unity of being. This synthesis was broken up in the late seventeenth century. The age of reason then demonstrated its genius in the univocal and idealist form of the neoclassic theatre. Degenerating into mechanistic materialism, this age revealed the inadequacy of its ruling idea. The romantic theatre of passion expressed the opposite and complementary—but still incomplete metaphysic—of the nineteenth-century poet or musician. This form too was univocal and idealist. It remained for the twentieth century to provide at least one dramatic poet whose art would dramatize the soul's discovery that its unity was to be found in neither reason nor passion but in recognition of the tragic completion of its cycle.

Shakespeare wrote at a time when the traditional synthesis of values was the background against which a vast variety of new secular careers was judged. Yeats wrote, so he felt, toward what is perhaps the end of this age of secularism, before the coming, perhaps, of some new synthesis—like or unlike the medieval one. He wrote in a country that had just had its own Renaissance and yet was nevertheless caught in the general decline. In one generation the conception of a synthesis was revived and exploded.

9. Cf. Fergusson, pp. 98–142, 234–36.

In his early plays, once he had turned away from the English Arthurian tradition embodied in *Vivien and Time,* Yeats attempted to evoke a national ideal through the revival of Celtic mythology. Later he felt that he, like Shakespeare, must exalt the individual who could personify a national ideal, since there could no longer be a "Holy City in the imagination."[10] Yet Yeats never really gave up that earlier dream. He wanted to express a national ideal so accepted by all that it was a part of the common consciousness.

These preoccupations have something to do with the development of his dramatic art. *The Countess Cathleen* and *The Land of Heart's Desire* accept traditional material and handle it in a traditional manner. In *Deirdre, The King's Threshold,* and *On Baile's Strand,* traditional material is subjected to the poet's private conception and a pattern is forced on the material, not discovered in it. Yeats is tending toward an exaltation of individualistic heroes patterned after his own purposes, not toward a ritualistic repetition of a national myth.

In Yeats's imitations of Japanese Noh and in his last plays, the two movements coexist. The middle and late plays dramatize the individual hero, repository of a nation's values when it does not have the moral strength to embody them throughout its structure. At the same time there is in these plays a rediscovery of sacred place and of perpetually recurring actions symbolic of place and nation, true actions which may be thought of as coming from the common consciousness.

Yeats felt that he could not in his age write a great poetic drama, realistic and analogical. He knew that his dream of a national synthesis of values was but a dream. Of his attempts to model plays upon the Japanese Noh drama he said:

Perhaps some day a play in the form I am adapting for European purposes may excite once more, whether in Gaelic or in English, under the slope of Slieve-na-mon or Croagh Patrick, ancient memories. . . . Yet I know that I only amuse myself with a fancy; for my writings if they be seaworthy will put to sea, and I cannot tell where they may be carried by the wind.[11]

10. *Autobiographies,* p. 494.
11. *Essays and Introductions,* pp. 236–37.

And in 1929 he wrote to Sturge Moore, "I always feel that my work is not drama but the ritual of a lost faith."[12]

There is no sense of defeat here, however. That would be contrary to his concept of the meaning of tragedy. In the same year he wrote:

The one heroic sanction is that of the last battle of the Norse Gods, of a gay struggle without hope. . . . Our literary movement would be worthless but for its defeat. . . . There is no improvement: only a series of sudden fires, each though fainter as necessary as the one before it. We free ourselves from obsession that we may be nothing. The last kiss is given to the void.[13]

12. *Yeats and Sturge Moore*, p. 156.
13. *Ibid.*, p. 154.

Appendix
A Description of the Manuscripts

Vivien and Time

National Library of Ireland Ms. 30,357 is a maroon notebook measuring 18 cm (7³⁄₃₂″) wide by 22.8 cm (8³¹⁄₃₂″) high and has on the cover in black ink in Yeats's hand, "Viven [*sic*] and Time/a dramatic poem/ January the 8th/1884." This stiff paper cover is textured with tiny diamond shapes (about .15 cm). On all four sides, about 1.1 cm in from the edge and parallel to each edge, a border line about .2 cm wide is impressed into the cover. At each corner two of these lines cross at right angles. In the center of the cover is impressed a monogram of the letters "M S S" superimposed one on another. In the lower right-hand corner the signature "W. B. Yeats" appears in the same black ink. The same signature, in a faded grey-brown ink, appears on the inside of the front cover.

The notebook paper is a rather heavy (20 lb.?) laid with line and chain marks but no watermarks. Sheets originally measuring 35.2 cm (13⅞″) wide were folded in the middle to make folios 17.6 cm (6¹⁵⁄₁₆″) wide. The height is 22.9 cm (9″). This white paper is lined every .9 cm (¹¹⁄₃₂″) in a violet blue, 23 lines to a page, with a top margin of about 2 cm (²⁵⁄₃₂″) and a bottom margin of about 1 cm (¹³⁄₃₂″). The sheets are sewn at the center fold. At present, counting some stubs, there are 42 folios. But folios 20–21 and 23–24 are detached from those with which they were originally joined and are loose in the notebook. This is significant in that it is just before folio 25 that the scene between Vivien and Time, now restored, would have appeared. The removal of the pages containing that scene has apparently caused the separation of the loose folios. Folios 8, 28, and 38–42 are mere stubs, the pages having been cut out. Marks on the stub of folio 8 show that both recto and verso had been written on, but there seems no break in the continuity.

We may assume that folio 8 was discarded because of a preferred version written on folio 9. There are no marks on the stub of folio 28, but the same situation may have existed there. There is now no break in the continuity between folio 27 and folio 29. Folios 29 and 30, on the other hand, give differing versions of the last lines of the play and Asphodel's exit.

Why folios 38–42 were cut out is unknown. The play ends with folio 30; the rest of the notebook is blank, except for a piece of pink stationery laid in between folio 30 and folio 31 which gives a slightly different version of folio 21, Vivien's curse on Asphodel and Clarin. The stationery is a paper of about 20 lb. weight, with some rag content, no line, chain, or watermarks. A sheet measuring 23 cm (9¹⁄₁₆″) wide has been folded to make two folios 11.5 cm (4¹⁷⁄₃₂″) wide. The height is 17.85 cm (7¹⁄₃₂″). The same grey-brown ink is used on this inserted paper as in most of the notebook. Divergences are noted.

This is a fair copy, probably one created for the rehearsal that J. B. Yeats mentions in his 7 January 1884 letter to Dowden. It is unlikely, considering the January 8th date, to be the manuscript lent to Dowden before January 7th. Yeats has carefully corrected his spelling errors by going over them with a black crayon wax pencil and in other places in black ink. He has also made a few changes of substance in both media.

The pages missing from Ms. 30,357, containing act II, scene 2, are found in National Library of Ireland Ms. 30,460. There are five leaves, six pages. The first leaf is folded to make two pages. The others are single, having been torn from their mates in the notebook, with which they match perfectly when the group is slipped in before folio 25. The paper, ink, and handwriting are all identical to those in the notebook. A red stain at the very bottom left of the last three pages matches the same stain on folios 25 ff. of the notebook. There is thus no doubt that the pages are from the notebook. They contain all of act II, scene 2, down to the stage direction "(*She dies.*)."

Both these manuscripts were until recently in the collection of Senator Michael Yeats, where they were catalogued as MBY 357 and MBY 460.

The Poet and the Actress

This description of *The Poet and the Actress* papers was made while the present National Library of Ireland MS 30,410 was still no. 410 in Senator Michael Yeats's collection.

A brown envelope 25.5 cm (10 in.) × 30.48 cm (12 in.) is marked on the flap in pencil "Poet & Actress (1916)/Mss & Typescript" in Mrs. W. B. Yeats's hand. The manuscript consists of twenty sheets, of two different types of stationery, on which Yeats has written in a dark blue ink, leaving all versos blank. After Yeats's death (or at least at some time when his help was not available) Mrs. Yeats wrote glosses in pencil over words hard to decipher. Pencil lines are drawn under other difficult words. Since Yeats never saw the glosses, which are often superseded in Mrs. Yeats's typescript, I do not detail them here.

Yeats has numbered the twenty sheets in the upper right hand corner. Page "(1" [SB22(1p192)] is on heavy, unlined, off-white (almost grey) stationery, with no line or chain marks, watermarked "MUDIE & SONS/15 COVENTRY St. w." The measurements are 17.8 cm (7$\frac{1}{32}$ in.) × 22.9 cm (9$\frac{1}{32}$ in.). The rusty paperclip stains in the upper left-hand corner match those on the verso of the final page. Page "(1a" [SB22(1p193)] is on a lighter weight (perhaps 20 lb.), unlined, off-white (cream-colored) stationery, with line and chain marks, watermarked "PIONEER/FINE". The measurements are 20.4 cm (8$\frac{1}{16}$ in.) × 26.6 cm (10$\frac{1}{2}$ in.).

Each of the twenty sheets is identical in size and paper to either page "(1" or page "(1a". I shall identify the page "(1" paper as "grey" and the page "(1a" paper as "cream." A table, with the Stony Brook numbers added for identification, will explain the sequence (cf. p. 270).

At least three stages of revision are represented in the manuscript. The original sequence was cream-colored pages "(1a" (probably without the "a"), "2", "(3", "4", "5", "~~5~~ 6", "~~16~~ 7", "8", "9.", "10", "~~11~~ 12", "13", and "14". (It is now impossible to explain the cancelled numbers on "~~5~~ 6" and "~~16~~ 7".) Then cream "3a/3.b" (although then the "3.b" had not been marked on it) was added after cream "(3" to provide a

Grey	Stony Brook No.	Cream
(1	SB22(1p192)	
	193	(1a
	194	2
2a	195	
2.b	196	
4.3	197	
3a	198	
	199	(3
	200	3a/3.b
	201	4
	202	5
	203	5 6
	204	10 7
	205	8
	206	9
	207	10
	208	11
	209	11 12
	210	13
14	211	

new version of a cancelled passage at the bottom of "10". (The last line of "10", "There cannot be real [or, new?] beauty without obsession," still leads on to the first line of "11 12", "just as there cannot be religious faith without doubt."

The grey pages represent the latest revisions. Yeats had completed the cream pages when he thought of the narrative frame provided in grey pages "(1" and "14" where the Poet speaks of having brought (or not brought) the Actress a mask from Fez. Cream "(3" speaks of "a mask with certain severe Egyptian lines" but does not mention Fez.

Grey "(1" is added before cream "(1a". Cream "2" follows, but the Actress's speech at the bottom is cancelled, and grey "2a" and "2.b" provide new material to be inserted before that speech. Then cream "(3" is removed from the sequence, and grey "4.3" and "3a" replace it. Cream "3a/3.b" follows (the "3.b" being added at this point), and then cream "4", "5", "$\cancel{6}$ 6", "$\cancel{16}$ 7", "8", "9.", "10", "11", "$\cancel{11}$ 12", and "13" follow in sequence. Grey "14" then completes the dialogue.

Mrs. Yeats's typescript is on lightweight (16 lb.?) white typing paper, 20.6 cm (8⅛ in.) × 26.1 cm (10⁵⁄₁₆ in.), no line or chain marks, watermark "SUMMIT/EXTRA STRONG." There are a title page ("THE POET AND THE ACTRESS"), a first page (beginning, "The Poet/I have just returned from the City of Fez and have in this box"), and pages numbered "2." to "13." The typing is black pica, ribbon copy, corrected in pencil by Mrs. Yeats. A very few further corrections are in black ink. Since there is no evidence that Yeats ever saw this typescript, I make no detailed description of it.

Bibliography

I have not been concerned to cite the very latest editions in this book first published in 1965. If an older edition is still satisfactory and accessible I have felt free to use it. The following abbreviations have been used for frequently cited works.

WORKS BY YEATS

Autobiographies: Autobiographies (London: Macmillan, 1955; reprinted 1977).

CL1: The Collected Letters of W. B. Yeats: Volume One, 1865–1894, ed. John Kelly and Eric Domville (London and New York: Oxford University Press, 1985).

Convegno di Lettere: Convegno di Lettere, 8–14 Ottobre 1934—XII, *Tema:* Il Teatro Drammatico. Reale Accademia d'Italia, Fondazione Alessandro Volta, Atti dei Convegne, 4 (Roma: Reale Accademia d'Italia, 1935–XIII).

Druid Craft: Druid Craft: The Writing of The Shadowy Waters, ed. Michael J. Sidnell, George P. Mayhew, and David R. Clark (Amherst: The University of Massachusetts Press, 1971; Dublin: The Dolmen Press, 1972; London: Oxford University Press, 1972).

Essays and Introductions: Essays and Introductions (New York: The Macmillan Company, 1961).

Explorations: Explorations, sel. Mrs. W. B. Yeats (New York: The Macmillan Company, 1962).

Fairy and Folk Tales: Fairy and Folk Tales of Ireland, ed. W. B. Yeats, foreword Kathleen Raine (Gerrards Cross: Colin Smythe, 1973). First published in *Fairy and Folk Tales of the Irish Peasantry* (London: Walter Scott, 1888).

John Sherman: John Sherman & Dhoya, ed. Richard Finneran (Detroit: Wayne State University Press, 1969).

Letters: The Letters of W. B. Yeats, ed. Allan Wade (London: Rupert Hart-Davis, 1954).

Letters on Poetry: Letters on Poetry from W. B. Yeats to Dorothy Wellesley, introd. Kathleen Raine (London: Oxford University Press, 1964).

Letters to Katharine Tynan: W. B. Yeats Letters to Katharine Tynan, ed. Roger McHugh (New York: McMullen Books, 1953).

Letters to the New Island: Letters to the New Island, ed. George Bernstein and Hugh Witemeyer (New York: Macmillan Publishing Company, 1989).

Mythologies: Mythologies (New York: The Macmillan Company, 1959).

Poems: The Poems: Revised edition, ed. Richard J. Finneran (New York: Macmillan, 1989).

Speckled Bird: The Speckled Bird, ed. William H. O'Donnell (Toronto: McClelland and Stewart, 1976).

Uncollected Prose: Uncollected Prose, I, ed. John P. Frayne (London: Macmillan; New York: Columbia University Press, 1970; II, coll. and ed. by John P. Frayne and Colton Johnson (London and Basingstoke: The Macmillan Press, 1975).

Variorum Plays: The Variorum Edition of the Plays of W. B. Yeats, ed. Russell K. Alspach, asst. by Catharine C. Alspach (New York: The Macmillan Company, 1966).

Variorum Poems: The Variorum Edition of the Poems of W. B. Yeats, ed. Peter Allt and Russell K. Alspach (New York: Macmillan Publishing Co., Inc., 1957).
A Vision, 1925: *A Critical Edition of Yeats* A Vision (1925), ed. George Mills Harper and Walter Kelly Hood (London and Basingstoke: The Macmillan Press, 1978).
A Vision, 1937: *A Vision* (London: Macmillan, 1962).
Yeats: Yeats: An Annual of Critical and Textual Studies, ed. Richard J. Finneran (Ann Arbor: University of Michigan Press).
YA: Yeats Annual, ed. Warwick Gould (London: Macmillan).
Yeats and Sturge Moore: W. B. Yeats and T. Sturge Moore, Their Correspondence 1901–1937, ed. Ursula Bridge (London: Routledge & Kegan Paul, 1953).

WORKS BY OTHERS

Ariosto: *Ariosto's Orlando Furioso,* sels. from trans. of Sir John Harrington, ed. Rudolf Gottfried (Bloomington and London: Indiana University Press, 1971).
Arnold: *Poetry and Criticism of Matthew Arnold,* ed. A. Dwight Culler (Boston: Houghton Mifflin Company, 1961).
Bentley: Eric Bentley, "Yeats as a Playwright," *Kenyon Review,* 10, No. 2 (Spring, 1948), 196–208.
Bradford, *Yeats at Work:* Curtis B. Bradford, *Yeats at Work* (Carbondale and Edwardsville: Southern Illinois University Press, 1965).
Burne-Jones: Burne-Jones, The Paintings, Graphic and Decorative Work of Sir Edward Burne-Jones 1833–98 (London: The Arts Council of Great Britain, 1975).
Dume: Thomas Leslie Dume, *William Butler Yeats: A Survey of His Reading* (unpublished dissertation, Temple University, 1950).
Eliot, *Poetry and Drama:* T. S. Eliot, *Poetry and Drama* (Cambridge: Harvard University Press, 1951).
Eliot, "The Poetry of W. B. Yeats": T. S. Eliot, "The Poetry of W. B. Yeats," *Southern Review,* 7, No. 3 (Winter, 1942), 442–54.
Ellmann, *Identity:* Richard Ellmann, *The Identity of Yeats* (New York: Oxford University Press, 1954).
Ellmann, *Man and Masks:* Richard Ellmann, *Yeats: The Man and the Masks* (New York: The Macmillan Company, 1948).
Fergusson: Francis Fergusson, *The Idea of a Theater, A Study of Ten Plays, The Art of Drama in Changing Perspective* (Princeton: Princeton University Press, 1949).
Harrison and Waters: Martin Harrison and Bill Waters, *Burne Jones* (New York: G. P. Putnam's Sons, 1973).
Henderson: Philip Henderson, *William Morris: His Life Work and Friends* (London: Thames and Hudson, 1967).
Hone: Joseph Hone, *W. B. Yeats 1865–1939* (London: Macmillan & Co. Ltd., 1962).
Johnson: *Burne-Jones All Colour Paperback,* introd. May Johnson (London: Academy Editions, 1979).
Murphy: William M. Murphy, *Prodigal Father, The Life of John Butler Yeats (1839–1922)* (Ithaca and London: Cornell University Press, 1978).

Myers: Frederic W. H. Myers, *Human Personality and Its Survival of Bodily Death,* 2 vols. (New York: Longmans, Green, and Co., 1903).

Newell: William Wells Newell, *King Arthur and the Table Round,* in 2 vols. (Boston and New York: Houghton Mifflin and Company; Cambridge: The Riverside Press, 1897).

'Noh' or Accomplishment: Ernest Fenollosa and Ezra Pound, *'Noh' or Accomplishment* (London: Macmillan, 1916).

Paton: Lucy Allen Paton, *Studies in the Fairy Mythology of Arthurian Romance* (Boston: Ginn & Company, 1903).

Sandys: Frederick Sandys 1829–1904 (Brighton Museum and Art Gallery, 1974).

Swinburne: Algernon Charles Swinburne, *Tristram of Lyonesse and Other Poems* (London: Chatto & Windus, Piccadily, 1882).

Tennyson: *The Works of Tennyson,* ed. Hallam, Lord Tennyson (New York: The Macmillan Company, 1913).

Ure, *Towards a Mythology:* Peter Ure, *Towards a Mythology* (London: Hodder & Stoughton Ltd., University Press of Liverpool, 1946).

Ure, *Yeats the Playwright:* Peter Ure, *Yeats the Playwright* (London: Routledge & Kegan Paul, 1963).

Vendler: Helen Hennessy Vendler, *Yeats's Vision and the Later Plays* (Cambridge, Massachusetts: Harvard University Press, 1963).

Wilson, *W. B. Yeats and Tradition:* F. A. C. Wilson, *W. B. Yeats and Tradition* (London: Victor Gollancz, 1958).

Wilson, *Yeats's Iconography:* F. A. C. Wilson, *Yeats's Iconography* (London: Victor Gollancz, 1960).

Wine: *Drama of the English Renaissance,* ed. M. L. Wine (New York: The Modern Library, 1969).

Indices

BY MARY F. CLARK

Author-Title Index

Cavalcanti, Guido (d. 1300), 166, 176, 183; "Io vengo il giorno a te infinite volte," 183
Chaucer, Geoffrey (1340?–1400), 89
Chrétien de Troyes, 96, 96n.111, 97, 99
Clark, David Ridgley, and George Mayhew, eds., *A Tower of Polished Black Stones: Early Versions of* The Shadowy Waters, 95n.110
Claudias, Matthias, 85n.63
Coleridge, Samuel Taylor (1772–1834), *The Best of Coleridge,* 86n.66; *The Rime of the Ancient Mariner,* 85n.63, 86, 87, 87n.68, ed. J. Noel Paton, 87
Comyn, Michael, "The Land of Youth" trans. Bryan O'Looney, 52
Congreve, William (1670–1729), 185
Cruikshank, George (1792–1878), 85n.63

D'Annunzio, Gabriele (1863–1938), 171
Dante Alighieri (1265–1321), *The Divine Comedy,* 176: *The Inferno of Dante Alighieri,* 186, 188, 190n.14, *The Purgatorio of Dante Alighieri,* 188, *The Paradiso of Dante Alighieri,* 188n.5
da Pistoia, Cino, "In verità questo libel di Dante," 183
de Chavannes, Puvis (1824–98), *Death and the Maidens (The Reaper),* 87
Delevoy, Robert L., *Symbolists and Symbolism,* 87n.70
De Morgan, Mary Augusta, *The Necklace of Princess Fiorimonde,* illus. Walter Crane, 79, 80
Donne, John (1572–1631), *The Complete Poems of John Donne,* ed. Roger E. Bennett, "The Undertaking: Platonic Love," 231n.44
Donner, Jörn, *The Films of Ingmar Bergman,* 85n.64
Dowden, Prof. Edward (1843–1913), 3n.4, 5, 7, 69, 268
Drama V, 18 (May 1915), 196n.15
Dume, Thomas Leslie, *William Butler Yeats: A Survey of His Reading,* 70n.15, 92n.91, 96n.111, 98n.126

Eglinton, John (William Kirkpatrick Magee), "Dublin Letter," 7, 70, 71n.15

Eliot, George (Mary Ann Evans 1819–80), *Daniel Deronda,* 85, 85n.65
Eliot, T. S. (1888–1965), 145, 244, 249; *The Cocktail Party,* 238; *Poetry and Drama,* 118, 118n.5, 143, 143n.38, 145n.44, 244n.11; "The Poetry of W. B. Yeats," 203n.32, 244n.10, 245n.12, 249nn.24–25; "Dante," *Selected Essays,* 190n.14
Ellmann, Richard, 7; *The Identity of Yeats,* 51, 51n.11, 166n.2, 235, 235n.57; *Yeats: The Man and the Masks,* 5n.9, n.11, n.16, 6, 6nn.19–20, 8n.29, 15n.58, 64n.64, 70n.18
Encyclopaedia Britannica (1962), 14n.56, 95
Euripides, *Hippolytus,* 185

Fenollosa, Ernest, and Ezra Pound, *'Noh' or Accomplishment,* 192nn.2–3, 193, 193nn.4–6, 195nn.12–15, 196nn.15–19
Fergusson, Francis, *The Idea of a Theater,* 118, 118n.3, 119n.7, n.9, n.10, 146n.1, 150, 150n.4, 189, 189n.8, 231, 236, 236n.9, 238n.70, 262n.6
Finneran, Richard J., 95n.108; "Farewell, 'Ha, ha!': New Revisions to Some Early Poems by W. B. Yeats," 3n.2; ed. *The Poems* by W. B. Yeats, *passim*
Flannery, Mary Catherine, *Yeats and Magic: The Earlier Works,* 6n.18
Ford, John (1586?–1693), *The Broken Heart,* 50
Fredeman, William E., *Pre-Raphaelitism: A Bibliocritical Study,* 78n.49
Friedman, John, 85n.64

García Lorca, Federico (1898–1936), *La Casa de Bernarda Alba,* 238
Gaunt, William, *The Restless Century: Painting in Britain 1800–1900,* 67n.5
Goethe, Johann Wolfgang von (1749–1832), 61n.54
Goldsmith, Oliver (1728–74), 112
Gonne, Maud, xiv, 6, 12, 13, 56, 60–61n.54, 96; "Yeats and Ireland," *Scattering Branches,* ed. Stephen Gwynn, 89n.80
Gregory, Lady Augusta (1859?–1932), xi, xiv, 50, 92, 95, 105, 109, 110, 112, 114, 166, 177, 184, 185, 195, 195n.15; *Cuchulain of Muirthemne* (1902), 56n.36, 69, 92,

Index of Titles by W. B. Yeats (1865–1939)

Subject Index

W. B. Yeats and the Theatre of Desolate Reality was composed in Granjon 11.5/14 by Keystone Typesetting, Inc., Orwigsburg, Pennsylvania; printed and bound by Braun-Brumfield, Inc., Ann Arbor, Michigan; and designed and produced by Kachergis Book Design, Pittsboro, North Carolina.